Modern Masters Volume Ten:

MODERN MASTERS VOLUME TEN:
KEVIN MAGUIRE

edited by Eric Nolen-Weathington and George Khoury
designed by Eric Nolen-Weathington
front cover art by Kevin Maguire
front cover color by Tom Ziuko
all interviews in this book were conducted by George Khoury
proofreading by Fred Perry and Christopher Irving

TwoMorrows Publishing
10407 Bedfordtown Dr.
Raleigh, North Carolina 27614
www.twomorrows.com • e-mail: twomorrow@aol.com

First Printing • January 2007 • Printed in Canada

Softcover ISBN: 978-1-893905-66-5

Dedication
To all the girls I've loved before. — George

*To my dad, John Weathington, for—among other things—letting me stay up late so many Sunday nights to watch James Bond movies with you.
And, as ever, to Donna, Iain, and Caper. — Eric*

Acknowledgements

Kevin Maguire, for his time and for letting us rummage through his closet for artwork.

Fabian Nicieza, for his invaluable input.

Terry Austin, for coming through once again.

Javier Soto, for having such a nice art collection and for allowing us to use it.

Special Thanks
Spencer Beck, John Cogan, Drew Geraci, Andy Helfer, Mark Ou, Joe Rubinstein,
Rick McGee and the crew of Foundation's Edge,
Russ Garwood and the crew of Capital Comics,
and John and Pam Morrow

KEVIN MAGUIRE

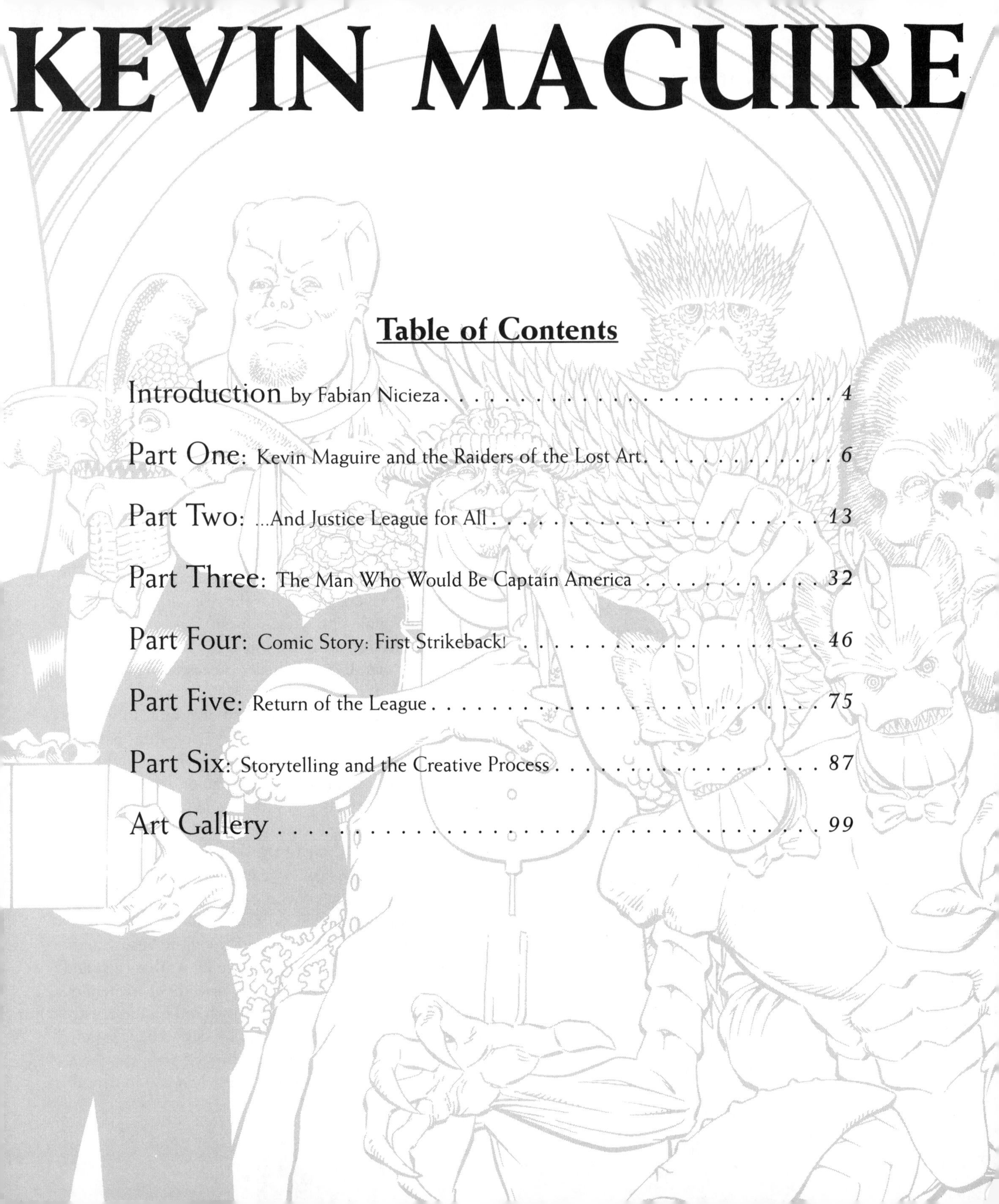

Table of Contents

Introduction by Fabian Nicieza 4

Part One: Kevin Maguire and the Raiders of the Lost Art 6

Part Two: ...And Justice League for All 13

Part Three: The Man Who Would Be Captain America 32

Part Four: Comic Story: First Strikeback! 46

Part Five: Return of the League 75

Part Six: Storytelling and the Creative Process 87

Art Gallery 99

Introduction

Genius Interrupted

When is it acceptable for commerce to cater to art? When is it understandable that art be asked to accede to commerce? We walk a very fine line in our industry. We always have, between art and commerce. Between the needs of the creator to create and the needs of the publisher to publish, there is often not just a fine line, but a very grand canyon.

But what if... all of that is just a smokescreen?

What if it's not in the least bit about art and commerce? What if, as good ol' Yoda once said, it's just a matter of, "Do or do not. There is no try."

And what does any of this have to do with Kevin Maguire?

Only in so much as it regards his life and his career.

I'm in a position to opine, since for twenty years—Jezus H. Christ, has it been that long?—Kevin's life and career have been very much intertwined with mine. We were young. We were poor. We worked at Marvel. We liked comics and movies and drinking after work with guys who liked comics and movies and girls who could care less, but were stuck with us because they worked at Marvel, too.

We have been friends and roommates, but we're not alike. We have very different mindsets and motivating forces. I am driven by insufferable ego, while he is stagnated by misplaced creativity. I type because I want to. He draws because he has to.

Kevin wants to be a film director, let's get that out in the open. He never really wanted to be a comic book artist. He doesn't have a passion for drawing—which is ironic considering his abilities are as much a gift from God as earned through formal training (which he has very little of). The "gift from God" line, coming from me, tells you how much I truly think of his talent, since I'm not much of a believer in God to begin with!

What does it mean that Kevin has spent the last twenty years of his life in a form of creative expression that fails to allow him to express himself creatively the way he really needs to?

It means he has been frustrated. It means that he has a hard time putting pencil to paper on a daily basis. It means his artistic output has suffered as a result, as has his earning potential.

And that's only part of the problem....

(It's so much fun psychoanalyzing one of your best friends in a public forum without his ability to interrupt you and tell you you're full of it.)

...the other part of the problem is that Kevin is a perfectionist, in a world that is imperfect. For an industry whose publishing requirements *demand* imperfection. A perfectionist who knows his work will be covered over by someone else in black India ink. A perfectionist who knows his panels and painstaking backgrounds will need to include word balloons and captions over them.

And what does that mean for Kevin? It means even when he does produce work—even when he does set a good, steady pace for himself—he is bound to be disappointed. It's a pretty vicious cycle, and yes, some might see some inherent nobility to that, some laudable pathos to the Greek tragedy, but I'm too close to the situation for that.

I see a friend I can't do enough to help. In fact, I'd guess that I've hurt him as often as I've helped in a wide variety of ways (never intentionally).

So we'll stay friends for the rest of our lives, I think... I certainly hope. We'll keep talking about movies and comics and things we'd like to do in comics and out. We have different priorities now. We're not quite young anymore. I have a family and the responsibilities suburbia burdens you with. Kevin doesn't have that. He has a dream of making movies. Hopefully, I'll be able to help him attain that dream. What're friends for, after all?

When you look through this book, look at his wonderful, magnificent, expressive art. Look at his panel compositions, his ability to draw just about anything under the sun (though he would rather draw black space with white stars between suns ;-) and marvel at what an incredible gift Kevin has.

I contend he is one of the best pure artists this industry has seen in the last 25 years. Certainly his style influenced an entire generation of artists to explore the possibilities of more photo-realistic art.

Look through this book and enjoy the beauty and emotion of his characters, but also know that each and every single image you see was not without tremendous effort. Each pencil line took its own toll on the artist.

If any comic book artist can be said to have suffered for his art, I think it is Kevin.

I think you need to know that when you look at this book.

But really, can this introduction *be* any more of a downer?

Cheer up, it's just comic books! And the new Bond movie kicked ass at the box office, so you know Kevin is happy about that....

(We go see a 1 p.m. showing the Friday *Casino Royale* opens up, we sit down in our seats at the Ziegfeld Theatre in Manhattan, and he looks at me and says, "I saw it last night. At a midnight show.")

...you see, one day, Kevin is going to be a director....

Fabian Nicieza
December 5, 2006

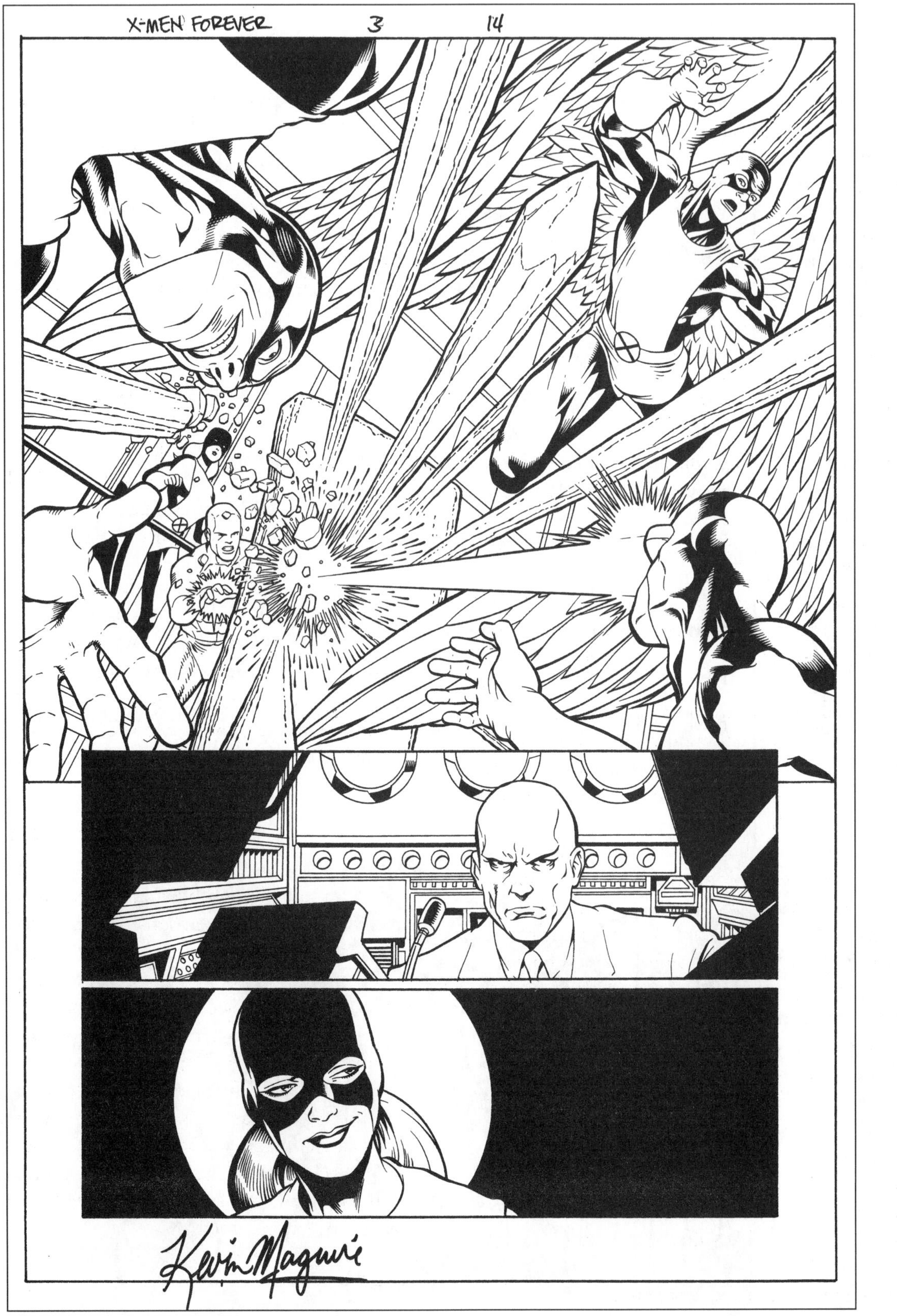
X-MEN FOREVER 3 14
Kevin Maguire

Part 1: Kevin Maguire and the Raiders of the Lost Art

Below: This recent line-up of Marvel characters includes a couple of Avengers along with a Defender—*The Defenders* being one of Kevin's all-time favorite books. **Next Page:** Take a super-hero comic, mix in a helping of the tongue-in-cheek eroticism of *Vampirella* and a dab of the monsters you'd find in the pages of *Creepy*, and you might get something like this scene from *Trinity Angels* #1.

MODERN MASTERS: Have you always kept a low profile, Kevin?

KEVIN MAGUIRE: I guess so. What do you mean by that?

MM: I was looking for material about you, and I didn't find many interviews.

KEVIN: Yeah. I don't go out and seek attention. I guess that means keeping a low profile.

MM: Where are you originally from?

KEVIN: New Jersey. I was born in Kearny, New Jersey. I lived there until I was, like, seven, and then moved to Edison, New Jersey, until I was 15, and then Long Island.

MM: What year were you born in?

KEVIN: 1960.

MM: Were you your parents' first child?

KEVIN: Yeah.

MM: Did you have other siblings?

KEVIN: Two brothers and a sister.

MM: What kind of household did you grow up in?

KEVIN: Ummm, more middle class. Semi-troubled, I guess. [*laughs*] I don't know how deep this interview is going to go.

MM: Who was the troublemaker in your family, you?

KEVIN: Oh, no, no, no, no, no. I was a hermit. My brothers used to tease me about it; they'd call me "the hermit."

MM: Right from early on you were into comics?

KEVIN: Yeah, pretty much.

MM: What kind of comics did you like? What was the one book that really sparked a connection?

KEVIN: Sparked a connection? I don't know that there was one in particular that sparked a connection.

MM: Were you more a Marvel fan or a DC fan?

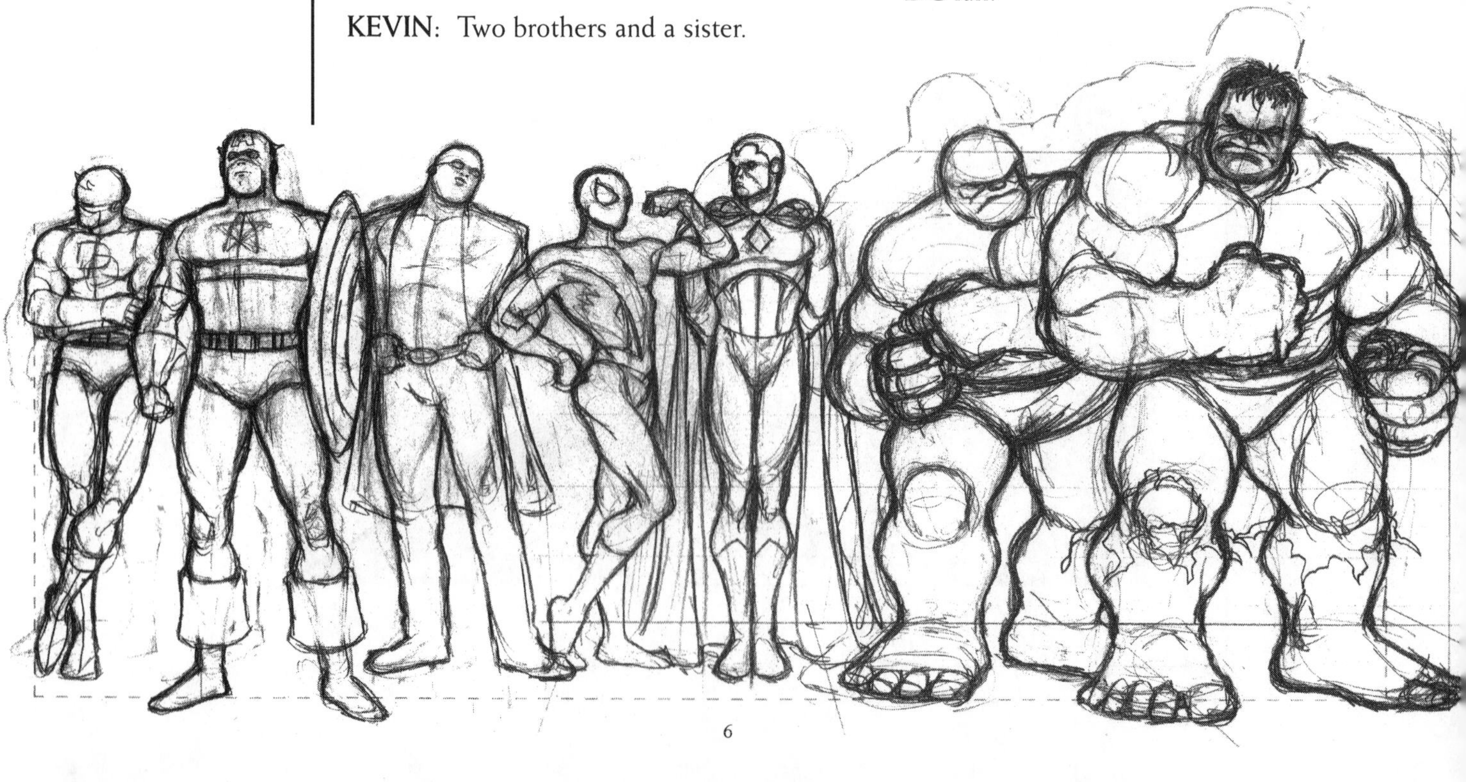

KEVIN: I was mostly into Marvel. I read pretty much all the stuff they put out. But I remember the Avengers/Defenders War was a monumental moment for me. You had to collect all the different issues of *Defenders* and *Avengers*. You had to buy both to keep up with the story, and I remember scrambling around to find that one issue that I couldn't find, and all that.

MM: About how old were when you started getting into comics?

KEVIN: I don't know. Early teens, I guess.

MM: What was all the rage back then? Neal Adams?

KEVIN: Well, yeah, Neal Adams was popular then. Barry Smith was starting to become popular.

MM: Was there a particular artist you'd gravitate to—a style that you liked more than the others?

KEVIN: I liked Frank Brunner. What was that guy's name who used to do *Vampirella*...? Esteban Maroto. Yeah, I remember *Vampirella* and *Creepy* magazine and stuff like that. I liked John Buscema's stuff when I was a kid.

MM: When you were in school were you starting to get inclined towards drawing?

KEVIN: Yeah.

MM: Had you always been artistically inclined?

KEVIN: Yeah, yeah.

MM: Who nurtured that?

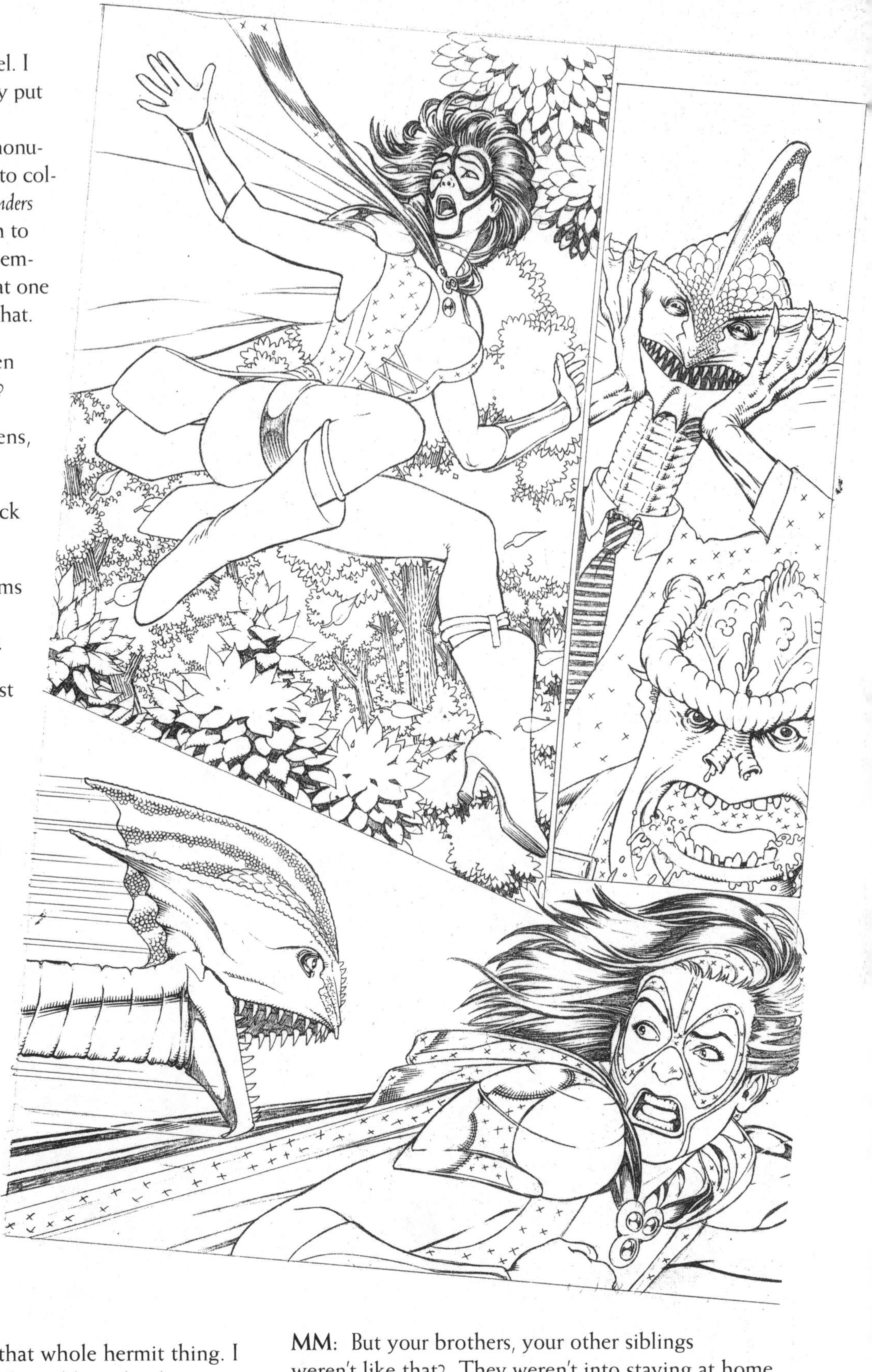

KEVIN: I think it was part of that whole hermit thing. I spent a lot of time in my room; I would just be drawing and stuff.

MM: Your parents just let you do your own thing?

KEVIN: I guess they encouraged it. I don't know how vociferously they were encouraging it. It wasn't like I was smoking crack and they were discouraging me from that.

MM: But your brothers, your other siblings weren't like that? They weren't into staying at home.

KEVIN: No, none of them wanted to do anything creative.

MM: And you weren't very athletic, I guess?

KEVIN: No, no.

MM: Did you have your own crowd that you would hang out with to talk about comics, or were you just all on your own?

KEVIN: I don't remember a lot of friends back then that were into comics. I don't remember having a lot of deep intellectual discussions around then. [laughs]

MM: Were you also becoming obsessive about film around this time?

KEVIN: Oh, yeah.

MM: That took a lot of your attention, as well?

KEVIN: Yeah, you could say that.

MM: What kind of movies were you into? Like, were you a horror buff, or just mainstream?

KEVIN: I liked horror, a big Bond fan, action... most of that kind of stuff.

MM: When you were a kid, what were you imagining that you would become? Did you aspire to be a filmmaker? Or a comic book artist?

KEVIN: Actually, wanting to be a filmmaker came a little bit later. When I was a kid I wanted to do comics. In my later teens I thought I preferred film.

MM: What was it about the medium of film that you like so much?

KEVIN: Visual storytelling. I just was fascinated by it. Which is why I don't like to do book illustrations or anything like that, I just like storytelling—visual storytelling.

MM: Would you imagine the type of films you wanted to do? I mean, would you actually write down storylines?

KEVIN: Yeah.

MM: Did you always keep a sketchbook handy in high school?

KEVIN: Well, not really. I just doodled a lot.

MM: Did you have a particular teacher when you were in high school who would push you, that liked your art? Was there anybody that really motivated you?

KEVIN: There was a teacher, Miss Viscardi, that I liked. She was fun. I don't know that she pushed me as much as kicked me in the ass when I needed it. And I kind of liked that. Not in an S&M kind of way, but sometimes I need the kick in the boot.

MM: When did you start working on your portfolio?

KEVIN: I can't really say I put together any sort of what one would call a portfolio. I just had a lot of unfinished things. I can't really say I had a portfolio.

MM: Did you consider going to art school after high school? You just went straight from high school to Marvel?

KEVIN: Well, no, I had jobs at shops like video stores and delis and places like that. I didn't go straight from high school to comics, no.

MM: How did you go about heading into that world, into Marvel and DC?

KEVIN: I don't know how old I was; I was in my twenties. Actually, I sent samples in to Marvel infrequently,

8

and there was one point where it took a long time for them to get back to me. I finally got a letter from Denny O'Neil saying that he thought he might have had something for me, but didn't, and blah, blah, blah. I don't know what year that was—it early to mid-80s—and up to that point, that was the closest I had gotten to actually getting into comics.

Then one night I was pulling an all-nighter with my buddies from the video store and the pizza parlor—this was when videos were just becoming popular, so we would stay up all night in the video store and bring over beers and stuff like that and watch whatever videos we wanted. Late in the night everyone was quite inebriated. They were telling me, "You're going to have to start banging on people's doors! They're not going to call you up and give you a job in comics! You have to go out there and grab it; you have to let them know you want it!" The next day I got a call from John Romita. [*laughter*]

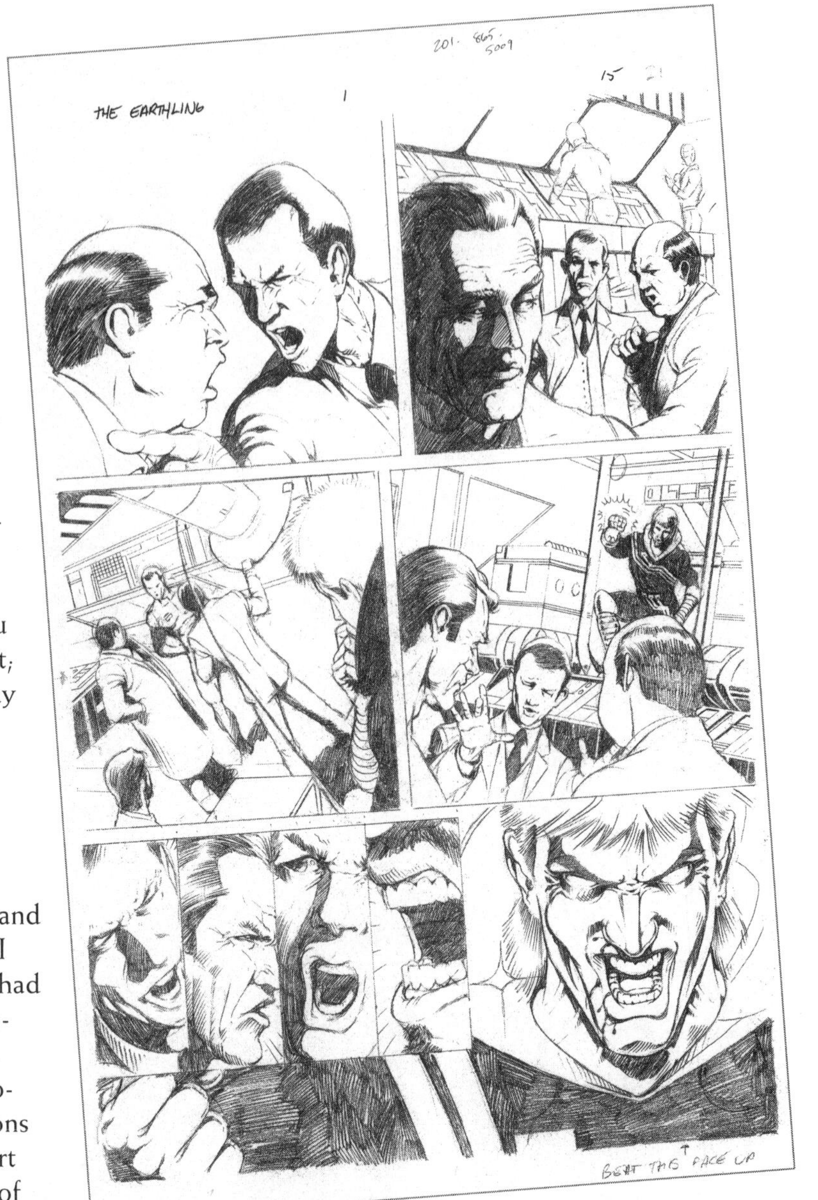
THE EARTHLING

MM: So when John Romita called, what happened? Did you show up the next day at Marvel?

KEVIN: Well, I don't know if it was necessarily the next day, but he called at, like, nine in the morning, and I had just hit the sack, so I was like, "What?" At first I thought it was someone pulling my leg. But, Marvel had the Romita's Raiders program where they hired people to work nine-to-five in the art corrections department to start getting the feel of comics—people who they felt had promise. And it was, I guess, minimum wage—I'm not sure. It wasn't high-paying at all, and I had to commute in and out of the city. At this point I was living in my own apartment, and I remember it was fairly tight, financially. And I was never really a good nine-to-fiver. Not commuting. I had to be on the train at, like, 7:30 in the morning to be there by 9:00. It was an interesting little experience.

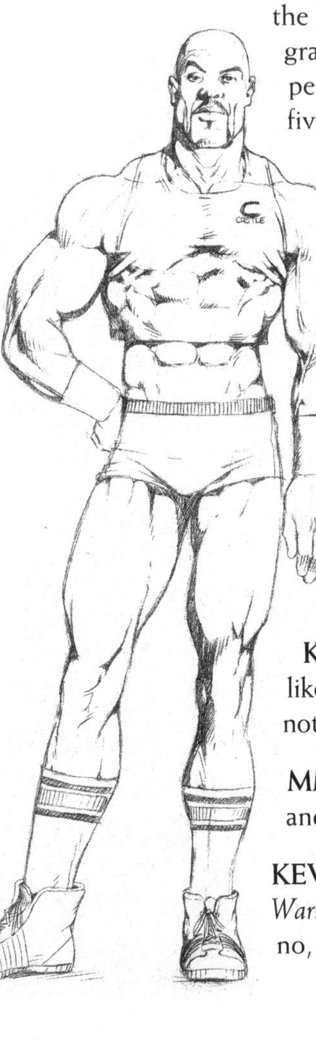

MM: What did John say to you? What was it that he liked about your samples?

KEVIN: Oh, I don't remember what he said about what he liked about it. At that point my mind was kind of swirling. I'm not sure exactly what it was about my stuff that he responded to.

MM: Did he personally teach you how to do art corrections and that sort of thing?

KEVIN: Yeah, he did. A lot of it was—for example, with *Secret Wars II* there was a character in the story that they'd say, "Oh no, we can't have it be that character." So this figure in the

Previous Page: While still serving in the Marvel Bullpen as part of the Romita's Raiders program, Kevin, along with Fabian Nicieza—who was working in the promotions department at the time—came up with a proposal for a comic entitled, *The Earthling*. Kevin even penciled a full issue on spec, of which this is page 2.
Left: One of *The Earthling*'s supporting cast.
Above: Page 15 of the unsold *The Earthling* #1.

THE EARTHLING

your own way?

KEVIN: It was what needed to be done, so that was the challenge. I was very, very hesitant to want to carry that over into my own stuff. I remember one of the guys there—it wasn't John, but one of the guys who had been there longer than me—would tell me, "All right, when you're drawing the hands, you have to draw the fingertips square." And I'm like, "Now, why would I be doing that? Maybe that's how *you* draw hands, and that's fine, that's your style, but that's not a helpful tip to me in terms of becoming a better artist. That's a tip to help make me draw more like you, which is not the goal." I was always looking for that line of what are you teaching me that makes my storytelling better versus what are you teaching me to make me draw with you, which I wasn't going to do.

MM: When were you there?

KEVIN: '85, '86—around there.

MM: And how quickly did you want to leave that job?

KEVIN: Oh, pretty quickly, yeah. Like I said, I was not a real nine-to-fiver and not into the whole everyday commute thing.

MM: And was it was kind of alienating, too, to be in that Marvel bullpen? I don't think a lot of those guys talked to each other. Or was it a friendly group?

KEVIN: No, it was okay. A lot of it all depends on the personality. I'm pretty low-key, quiet, until people get to know my style. I made some friends there.

MM: Who were some of the people you worked with that were Romita Raiders at that point?

KEVIN: I think Steve Geiger was either still there or had just left. Mark McKenna; Tom Morgan, I think. Was [James] Fry there before me? I think those are the people that were there around that time.

panel would have to be redrawn and then statted in. A lot of it was drawing like other artists so that no one could tell the difference—that kind of patchwork.

John would always give us tips about how to make the storytelling clearer or crisper, how to keep things clean, and stuff like that.

MM: Did you feel that you were competent as an artist, at this point? Did you feel comfortable drawing in somebody else's style when maybe you were just finding

MM: Did you see this as an opportunity, once you were there at Marvel, that you could show your work to the other editors?

KEVIN: Oh, yeah. That was the point of the whole program was they would pick people that they think had potential and give them an opportunity for their stuff to be shown while learning the tricks of the trade.

MM: Yeah, but you had to do the rounds on your own, right? I'm guessing that Romita wouldn't do this for you.

KEVIN: Occasionally he would. If something was needed, he would assign it to somebody in the group. That's how I got my first cover.

MM: Do you remember drawing that *Power Man/Iron Fist* cover? I can imagine that you were under a lot of stress having to do it.

KEVIN: It was extremely easy. It was a big close-up of Power Man's face pissed off. [*laughs*] You know, so it wasn't that tough.

MM: Every time I see it, it reminds me of how John Byrne used to draw Power Man. I don't know if you were using that as a reference or anything.

KEVIN: No, but I think that was one of those episodes where people were coming in and telling me to draw things in a certain way. Yeah, I remember feeling like, "Okay, it's not exactly me, but I have a comic book cover! So who cares?"

MM: What did your parents make of all this, once you started getting more serious about comics?

KEVIN: Well, my father passed away when I was younger, but my mother was proud.

MM: Do you remember showing her that first *Power Man* cover?

KEVIN: Yeah, yeah.

MM: "I'm in print!"

KEVIN: Oh, yeah.

MM: Was any part of this experience overwhelming?

KEVIN: It's like any sort of new experience, where you're coming into the city and you're working at the big office.... I'm trying to remember that first day of saying, "Hi, I'm an employee of Marvel Comics," and getting buzzed through the door. That must have been a pretty special moment.

MM: Working under John Romita must have been pretty cool.

KEVIN: Oh, yeah.

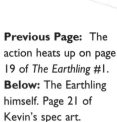

Previous Page: The action heats up on page 19 of *The Earthling* #1. **Below:** The Earthling himself. Page 21 of Kevin's spec art.

The Earthling ™ and ©2007 Fabian Nicieza & Kevin Maguire.

more freewheeling, a lot less corporate, so it was a much more casual atmosphere.

MM: Because when I was at Marvel it seemed that the art corrections guys hung together, and the colorists are a separate group.

KEVIN: Yeah, that's just cliques like in anything.

MM: It seemed to me like the editors and assistant editors didn't talk to those guys. I thought it was strange that you and Fabian developed a friendship.

Above: Artwork for the Garokk bio in *The Official Handbook of the Marvel Universe*. Kevin drew several entries throughout the series, thanks to Joe Rubinstein, who was one of Kevin's early champions.

Next Page: More early work for Marvel—this one of GI Joe's leader, Hawk. Inks by Joe Rubinstein.

MM: And he was a good teacher, I guess?

KEVIN: And a great guy. He's just the sweetest guy in the world. He really is.

MM: So you met Fabian Nicieza at Marvel early on? He was already there when you started?

KEVIN: Yeah. He was working in the promotional department.

MM: Oh, he was still trying to become a writer at that point?

KEVIN: Yeah, he was trying to get in. While I was a Romita Raider, we were actually putting together a comic book proposal called *The Earthling*. He would describe these characters and I'd do the drawings of them and stuff like that. It never went anywhere.

MM: How exactly did you two meet?

KEVIN: Well, I think he was friends with Mark McKenna. People were always wandering around. Back then Marvel was a lot

KEVIN: Fabian wasn't an editor. Fabian was—

MM: Even the Marvel sales guys seemed to look down on everybody.

KEVIN: Well, I don't know. I don't know. I would assume Fabe saw in me the same thing he saw in himself: someone who was about to start a career, you know, who was on the launching pad to do so.

MM: In those early days at Marvel, could you see yourself working on *X-Men* at some point? Is that what you wanted to do?

KEVIN: Oh, sure, sure.

MM: Well, did you try?

KEVIN: Not specifically, no. I mean, you're probably gleaning from this whole conversation that I wasn't the most aggressive guy as far as seeking out the work. The opportunities generally kind of fell to me or came to me.

Part 2: ...And Justice League for All

MM: So how did you get to DC?

KEVIN: While you were killing time at the office, in between assignments, you'd do your own little drawings and stuff. Kurt Busiek saw me doing—was it Kurt or Joe Rubinstein? I don't know, but one of them saw me drawing something and suggested me for a book at DC Comics called *Wildcard*, which I still have. I think it was Kurt. I think Joe was trying to get me other stuff, but it was Kurt that got me an interview with Andy Helfer up at DC. I went up there and I showed Andy my stuff and he essentially gave me the gig.

MM: What kind of reaction did you get when people saw your work the first time? Because it wasn't from the John Buscema school; it was more subtle.

KEVIN: Well, maybe. I did do a monthly book for two years.

MM: I notice that you take a lot of time to show the characters moving around. It's not like you're jumping from panel to panel.

KEVIN: Oh, a lot of that is the scripts I get, too, where they're sitting around strip malls and talking for hours on end.

MM: What kind of reaction did you get about your art from editors? "This isn't going to work in comics."

KEVIN: No, they were always fairly positive. I wasn't in Romita's Raiders for that long; it was only a few months. I think I broke the record for getting out of there the quickest. [*laughs*] For someone who wasn't actually banging on doors looking for work, it didn't take me too long to start getting jobs.

Oh, right, Joe was getting me the [*Official Handbook of the*] *Marvel Universe* figures—that's right. I was doing several of those.

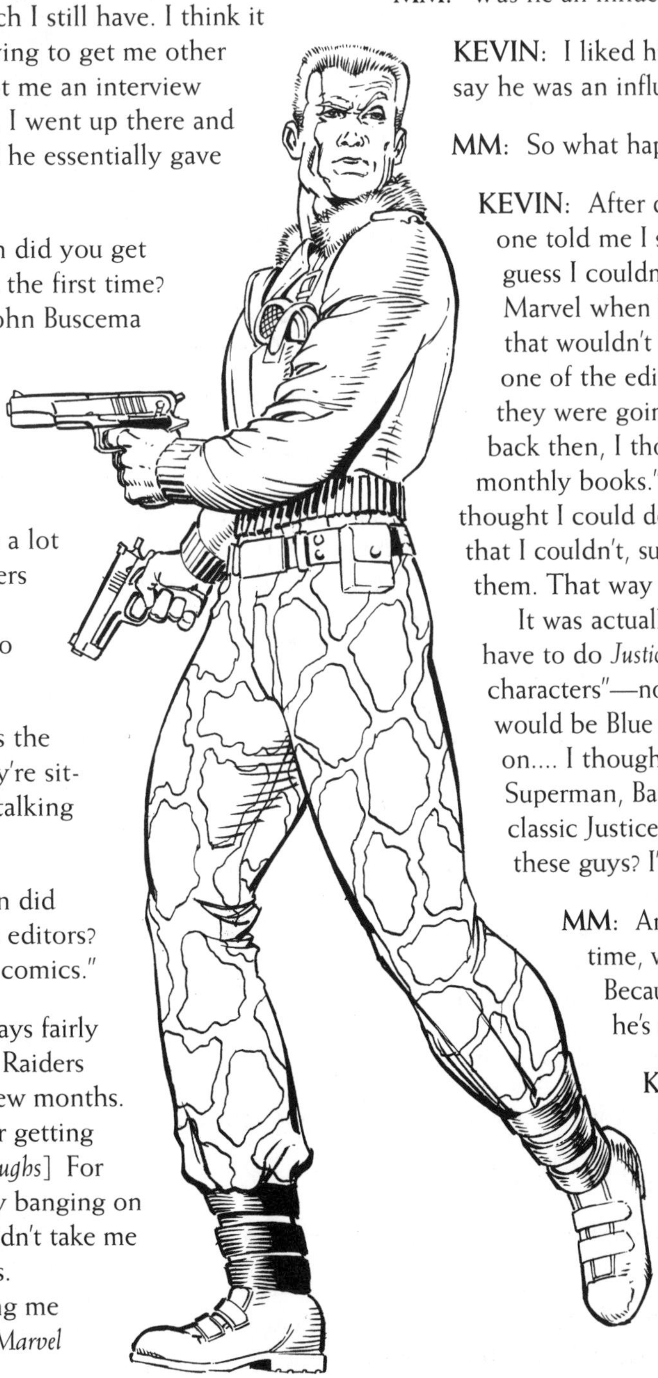

MM: When I look at your artwork, especially from back then, it reminds me a lot of the stuff Paul Smith was doing.

KEVIN: Yeah, I've heard that.

MM: Was he an influence?

KEVIN: I liked his stuff, but I wouldn't actually say he was an influence.

MM: So what happened with *Wildcard*?

KEVIN: After doing the first issue, I think someone told me I should show it around Marvel. I guess I couldn't have still been working at Marvel when I penciled the book for DC—that wouldn't have been right. But at that point one of the editors offered me *Silver Surfer*, which they were going to relaunch. And silly as I was back then, I thought, "Well, I can do two monthly books." [*laughter*] I laugh now. But I thought I could do both. Andy Helfer, knowing that I couldn't, suggested that I do *Justice League* for them. That way I would stay over there.

It was actually Fabian Nicieza who said, "You have to do *Justice League*. There are all the cool characters"—not knowing at the time that it would be Blue Beetle, Booster Gold, and so on.... I thought going in, "Oh, cool! Hawkman, Superman, Batman, and Aquaman! Flash! The classic Justice League!" Then it was, "Who are these guys? I've never heard of these guys."

MM: And meeting Andy for the first time, was that an interesting experience? Because he seems a little out there, but he's one of the best editors DC had.

KEVIN: He's a character, yeah.

MM: Did you trust him right away?

KEVIN: I don't really recall having any sort of *dis*trust of him. I thought he was on the up-and-up.

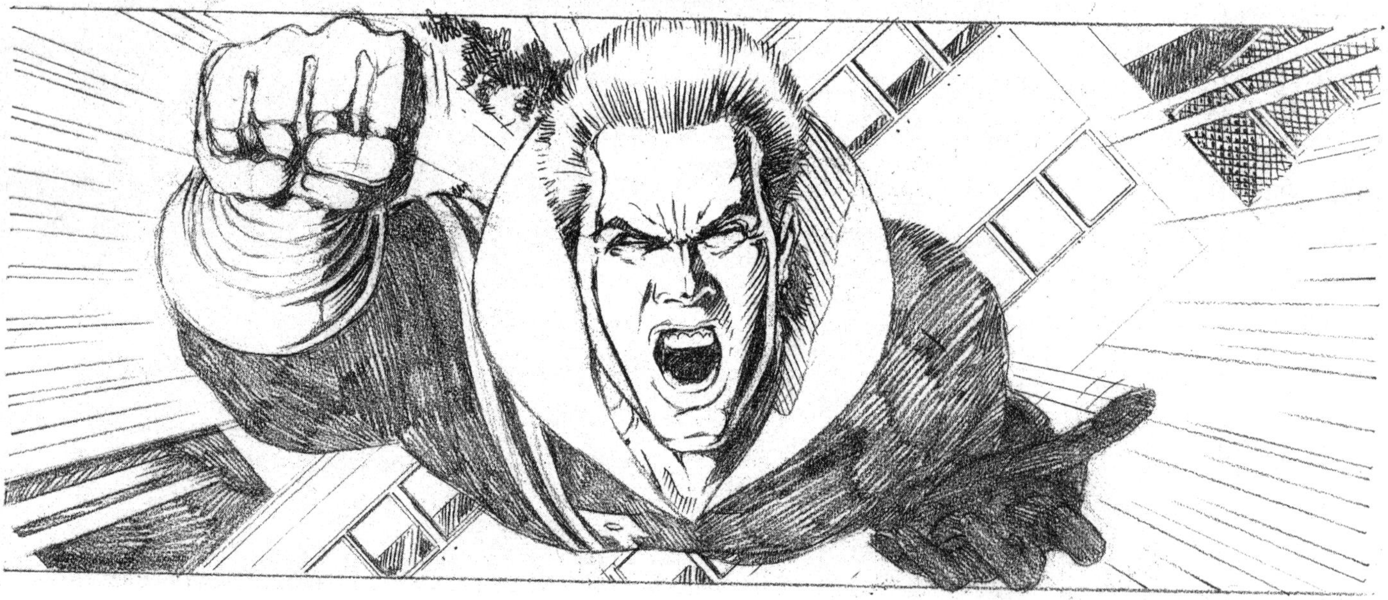

Above: This panel from page 6 of *Wildcard*, shows a similar design to The Earthling, which Kevin had just recently been drawing. **Below and Right:** Kevin's early character designs for Wildcard. Doug Richter is the alter ego of the title hero. At right are love interest, Carrie Brooke; the conniving Vivian Harding; and bad guy, Gentleman Jack. **Next Page:** Page 12 of *Wildcard* #1.

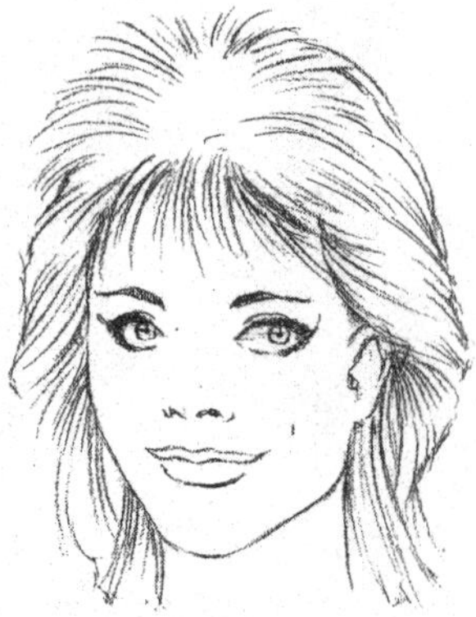

MM: He seems like a really easygoing guy. He's not what you expect in an editor; you expect somebody serious and poker-faced.

KEVIN: Yeah, but for comics? At Marvel the editors had their own offices, and they would decorate them in weird, funky ways, so I didn't look at editors as these imposing school principal sort of characters. They were geeks with jobs.

MM: Yeah, I'm sure, but most artists are not completely trusting of them. They're the editors, and they stick together.

KEVIN: No, I didn't have any of those sorts of conceptions going on.

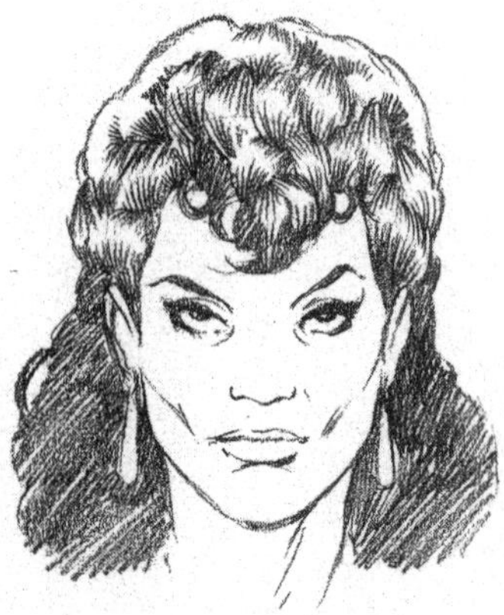

MM: That's funny. I got that vibe right away from some editors: a "you don't know what these guys are saying about you behind your back" type of thing. It always seemed to me that writers and artists were kind of weary of their editors.

KEVIN: Well, I think you get that over time. Maybe I was just a little Pollyanna about the whole thing. I encountered that kind of stuff later, but not up to that time, no.

MM: So *Wildcard* never came out?

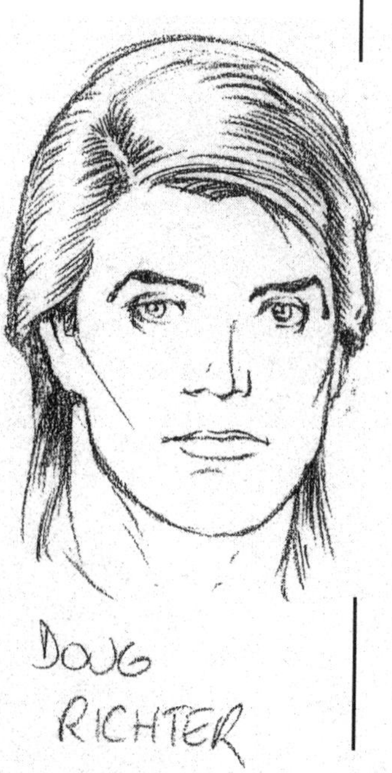
DOUG
RICHTER

KEVIN: No, I think a legal problem came about because there was also the series of super-hero books called *Wild Cards*. [*Note:* Wild Cards *was an anthology book series, edited by George R.R. Martin, consisting of stories by various science-fiction and fantasy authors, some of which were adapted by Marvel into comic book format in the early '90s.*]

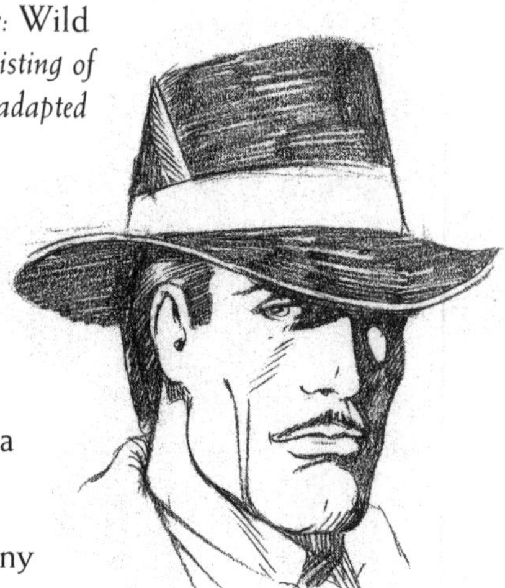

MM: What kind of character was Wildcard?

KEVIN: You know, a teenager gets super-powers.

MM: Did you design it?

KEVIN: In heavy conjunction with everyone else. I wasn't in a position to be given free rein.

MM: Did Andy like what he saw right away, or did he have any complaints? Did he like what he saw in those pages?

KEVIN: Well, yeah. Enough to give me *Justice League* #1. I have to assume so, because if he didn't, he could have just said, "Hey, go and do *Silver Surfer*. Have fun."

MM: Did you have any regrets in not doing that *Silver Surfer* book?

KEVIN: Only in the fact that I looked at the book and the first five pages or so were just big, empty shots of space—and he got *paid* for that? [*laughter*] He got paid the same amount I did for drawing roomfuls of people?

MM: How seriously did you consider going to film school?

KEVIN: I was never a very good student in high school, so I didn't really. I'm, like, major league ADD—at the time no one really knew what it was—and focus has always been a problem. So I would have liked to, but I didn't really pursue it that heavily. I looked into it, but I didn't follow through with it.

MM: Once, there was blip in the DC news bulletin that mentioned you took some time off to work on a film.

KEVIN: What that was, was a friend of mine in a mutual film class got money to make an independent film, so I took a month off to help him out with it—you know, be on the set every day. So it was just to make one little independent film, that's what I took the time off for.

MM: Do you remember in what sort of place you were when the *Justice League* book came to you?

KEVIN: No. First off, I've never done well financially, so let's get that out of the way right off the bat. Where was I?

MM: In terms of yourself, where were you emotionally?

KEVIN: I'm always struggling.

MM: But you were ready for the monthly book? You thought you were ready?

KEVIN: Well, I did it, you know, for a couple years. For the most part.

MM: When Andy asked you about doing the book, what type of deadline did he give you? How much time was there between getting the job and doing the actual work?

KEVIN: Well, not long. Actually, I think there was a lag time, but I'm not sure why. Maybe it was because they were still formulating the book. But I did a Deadman origin story, for *Secret Origins*.

MM: With Andy.

KEVIN: Yeah, Andy was the writer. I remember him giving me that as something to do to kill time until *Justice League* was ready.

MM: Terry Austin remembered seeing your work for the first time and he was really attracted to it. Andy assigned *Justice League* to him and it took three months just to see the book get lettered. He said they just gave him pencils and then he inked it. He prefers the pages to be lettered before he inks, so this might have been a sign that the script wasn't ready or something. It annoyed him a little bit, because he likes to work around the lettering.

KEVIN: So do I.

MM: Do you remember what was going on? Were they just trying to find the tone of it or something?

KEVIN: I don't know. That was so long ago.

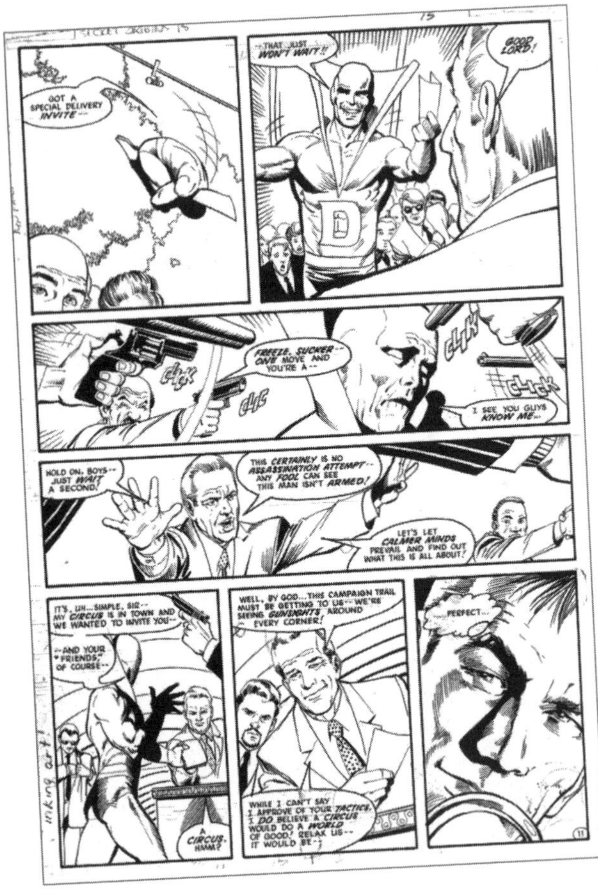
GOT A SPECIAL DELIVERY INVITE--
--THAT JUST WON'T WAIT!!
GOOD LORD!
FREEZE, SUCKER--ONE MOVE AND YOU'RE A--
I SEE YOU GUYS KNOW ME...
HOLD ON, BOYS--JUST WAIT A SECOND!
THIS CERTAINLY IS NO ASSASSINATION ATTEMPT--ANY FOOL CAN SEE THIS MAN ISN'T ARMED!
LET'S LET CALMER MINDS PREVAIL AND FIND OUT WHAT THIS IS ALL ABOUT!
IT'S, UH...SIMPLE, SIR--MY CIRCUS IS IN TOWN AND WE WANTED TO INVITE YOU--
--AND YOUR "FRIENDS," OF COURSE--
A CIRCUS. HMM?
WELL, BY GOD...THIS CAMPAIGN TRAIL MUST BE GETTING TO US--WE'RE SEEING GUNSIGHTS AROUND EVERY CORNER!
WHILE I CAN'T SAY I APPROVE OF YOUR TACTICS, I DO BELIEVE A CIRCUS WOULD DO A WORLD OF GOOD! RELAX US--IT WOULD BE--
PERFECT...

That was 20 years ago. Maybe Helfer knows, but I don't. You know, everybody has different memories. It's *Rashomon*. We all remember things a little differently. But I don't remember it at all, so.... [*laughter*]

MM: There was a lot of build-up. Was Andy treating this like it was going to be a big event?

KEVIN: Well, it was a relaunching of their little franchise, there, so there was certainly promotional value to it.

MM: And there was no pressure for you?

KEVIN: I don't recall any more pressure than, you know, any other job. I thought my career was over. [*laughter*] I remember I was going to a party that Howard Chaykin was having, and I was talking to an editor, Greg Weissman. He and I were talking there—and this was some time before the issue came out. Once again, I said, "It's ridiculous, it's silly." [*laughs*] "You know, it's not the big super-hero characters. This is going to be a bomb."

MM: But you believed in this thing a little, didn't you?

KEVIN: No, not really. Not really.

MM: Were you living at Fabian's house in New Jersey there for a time?

KEVIN: Yeah. It was around that time. It was for a year around that time, so.... I know the book came out while I was living there.

MM: He said that the book wasn't his cup of tea.

KEVIN: Yeah, yeah. That's fine. I didn't write it, so I don't take credit. The comedic success of it is the work of the writers and the editor. I understand that some people don't like that style, and I understand that.

MM: How were you pitched in terms of working on the book? Right from the beginning they told you were going to work over Giffen's layouts?

KEVIN: Yeah.

MM: Did that present any problem for you?

KEVIN: No, not really. I thought, "All right, I gotta learn something here." I do remember that there was a fight—I don't know if it was

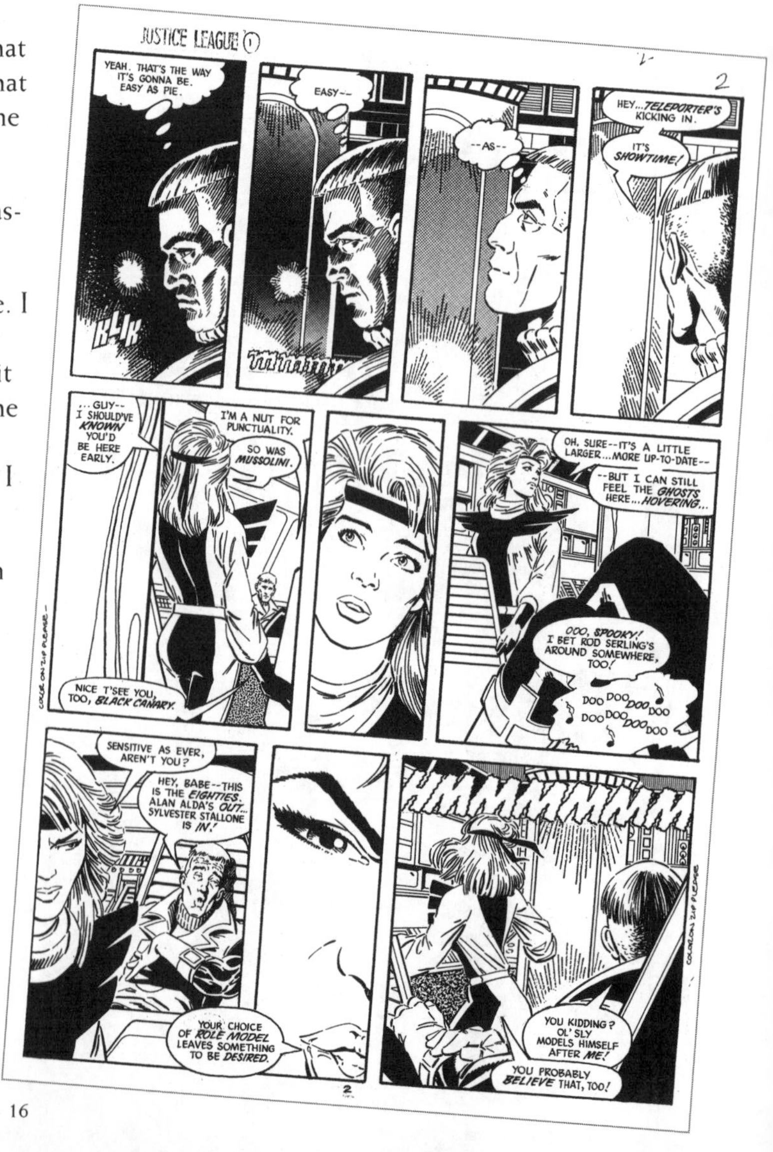
JUSTICE LEAGUE 1
YEAH. THAT'S THE WAY IT'S GONNA BE. EASY AS PIE.
KLIK
EASY--
--AS--
HEY...TELEPORTER'S KICKING IN.
IT'S SHOWTIME!
...GUY--I SHOULD'VE KNOWN YOU'D BE HERE EARLY.
I'M A NUT FOR PUNCTUALITY.
SO WAS MUSSOLINI.
NICE T'SEE YOU, TOO, BLACK CANARY.
OH, SURE--IT'S A LITTLE LARGER...MORE UP-TO-DATE--
--BUT I CAN STILL FEEL THE GHOSTS HERE...HOVERING...
OOO, SPOOKY! I BET ROD SERLING'S AROUND SOMEWHERE, TOO!
DOO DOO DOO DOO DOO DOO DOO DOO
SENSITIVE AS EVER, AREN'T YOU?
HEY, BABE--THIS IS THE EIGHTIES. ALAN ALDA'S OUT... SYLVESTER STALLONE IS IN!
YOUR CHOICE OF ROLE MODEL LEAVES SOMETHING TO BE DESIRED.
HMMMMMMM
YOU KIDDING? OL' SLY MODELS HIMSELF AFTER ME!
YOU PROBABLY BELIEVE THAT, TOO!

Above: Page 11 of Kevin's "Deadman" story from *Secret Origins* #15. Inks by Dick Giordano. **Right:** The new League is introduced, even though it wasn't who Kevin was particularly hoping for. Pages 2 and 3 of *Justice League* #1. Inks by Terry Austin. **Next Page Top:** In *JL* #4, Kevin had the opportunity to orchestrate Booster Gold's fight scene himself.

issue four or five—where Booster Gold first shows up and he fights the Royal Flush Gang [*Justice League #4*], and there's the sequence where he's fighting the Royal Flush Gang alone. I think that was one of the first things I got to lay out myself, because I really wanted to do the action sequence myself. I remember having a particular pride in that.

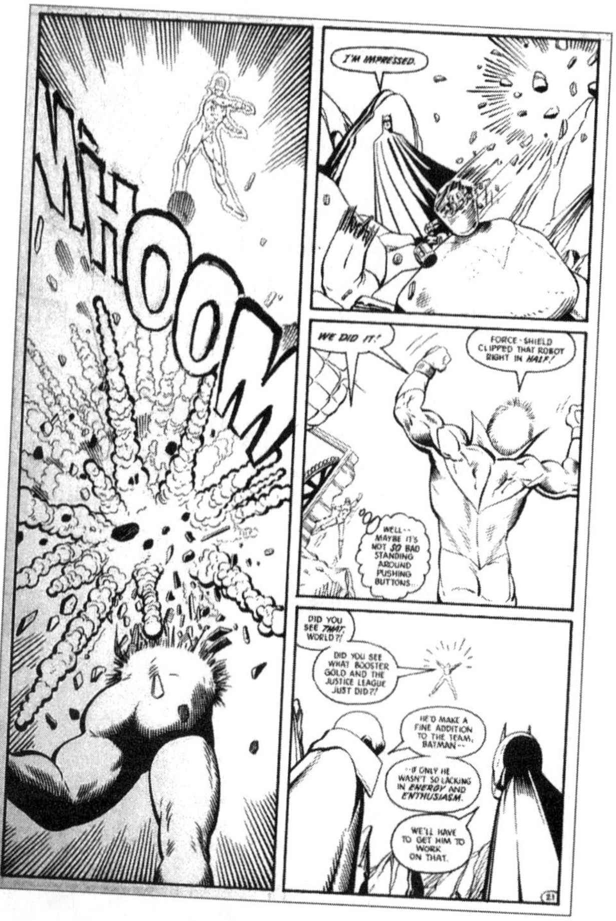

WHOOOM
I'M IMPRESSED.
WE DID IT!
FORCE-SHIELD CLIPPED THAT ROBOT RIGHT IN HALF!
WELL-- MAYBE IT'S NOT SO BAD STANDING AROUND PUSHING BUTTONS...
DID YOU SEE THAT, WORLD?!
DID YOU SEE WHAT BOOSTER GOLD AND THE JUSTICE LEAGUE JUST DID?!
HE'D MAKE A FINE ADDITION TO THE TEAM, BATMAN--
--IF ONLY HE WASN'T SO LACKING IN ENERGY AND ENTHUSIASM.
WE'LL HAVE TO GET HIM TO WORK ON THAT.
21

MM: Was it an advantage working over Giffen's layout?

KEVIN: Ummm... I suppose so. I mean, it was early in my career, so it was the old veteran helping the new guy along. I don't think it was a hindrance by any stretch of the imagination. It wasn't like I was forced to do that for my entire career.

MM: But you didn't feel trapped by the time you got to the end? By the time you left the series with issue #24.

KEVIN: Oh, no, by that time I had been given more free rein. It wasn't like that for the entire run. I mean, the main reason that was done was less to sort of guide me and more because at that point Keith was a penciler and didn't tell stories verbally, he told them visually, which is why DeMatteis was doing the dialogue. Giffen would just, rather than write, you know, "Superman walking across a room," he would draw little stick figures, and that's how he communicated that. So, I mean, it wasn't just me that was getting the layouts. Anyone doing a *Justice League* book was getting those layouts, because that's how Keith "wrote" at that time. Then he became more proficient at writing, and now he's a full script kind of guy.

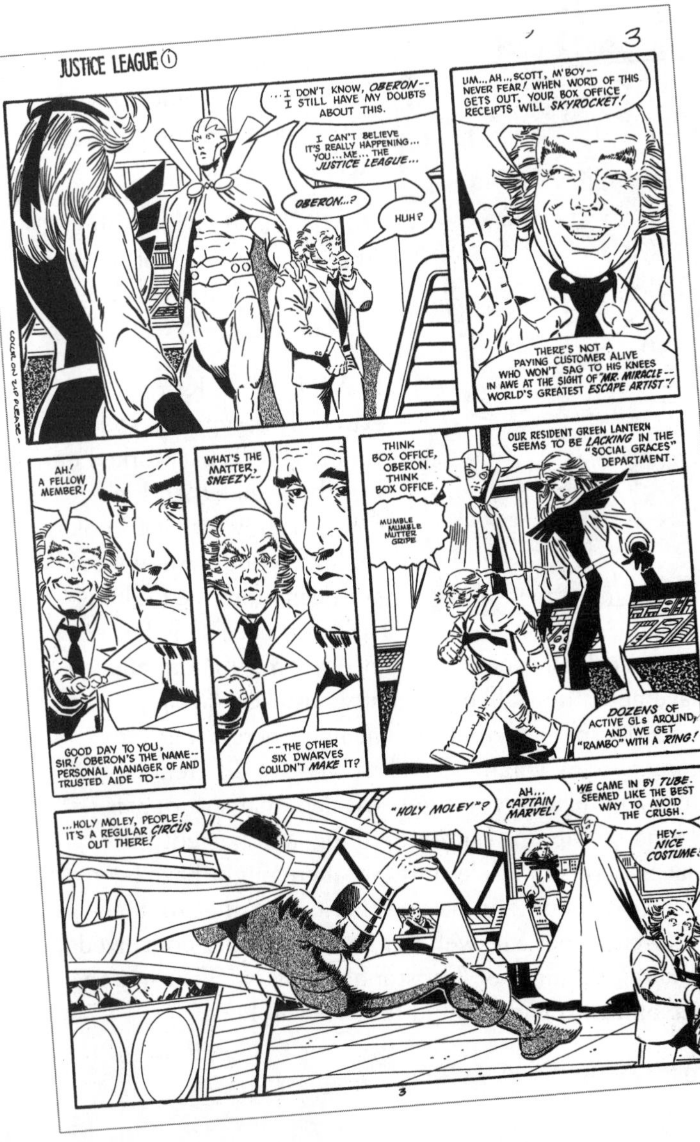

JUSTICE LEAGUE ①
3
...I DON'T KNOW, OBERON-- I STILL HAVE MY DOUBTS ABOUT THIS.
I CAN'T BELIEVE IT'S REALLY HAPPENING... YOU... ME... THE JUSTICE LEAGUE...
OBERON...?
HUH?
UM...AH...SCOTT, M'BOY-- NEVER FEAR! WHEN WORD OF THIS GETS OUT, YOUR BOX OFFICE RECEIPTS WILL SKYROCKET!
THERE'S NOT A PAYING CUSTOMER ALIVE WHO WON'T SAG TO HIS KNEES IN AWE AT THE SIGHT OF "MR. MIRACLE-- WORLD'S GREATEST ESCAPE ARTIST"!
AH! A FELLOW MEMBER!
GOOD DAY TO YOU, SIR! OBERON'S THE NAME-- PERSONAL MANAGER OF AND TRUSTED AIDE TO--
WHAT'S THE MATTER, SNEEZY--
--THE OTHER SIX DWARVES COULDN'T MAKE IT?
THINK BOX OFFICE, OBERON. THINK BOX OFFICE.
MUMBLE MUMBLE MUTTER GRIPE
OUR RESIDENT GREEN LANTERN SEEMS TO BE LACKING IN THE "SOCIAL GRACES" DEPARTMENT.
DOZENS OF ACTIVE GLs AROUND, AND WE GET "RAMBO" WITH A RING!
...HOLY MOLEY, PEOPLE! IT'S A REGULAR CIRCUS OUT THERE!
"HOLY MOLEY"?
AH... CAPTAIN MARVEL!
WE CAME IN BY TUBE. SEEMED LIKE THE BEST WAY TO AVOID THE CRUSH.
HEY-- NICE COSTUME!

MM: Did you see the full script or did you just get Keith's plot most of the time?

KEVIN: Mostly I just got Keith's plot, which I'm not really too keen on that system. I like to know what the characters are going to say.

MM: Would you have to talk to him sometimes just to figure out what was going on in those drawings?

KEVIN: Well, at that time I was actually working in Andy Helfer's office. That's part of the reason why I got a monthly book on this; he set up a drawing table next to his desk, so I would come in every day and sit there and draw. If I would get up, he'd say, "Sit down. Get back to work." [*laughter*]

MM: So you had to punch the clock?

KEVIN: Well, not, a check in, nine-to-five sort of thing, but for me it was good that I got out of the house rather than sitting in the apartment all day. I got to interact and make friends up there, so, you know, I liked that.

MM: But that must have felt strange. Did you feel any pressure having Andy stare at you, waiting for you to work?

KEVIN: No, not really. I mean, the pressure that comes with any deadline, I suppose. But I welcomed the opportunity to.... The thing is, it changed at Marvel and DC. It became more corporate, and they just started cracking down, saying, "You know what? Freelancers are not allowed to work in here anymore for insurance reasons. They're not actual employees." Otherwise I'd go up there and work all the time, given the opportunity, because like I said, it's just....

1ST ISSUE!
A RETURN TO GREATNESS FOR THE ALL-NEW
JUSTICE LEAGUE
1
75¢
CAN. $1.00
U.K. 40p
MAY 87
STORY BY GIFFEN & DeMATTEIS
ART BY MAGUIRE & AUSTIN
WANNA MAKE SOMETHIN' OF IT?
THE HISTORY OF THE DC UNIVERSE is must reading

MM: More nurturing.

KEVIN: Well, not nurturing as much as there are people around. It's not sitting alone and....

MM: ...wandering or something?

KEVIN: Yeah.

MM: [*laughs*] How long did this go on, working in the office?

KEVIN: A couple of years.

MM: How did you get Al Gordon to ink your stuff?

KEVIN: That was Andy Helfer.

MM: Did you have any say in that?

KEVIN: No. I'm sure I was given a look at samples of stuff, but I trusted his opinion on it, because I didn't know who was out there inking and what their styles were and all that stuff.

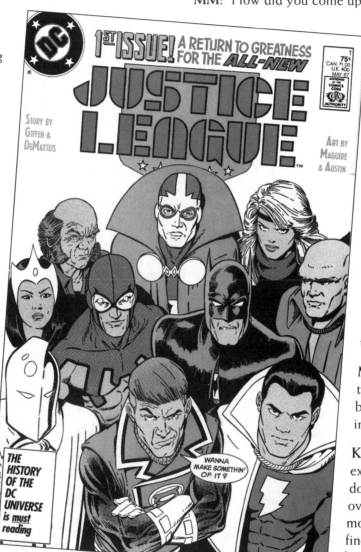

MM: But you didn't have any problems when you saw the results?

KEVIN: No, not really, not any more than usual. A lot of times there were—I get a lot of cross-eyes. That drives me nuts sometimes. Like, if eyes are drawn too close together or something, it looks like they're... "That's not how I did it!"

MM: Do you remember seeing the first issue completed? Were you thinking that you could have done better? Were you satisfied?

KEVIN: Gee, I don't know. I can't remember the first time I actually held that issue in my hand. I'm sure there was some joy and satisfaction.

MM: When you got this gig, you weren't in the mindset of "I'm going to draw 200 issues of this" were you?

KEVIN: No, not at all.

MM: How did you come up with that cover design for issue one?

KEVIN: Oh, that was probably Helfer. I'm sure a lot of people weighed in on that. It was *Justice League* #1, so there was going to be some concern about what the cover looked like. But I would imagine, again, there's probably a lot of people involved with that—the art directors and all that stuff, everyone throwing out ideas—but I don't remember who exactly it was that came up with the concept of the characters looking up.

MM: Was there anything that Keith might not have been happy with, or Andy, in your pages?

KEVIN: Well, Keith is extremely easygoing, so he doesn't get all that worked up over things like that. He's more, "Yeah, whatever. Looks fine." If anybody, Andy would have been more focused on changes, if necessary. But I don't recall any specific instance where.... There might have been things like continuity mistakes. "Well, his costume doesn't have that." I remember there being something about Captain Marvel having two different costumes—one where he's got that flap, that sort of *Star Trek II* kind of flap, the button-up thing; and he's got the regular Superman muscle shirt. So, there might have been concerns about that, but nothing that springs to mind.

I remember Maxwell Lord was originally conceived as along the lines of Christopher Walken. That was the person Keith had in mind for Maxwell Lord.

MM: Who did you use?

KEVIN: I ended up using Sam Neill.

MM: That is him.

KEVIN: The first issue I was thinking Christopher Walken. The second issue—it was around the time where they were trying to decide who was going to be the next James Bond, and it was between Timothy Dalton and Sam Neill. And considering Maxwell Lord was supposed to be this sort of sinister guy, I was thinking of Sam Neill from the *Omen* movie.

MM: That's what he looks like. I was going to say that, that he looks a lot like Neill looked in *Omen III*.

KEVIN: In one panel, I actually used Sam Neill as a reference, which is why I don't like using known people as reference—"Is that supposed to be him? Is that supposed to be him?" But for one panel I actually drew him off from a picture of Sam Neill. The rest was all off that sort of template.

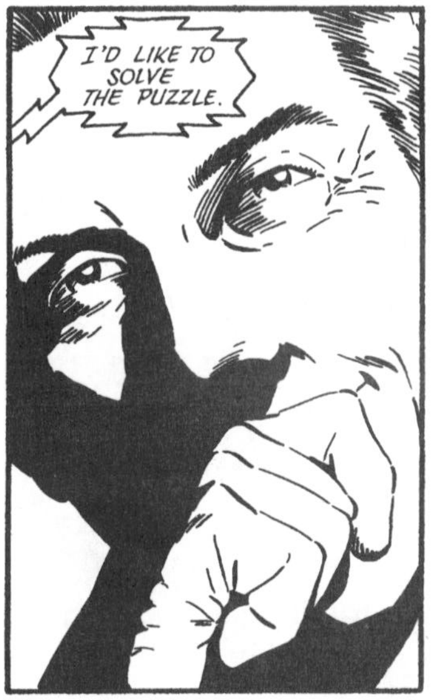

I'D LIKE TO SOLVE THE PUZZLE.

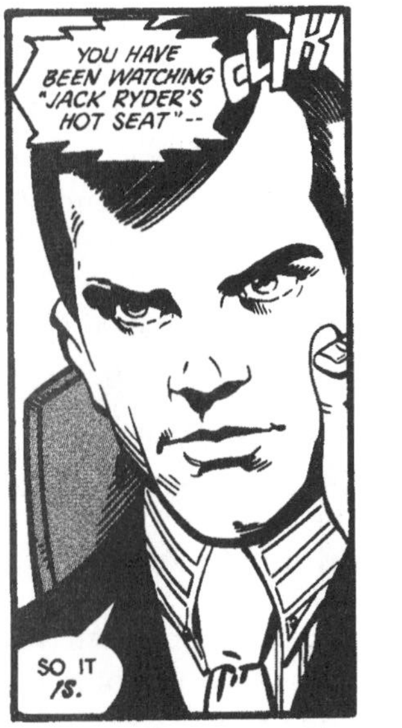

YOU HAVE BEEN WATCHING "JACK RYDER'S HOT SEAT"--
CLIK
SO IT IS.

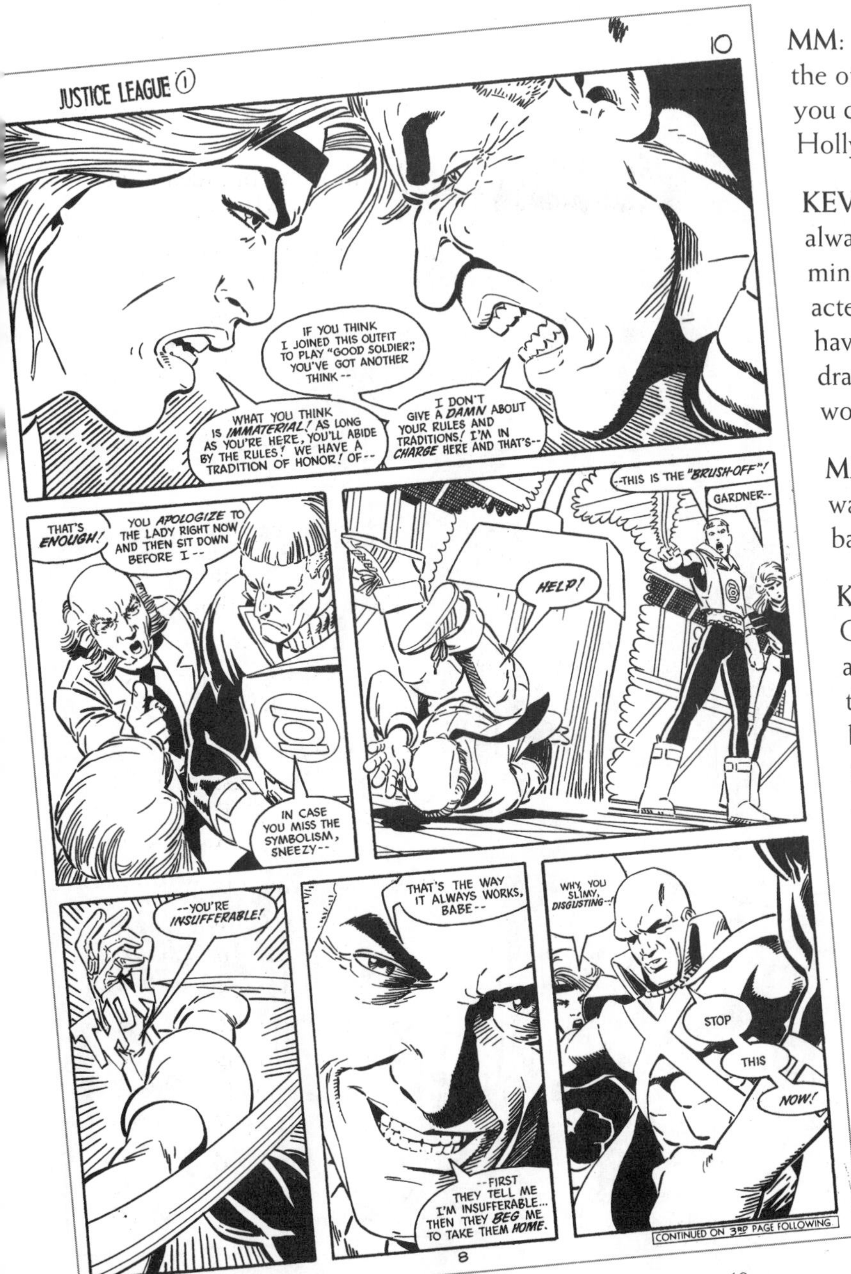

10
JUSTICE LEAGUE ①
IF YOU THINK I JOINED THIS OUTFIT TO PLAY "GOOD SOLDIER", YOU'VE GOT ANOTHER THINK --
WHAT YOU THINK IS IMMATERIAL! AS LONG AS YOU'RE HERE, YOU'LL ABIDE BY THE RULES! WE HAVE A TRADITION OF HONOR! OF--
I DON'T GIVE A DAMN ABOUT YOUR RULES AND TRADITIONS! I'M IN CHARGE HERE AND THAT'S--
THAT'S ENOUGH!
YOU APOLOGIZE TO THE LADY RIGHT NOW AND THEN SIT DOWN BEFORE I --
IN CASE YOU MISS THE SYMBOLISM, SNEEZY--
--THIS IS THE "BRUSH-OFF"!
GARDNER--
HELP!
--YOU'RE INSUFFERABLE!
THAT'S THE WAY IT ALWAYS WORKS, BABE--
--FIRST THEY TELL ME I'M INSUFFERABLE... THEN THEY BEG ME TO TAKE THEM HOME.
WHY, YOU SLIMY, DISGUSTING--!
STOP
THIS
NOW!
CONTINUED ON 3RD PAGE FOLLOWING
8

MM: Did you do that for the other characters? Did you cast them from Hollywood types?

KEVIN: I don't do that. I always have people in my mind for some of the characters, but I don't actually have photos of them to draw from, because that wouldn't work for me.

MM: Guy Gardner, who was your Guy Gardner based on?

KEVIN: Well, Guy Gardner, I mean, he's actually more attitude than any particular actor, but if I were to cast one actor, the person I always had in my mind was John Cassavetes from *The Dirty Dozen*—his Franco character. That to me was Guy Gardner!

MM: How do you get all those expressions in your art? Do you usually work with a mirror close by or something?

Previous Page: Regarding the cover design for *Justice League* #1, Editor Andy Helfer says, "I guess you could say Kevin and I designed it—I gave him a sketch of circles showing the angle of the shot. The slight down-shot with the characters looking up—the angle, I figured, would make the characters seem more human and less traditionally heroic. Levitz made me change the original word balloon, which had Guy Gardner saying 'Big deal.' Levitz felt it was, uh... disrespectful to the characters. Personally, I thought it conveyed the idea of the series a lot better than the tough-guy second choice." **Above:** Max Lord in his Christopher Walken look from issue #1, and his Sam Neill/*Omen III* look from issue #2. **Left:** Guy shows his true colors right off the bat. *Justice League* #1, page 10. Inks by Terry Austin.

KEVIN: No. I just imagine it as I'm working on it. I mean, a lot of times I'll notice that, as I'm penciling it, my face is making—like, if Guy is scrunching up his nose, I'm scrunching up my nose. I'm not looking at myself, but I'm kind of doing it. [*laughter*] So when I'm drawing in public, I look ridiculous.

MM: Could you tell these stories were going to be so dialogue heavy?

KEVIN: Well, it wasn't dialogue heavy back then, because Andy Helfer cut out a lot of dialogue.

MM: He did?

KEVIN: Oh, yeah. It wasn't that dialogue heavy until the last couple of mini-series. That's where I really noticed it.

MM: That's interesting. I thought that they lightened up in the newer books. If you look at the first seven issues of the regular series, and then you look at issue #8 and #9, with #8 and #9 you could see a lot more of the artwork—it's more open. Do you remember if was that a conscious decision from Andy, to allow you breathing room?

KEVIN: I don't know. I would imagine the first few issues were more establishing things, and then later on they're given to more action, so there would probably be less dialogue.

MM: But the artwork was a lot better; you had bigger panels, you could do more. By the time that you got to the "Millennium" crossover issue, you could really see your style.

KEVIN: Yeah, I don't know why. It's the evolution of a creative process. If you look at the first couple episodes of *Seinfeld*, they're like, "Eh, they're okay," but then you see it later on, "Okay, now they're—". I guess it's finding your groove?

MM: But at the same time you still get fans coming up saying, "Oh, you're best stuff was your first issue."

KEVIN: No, they've never said that, my "best stuff."

JUSTICE LEAGUE INT.
VE-RY, VE-RY QUIETLY--
PICK
UP
THE
DOOR!
UH...SO SORRY FOR INTERRUPTING... WE...AH... WE...UM--
WE HAD THE WRONG ADDRESS?
RIGHT! RIGHT! WE HAD THE WRONG ADDRESS!
'BYE, NOW!

AH--THERE YOU ARE! SO DARK I CAN HARDLY--
GOT IT-- I THINK--ON THE TIP OF MY FINGERS! IF I CAN JUST--
HMM! NOW IT FEELS LIKE SOME KIND OF FUR! IT--
YEOW!
WONK
GAK!
GLK-KK...
21

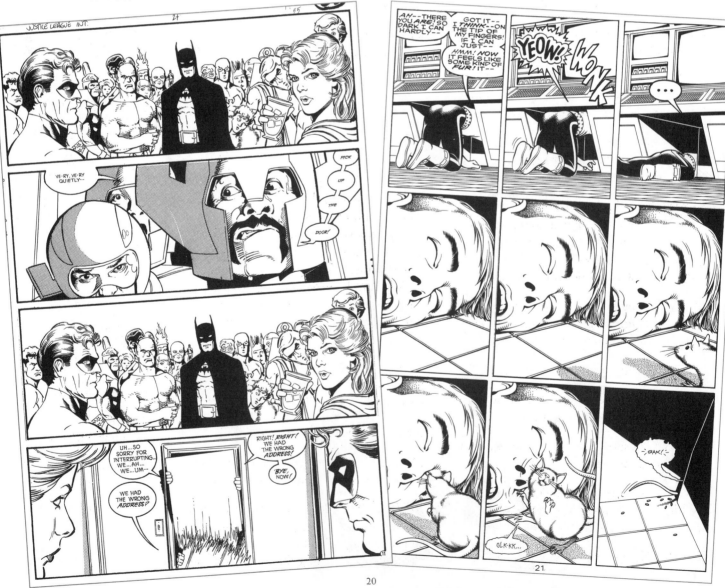

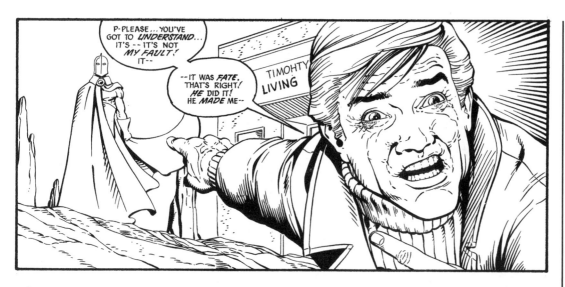

P-PLEASE... YOU'VE GOT TO UNDERSTAND... IT'S -- IT'S NOT MY FAULT! IT--
--IT WAS FATE, THAT'S RIGHT! HE DID IT! HE MADE ME--
TIMOHTY
LIVING

Previous Page: The gags in *Justice League* often relied more on Kevin's artwork than on the dialogue. Inks by Joe Rubinstein (left) and Karl Story (right).
Left: The Gray Man tries to pin the rap on Dr. Fate. Inks by Al Gordon.
Below: Captain Marvel pencils from *Justice League* #5.

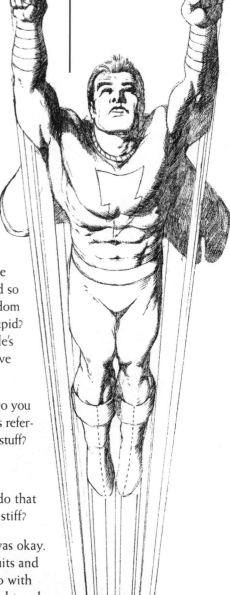

Maybe it's what they remember the most, but I wouldn't call it my best stuff.

MM: Were you close with your inkers, like when Al Gordon was inking you, or Joe Rubinstein?

KEVIN: No, Al was in California.

MM: But you didn't talk on the phone or anything?

KEVIN: No, no. I'd try to have the attitude of, "Well, it's out of my hands, it's out of my hands. It's someone else's responsibility now."

MM: You would get excited, I guess, when you'd see the inked pages coming in, since you were in Andy's office?

KEVIN: Yeah, but, again, you're looking at someone's impression of you, so sometimes you're like, "That didn't capture what I was looking for," and sometimes—I'd have to say not often—"Wow, it's better than I expected."

MM: Did you enjoy the "country club" aspect of *Justice League*, these super-heroes hanging out and talking and bickering?

KEVIN: I had no problem with that.

MM: Did you ever find yourself cracking up while you were drawing these?

KEVIN: I'm sure there were times where I found things amusing.

MM: Were there ever things that you couldn't wait to draw? Maybe the scene when Batman punches out Guy?

KEVIN: No, no one had any idea. It's just one of those things; no one had any idea that that would resonate with people. It was just someone punching out a character in a comic. That happens all the time.

MM: But they were fellow super-heroes on the same team.

KEVIN: I remember a lot of debates about certain things, like when Guy Gardner became a nice guy. We let that go on way too long. [*laughter*]

MM: I think it lasted about a year!

KEVIN: I remember being frustrated by it. I always had debates with Andy Helfer about Captain Marvel, because we'd argue about Captain Marvel being played so naïve. I'd say, "S stands for the wisdom of Solomon? How can he be so stupid? He has the wisdom of Solomon. He's not 'Hazam'." So, there were creative differences.

MM: Would you act out scenes? Do you have any photographs of yourself as reference? Did you ever do that kind of stuff?

KEVIN: I tried that later on.

MM: Did you find it difficult to do that and keep your art from becoming stiff?

KEVIN: Umm, no, I thought it was okay. I mean, a lot of it was people in suits and stuff like that, so that's easier to do with photographs—getting the folds right and

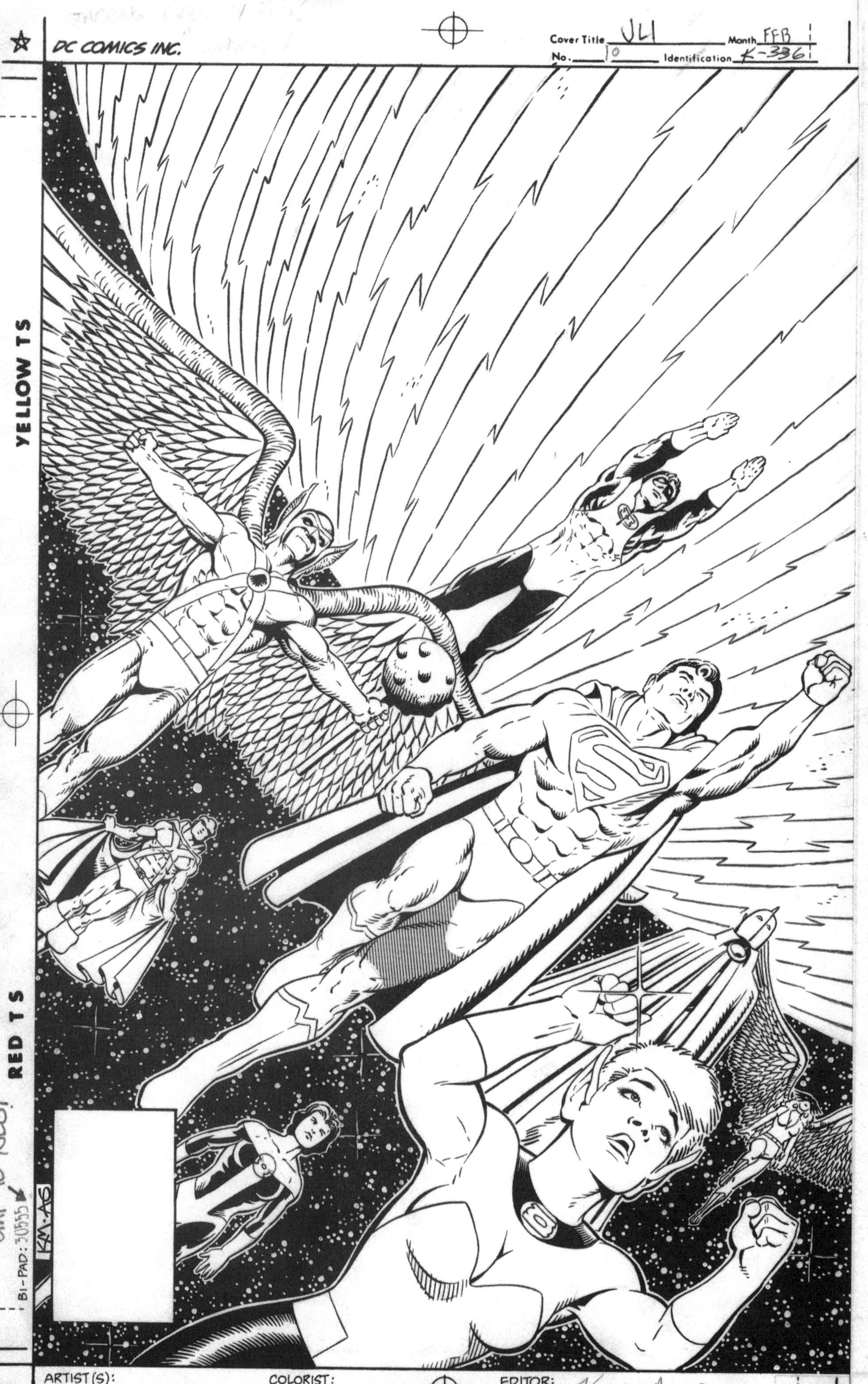
DC COMICS INC.
Cover Title JLI Month FEB
No. 10 Identification K-336
YELLOW TS
RED TS
STAT TO NEG!
BI-PAD: 30555
KM-AG
ARTIST(S):
COLORIST:
EDITOR:
Kevin Maguire

all that. I suppose I should use more photos. I just bought that computer program, Poser. Do you know what that is?

MM: Is that the one with the figure that you can move around however you want?

KEVIN: Yeah, but they have a ton of figures. They also have a ton of poses you can start with. Like, there's a comic book section, so you'll have every comic book pose a character could have: punching, kicking, flying, shooting. You can move the camera anywhere you want, you can move the lighting any way you want. I've been playing with that just recently. But I don't usually use photos, no.

MM: Have you ever used action figures for moving these guys around? Say, if you've got ten super-heroes that you want to have in interesting poses?

KEVIN: No, no.

MM: Composing group shots never presented a challenge? Like, "What am I going to do to make this interesting," when you've got the whole Justice League in one panel?

KEVIN: Well, yeah, yeah. I mean, you always want it to be visually interesting, but I don't know that photos or action figures helped in clearing that up.

MM: [*laughs*] I was thinking of Alex Ross. I think he does that a lot; he uses action figures, to move them around and pose.

KEVIN: I thought he uses reference for everything.

MM: He does.

KEVIN: You know, I have mixed feelings about that, because in some ways I feel like it's cheating. It's like tracing, you know? I remember seeing that *Anastasia* animated movie, and they shot actors doing these things and they just traced them onto the cells and called that animation. Animation should come out of your head. That should be it: imagination—like Chuck Jones.

MM: That's what you think of as a comic book artist: A guy with a board and some pencils and a blank piece of paper in front of him.

KEVIN: Yeah. I can see how it definitely helps, but I remember when I was a kid being kind of amused and distracted by *Master of Kung Fu*, when Paul Gulacy would have Sean Connery and Marlon Brando and David Niven and Bruce Lee. Sometimes it takes you out of the experience, because you're like, "Oh, that's a picture of Bruce Lee from this movie," or, "Oh, that's Sean Connery from this movie."

MM: It's like when you see a *Star Wars* comic and they keep swiping the same pictures from the publicity stills.

KEVIN: Yeah, it looks nice, but to a degree it takes you out of the reading experience. To me it does.

MM: What was your favorite aspect of working on the book? Do you have any fond memories of working with Andy or Keith?

KEVIN: Umm, dollar beer night—I remember that being a fond memory of working on *Justice League*. [*laughter*] No, it was nice. It was a little family community at DC. I'd go up there all the time and had a lot of friends there. It was a nice experience.

Previous Page: Cover art for *Justice League International* #10. In the top left corner of the page is written, "Starring Gregory Peck as Superman." Inks by Al Gordon.
Below: Panels from *Justice League International* #17 featuring a rather animated fellow in his own right—the Green Lantern, G'nort.

WHAT IS IT WE'RE DOING AGAIN, COMRADE BARDA?
HOOKING MY POWER WAND INTO THE SHIP'S WARPDRIVE.
AND WHY ARE WE DOING THIS?
THE WAND HAS BOOM TUBE CAPACITY--
BOOB TUBE?
BOOM TUBE! A UNIQUE STYLE OF INTER-SPATIAL TRANSPORTATION CREATED BY METRON HIMSELF.
THIS SHIP ISN'T CAPABLE OF GOING INTO HYPER-DRIVE... BUT THE WAND IS THE NEXT BEST THING.
HELL -- IT'S TEN TIMES BETTER!
WHAT IS IT WE'RE DOING AGAIN?
OH... NEVER MIND!

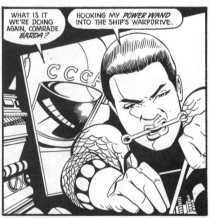

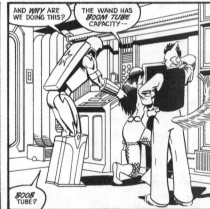

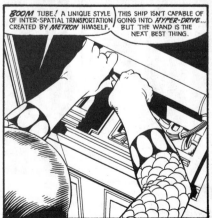

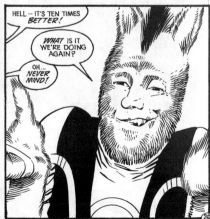

Below: Batman makes a dramatic entrance. Opening splash page from *JLI* #16 with inks by Al Gordon. **Next Page Top:** Kevin takes on Superman. Page one of *Superman* #177. Inks by Cam Smith. **Next Page Bottom:** Cover layout for *Green Lantern* #18.

MM: Along with that, you got a lot of respect from fans pretty quickly, too. The instant you started the series.

KEVIN: Yeah, I kind of got out there pretty quick.

MM: Did it ever go to your head?

KEVIN: No, I'm not—I have too many self-esteem issues for that.

MM: Did you ever tell Andy, "I want to take over Batman," or anything like that?

KEVIN: No, no. If anything, I was threatening to go the other route. It's like, "I'm just going to give it up and go back to making pizza." Helfer will tell you that. He's always holding that over my head.

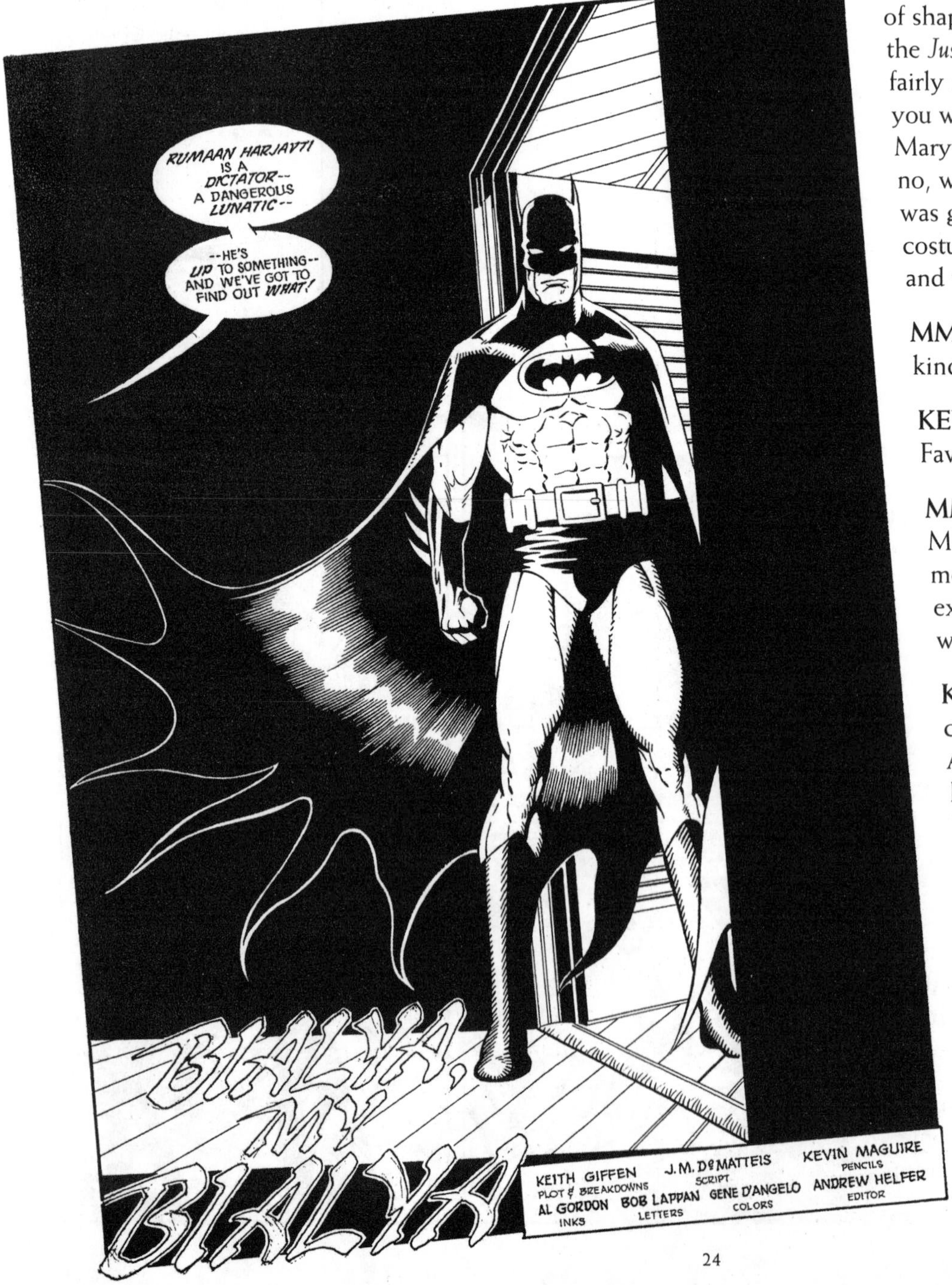
RUMAAN HARJAVTI IS A DICTATOR-- A DANGEROUS LUNATIC--
--HE'S UP TO SOMETHING-- AND WE'VE GOT TO FIND OUT WHAT!
BIALYA, MY BIALYA
KEITH GIFFEN PLOT & BREAKDOWNS
J.M. DeMATTEIS SCRIPT
KEVIN MAGUIRE PENCILS
AL GORDON INKS
BOB LAPPAN LETTERS
GENE D'ANGELO COLORS
ANDREW HELFER EDITOR

MM: Now, Andy was nurturing wasn't he?

KEVIN: Yeah, yeah, yeah.

MM: Was he the best editor you ever had?

KEVIN: Ummm....

MM: Was he the most patient one?

KEVIN: Well, every editor who works with me has to be patient. [*laughter*] That's just a given. Yeah, I guess so. I guess he was the best. You know, it was early in my career and he was very hands-on in terms of shaping the whole thing. You know, for the *Justice League* mini-series I was given fairly free rein. Two mini-series, whatever you want to do. Keith wanted to have Mary Marvel lose her virginity. Well, no, no, we're not going to do that. I mean, he was going to have her wearing her white costume, and then she loses her virginity and wears the red one. [*laughter*]

MM: I thought DC liked doing that kind of stuff nowadays?

KEVIN: Well, maybe not with Fawcett characters. [*laughter*]

MM: Did you try to bring a lot of the Marvel sensibility to your work? To me, your work was visually more exciting than the rest of what DC was doing at that time.

KEVIN: I wouldn't have known to consider it a kind of Marvel style. Again, a lot of it was following Keith's layouts, so, I mean, I didn't have that much latitude in terms of layouts.

MM: When I was a kid I always thought that DC's stuff was kind of stiff and boring, and it seemed like this was a much looser book, more fun—just like reading an issue of *Spider-Man*.

KEVIN: Well, again, a lot of that was Helfer. A lot of that was agreeing to that tone.

MM: Did you ever talk about, say, "We've got to change the way DC is perceived with this book?"

KEVIN: Do you mean an editorial decision?

MM: Yeah.

KEVIN: Oh, I don't know what the decisions were between Helfer and the other DC editors in terms of which direction this book would go. I mean, the only thing I knew was that we weren't allowed to have certain characters because there was more reverence with them.

MM: But eventually you got all those guys. You had Superman pop up and Hal Jordan and characters like that.

KEVIN: But those were "Millennium" crossovers. They had to be there. That was the only time Superman was in the book while I was on.

MM: Were the royalties good on this book?

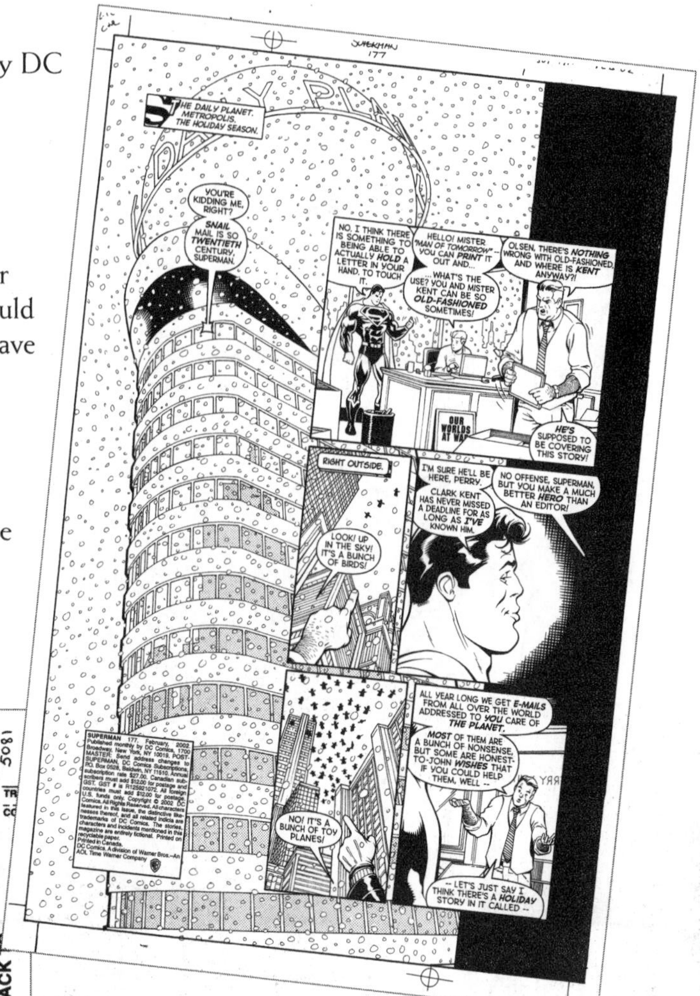

SUPERMAN
177
THE DAILY PLANET. METROPOLIS. THE HOLIDAY SEASON.
YOU'RE KIDDING ME, RIGHT?
SNAIL MAIL IS SO TWENTIETH CENTURY, SUPERMAN.
NO, I THINK THERE IS SOMETHING TO BEING ABLE TO ACTUALLY HOLD A LETTER IN YOUR HAND, TO TOUCH IT.
HELLO! MISTER "MAN OF TOMORROW"-- YOU CAN PRINT IT OUT AND...
...WHAT'S THE USE? YOU AND MISTER KENT CAN BE SO OLD-FASHIONED SOMETIMES!
OLSEN, THERE'S NOTHING WRONG WITH OLD-FASHIONED. AND WHERE IS KENT ANYWAY?!
HE'S SUPPOSED TO BE COVERING THIS STORY!
OUR WORLDS AT WA
RIGHT OUTSIDE.
LOOK! UP IN THE SKY! IT'S A BUNCH OF BIRDS!
I'M SURE HE'LL BE HERE, PERRY.
CLARK KENT HAS NEVER MISSED A DEADLINE FOR AS LONG AS I'VE KNOWN HIM.
NO OFFENSE, SUPERMAN, BUT YOU MAKE A MUCH BETTER HERO THAN AN EDITOR!
NO! IT'S A BUNCH OF TOY PLANES!
ALL YEAR LONG WE GET E-MAILS FROM ALL OVER THE WORLD ADDRESSED TO YOU CARE OF THE PLANET.
MOST OF THEM ARE A BUNCH OF NONSENSE, BUT SOME ARE HONEST-TO-JOHN WISHES THAT IF YOU COULD HELP THEM, WELL --
-- LET'S JUST SAY I THINK THERE'S A HOLIDAY STORY IN IT CALLED --

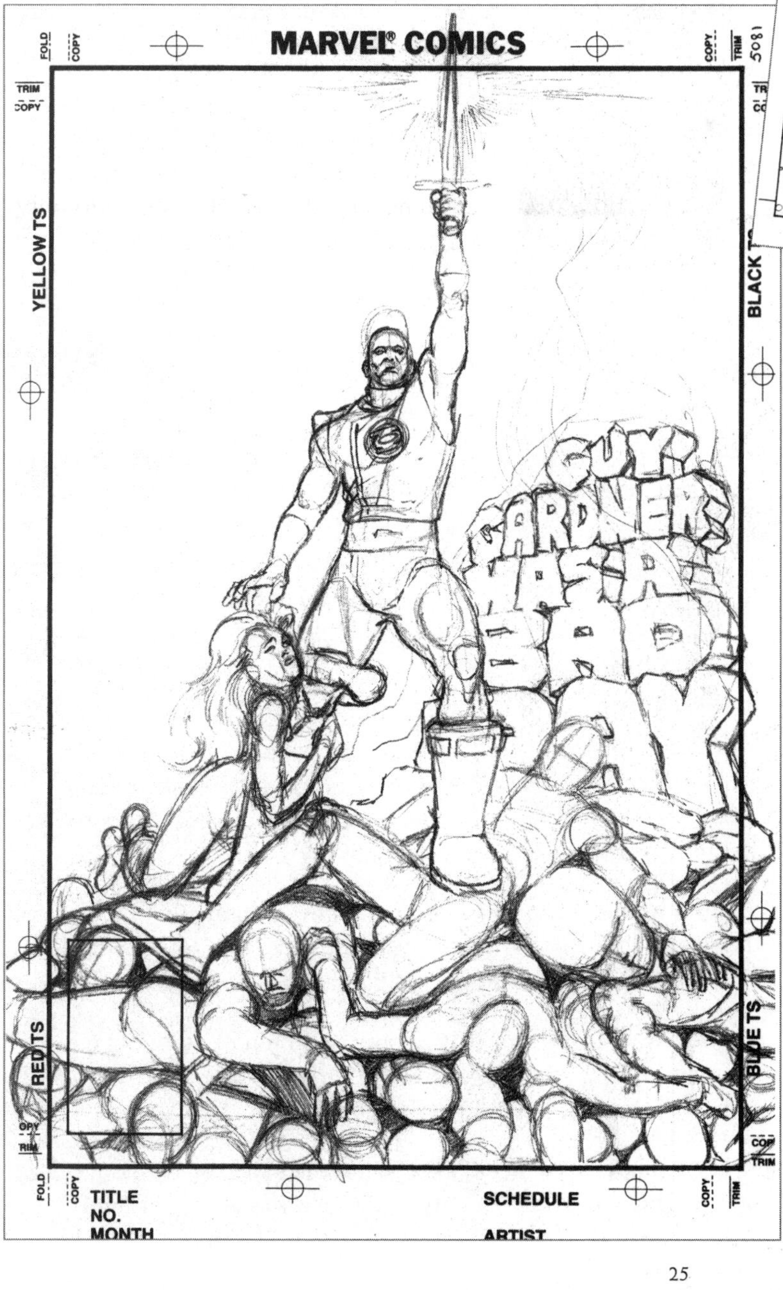

MARVEL® COMICS
YELLOW TS
BLACK TS
RED TS
BLUE TS
TITLE
NO.
MONTH
SCHEDULE
ARTIST

KEVIN: For the time they were, yeah. In fact, the first issue sold, like, 180,000, which nowadays people would be going nuts for.

MM: Did you make character sheets for yourself—style sheets?

KEVIN: No.

MM: So how did you separate each character for yourself and keep them consistent? You know, their little personal quirks and characteristics?

KEVIN: I don't know that I was 100% successful in that department.

MM: I think you were. You said Guy had this certain attitude and Captain Marvel had his little quirks.

KEVIN: Well, Guy's an extreme character, as is Batman. But between Blue Beetle, Mister Miracle, and Booster Gold, I don't know that I did all that much to—being successful in that would have been if I started drawing Blue Beetle wearing Booster Gold's outfit and people could tell the difference. I don't know that I got to that level.

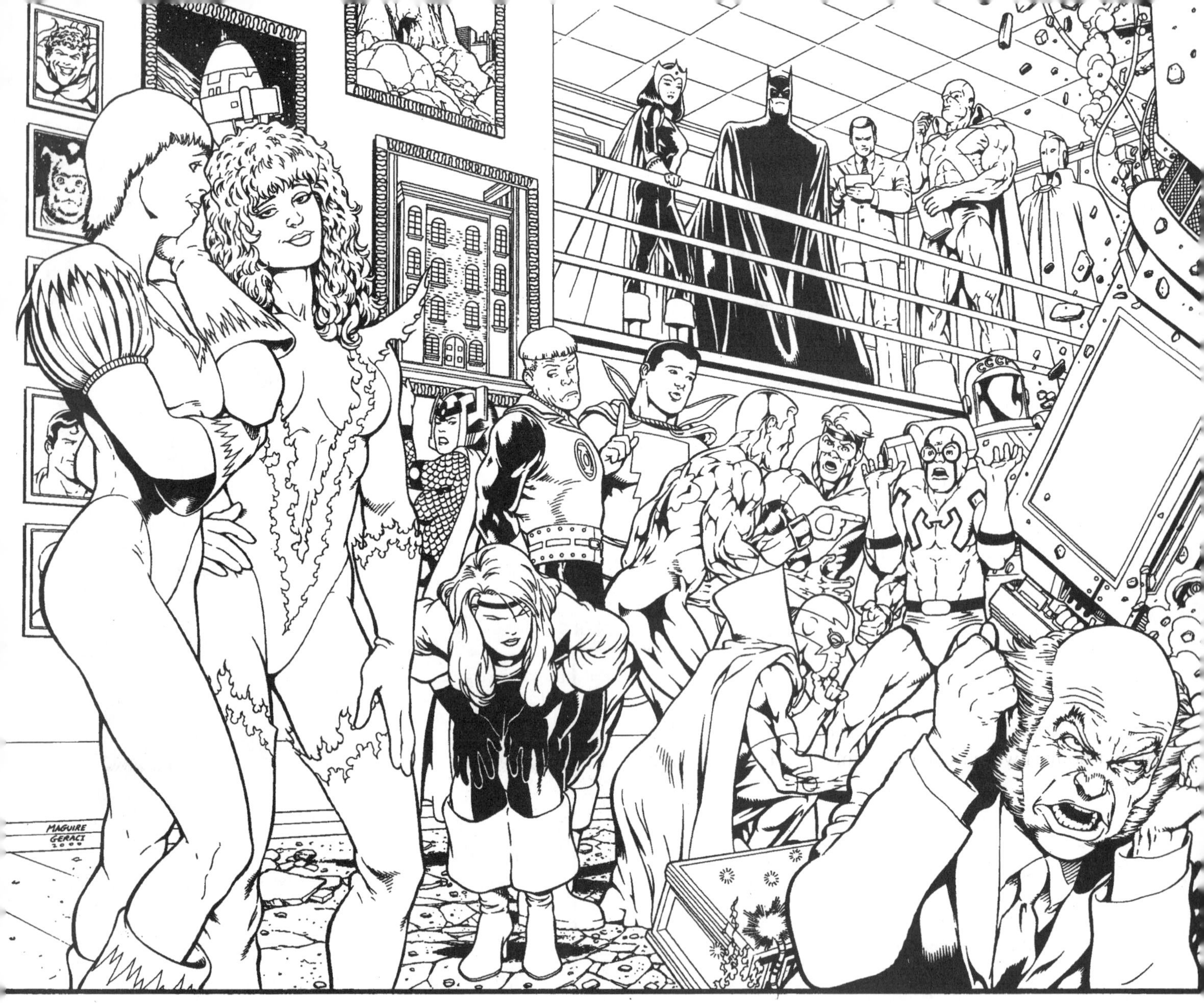
MAGUIRE
GERACI

Above: Pin-up from *JLA Secret Files* #3. Inks by Drew Geraci.
Next Page: Ladies of the Justice League—Crimson Fox, Maxima, and, of course, Wonder Woman. Pin-up from *Martian Manhunter Special* #1, inked by Kevin himself.

MM: I think you got there. Blue Beetle was kind of a self-doubter, and Booster Gold, the confident, handsome guy.

KEVIN: Right, but I don't know if I feel like visually, in terms of facial structure, that I've done that much variety. It seemed to be more of a template heroic facial feature for a lot of the characters. I didn't give one a pointy nose and one a round nose, or one a clearly square jaw. Although, I think I did make Blue Beetle more round.... Yeah, his jaw was rounder. Booster had more of a square jaw.

MM: It seemed like Blue Beetle was a little out of shape. [*laughter*]

KEVIN: That became a running gag, that Blue Beetle was getting fat and getting out of shape, and then sort of mining that for comedy.

MM: Did these characters grow on you—like Booster Gold and Blue Beetle—after a while?

KEVIN: Yeah, oh, yeah.

MM: Do you have a favorite? Is there one you enjoy drawing more than the others?

KEVIN: Guy Gardner, because he's the most extreme guy to animate—a lot of colors to play with with him, other than just green.

MM: At the beginning you didn't really have a lot of girls to illustrate. You eventually got Fire and Ice—was that your doing?

KEVIN: They had Doctor Light and Black Canary. Big Barda was always around.

MM: But these two were actually sexy. [*laughter*]

KEVIN: Yeah, they're more babes, yeah.

MM: Doctor Light always looked like a nun or something.

KEVIN: Yeah, she was fairly prissy, and Black Canary was fairly tough. And Big Barda was just a big gal.

MM: Was there anything you had to complain about when you were working on *Justice League*?

KEVIN: Oh, there were a million things I complained about!

MM: Did you talk to Andy about this?

KEVIN: Oh, absolutely.

MM: Would they listen?

KEVIN: Ah, sort of. But you know, a lot of it was just personal frustrations.

MM: Did you feel like you had the chance to strut your stuff on this book?

KEVIN: No, but I didn't think I should at that point. I was just starting, and this was a team of established DC characters, so it wasn't my playground to dictate terms. I just got my scripts and did what was asked of me, I suppose.

MM: Did you see a difference between working at DC and Marvel at that point? I mean, were you more comfortable one place or the other?

KEVIN: It was a looser sort of place at Marvel at that time, but with my being up at DC every day, like I said, I just became friends with a lot of people there, so I just felt more... not so much more respected, because it sounds kind of trivial to put it that way, but when I was working at Marvel in the bullpen, I was thought of as an art corrections guy. That's kind of like the little pat on the head, little kid, go away, type of job, whereas at DC I was penciling *Justice League*. I was penciling one of their better-selling books, so it was like, "Hey, Kevin!"

MM: While you were there, *Justice League* was never late, right?

KEVIN: It might have been. I know there were a couple of fill-ins, but I don't think I've ever shipped late. I don't know. I don't think so.

MM: Were you always working really close to the deadline, or did you have a lot of space?

KEVIN: That there was plenty of. There was a lot of "ahead time"—a decent amount.

MM: What did you think of Templeton's stuff when he would do a fill-in for you? Because he seemed like an odd choice. He's not anywhere necessarily close to your style.

KEVIN: Which would be my preference.

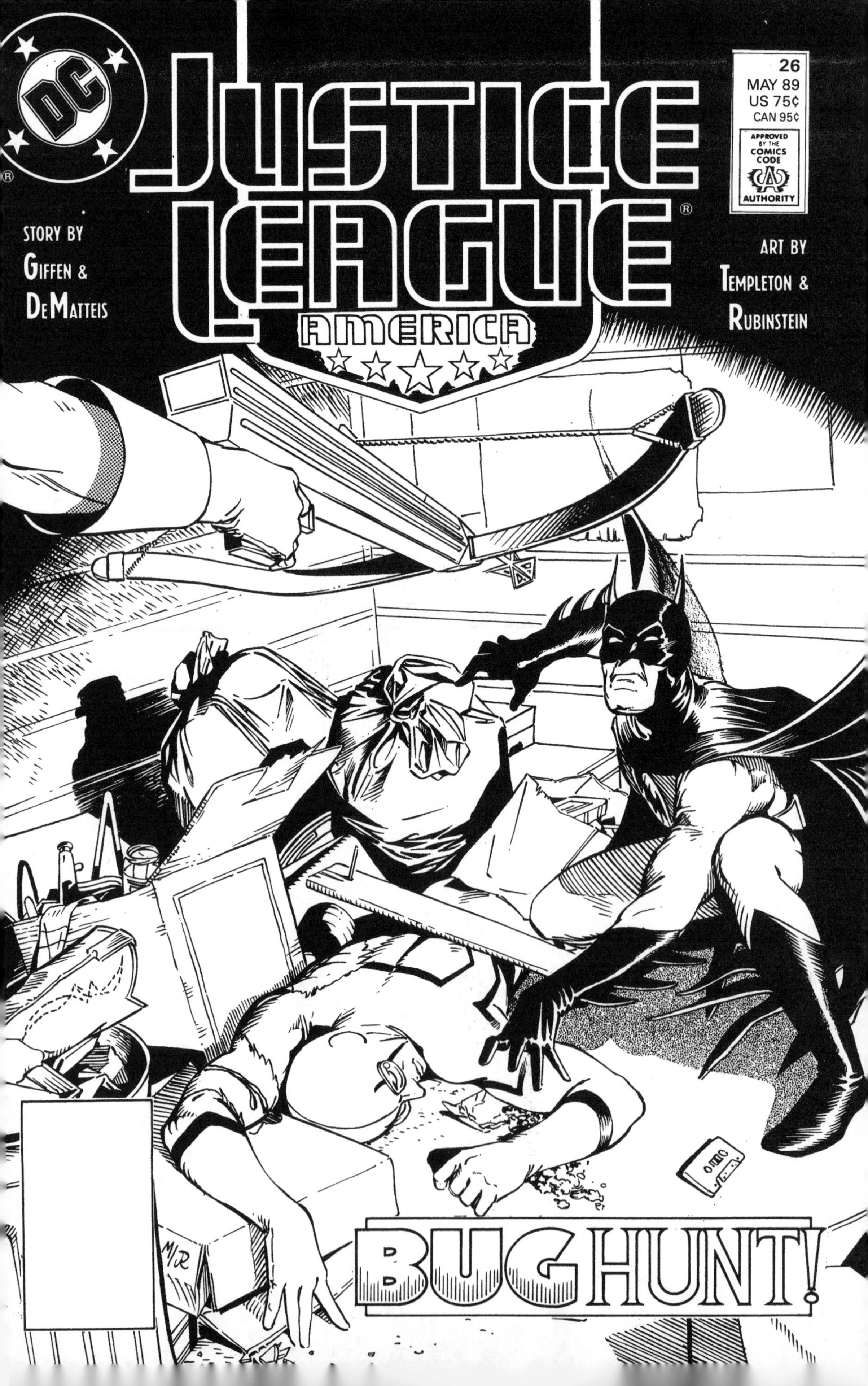
DC
JUSTICE LEAGUE
AMERICA
26
MAY 89
US 75¢
CAN 95¢
APPROVED BY THE COMICS CODE AUTHORITY
STORY BY
GIFFEN &
DEMATTEIS
ART BY
TEMPLETON &
RUBINSTEIN
BUG HUNT!
M/R

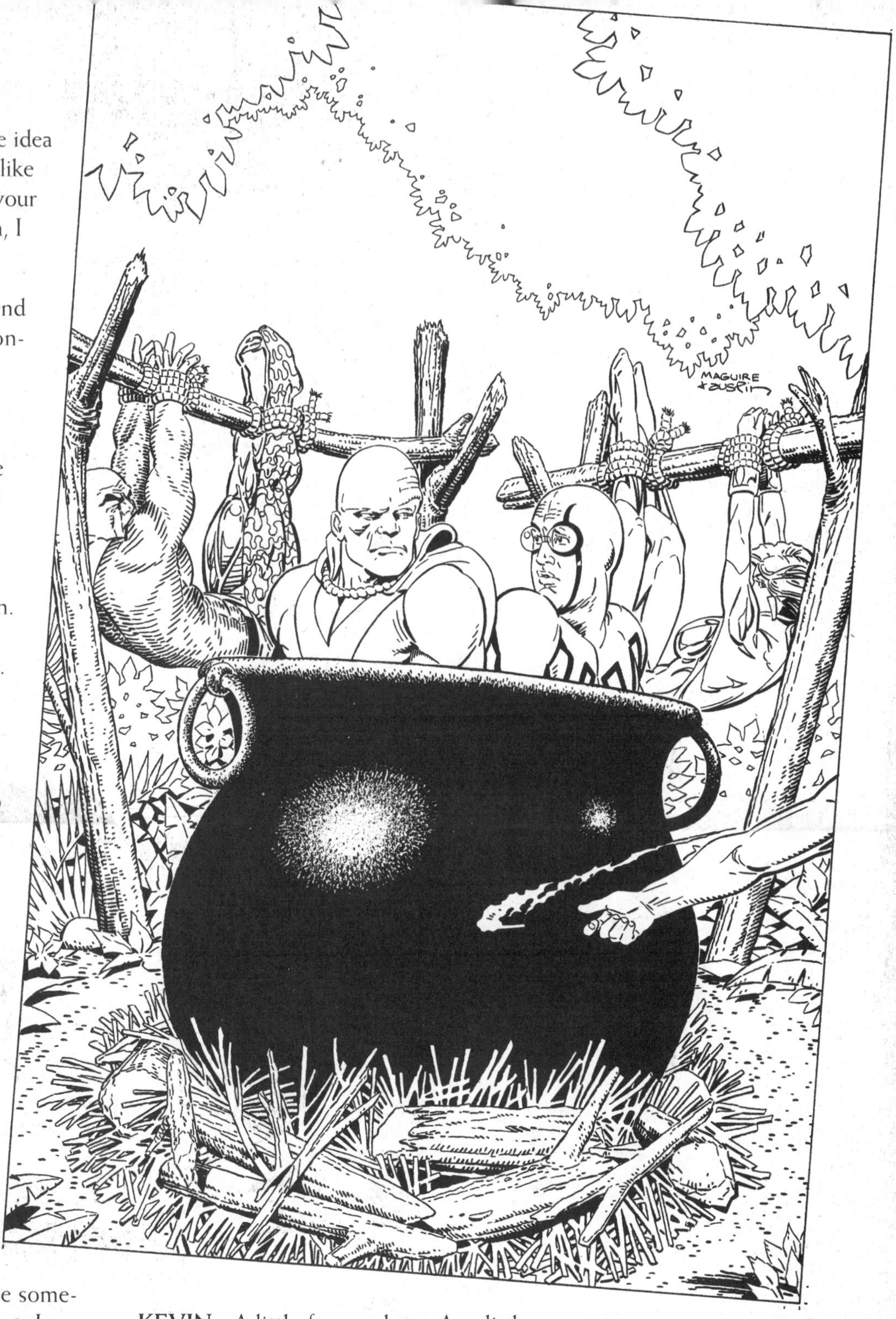
MAGUIRE

MM: Oh, really?

KEVIN: Oh, yeah. I never liked the idea of someone coming in and drawing like me. I'd rather it be come in and do your own voice, do your own thing. Yeah, I mean, I prefer different to similar.

MM: By the time you got to the end of the series, would they let you contribute to the plot?

KEVIN: Not really, no.

MM: By the end of your run, were you ready to spread your wings, or did you want to stay?

KEVIN: No, I was eager to go. A couple of years... that's a decent run. Even with fill-ins, that's a decent amount of time spent on one thing. I was eager to try different things.

MM: What did you have in mind when you were leaving? Do you have any regrets or any ill feelings?

KEVIN: No, not really. As far as starting a career in comics, it certainly could have gone a lot worse. It was a pretty good way to start.

MM: And when you look at this art, what do you see in it?

KEVIN: Oh, I hate it.

MM: The whole thing?

KEVIN: Most of it. I haven't looked at it in detail in a long time, but, for the most part, it just annoys the hell out of me. There are very few times that I'll see something that I'll say, "Oh, I still like that, I still like that, that still looks fine."

MM: When you think about all the guys you've influenced, that loved your stuff—like, I thought when Adam Hughes came along that he was doing a lot of your stuff.

KEVIN: I would say a lot of that was at the insistence of Andy Helfer, who wanted to keep that kind of consistent look to it.

MM: Were you flattered, or were you just disturbed?

KEVIN: A little from column A, a little from column B. I'm just into doing your own thing, so, yes, it's flattering that people say that I was an influence—of course that's flattering—but sometimes it's like, "All right, now do your own thing."

The best compliment I got from a creative guy, one of the best, was actually a couple of years ago, from Darrick Robertson, who said that something I did changed the way he thought about comics. The page where Batman punches out Guy Gardner, in the last panel there's a shot of Blue Beetle

Previous Page: Cover art for *JLA* #26. Inks by Joe Rubinstein.
Above: Kevin came back to *Justice League* after a long absence and penciled this cover [*JLA* #59] as well as the entire following issue. Inks by Terry Austin.

laughing so hard that he reaches up under his mask to wipe tears from his eyes. Darrick said that panel of Blue Beetle reaching up under the mask just made him think, "Oh, yeah, they're people. They're not action figures." I guess as a kid that becomes a revelation. I'm not sure he was a kid when he read it, but, it's just one of those things you just never know. You never think that, "This figure, this panel I'm drawing now will change the way people think about comics." You just don't think that way.

MM: And for you that was just work, just part of the job?

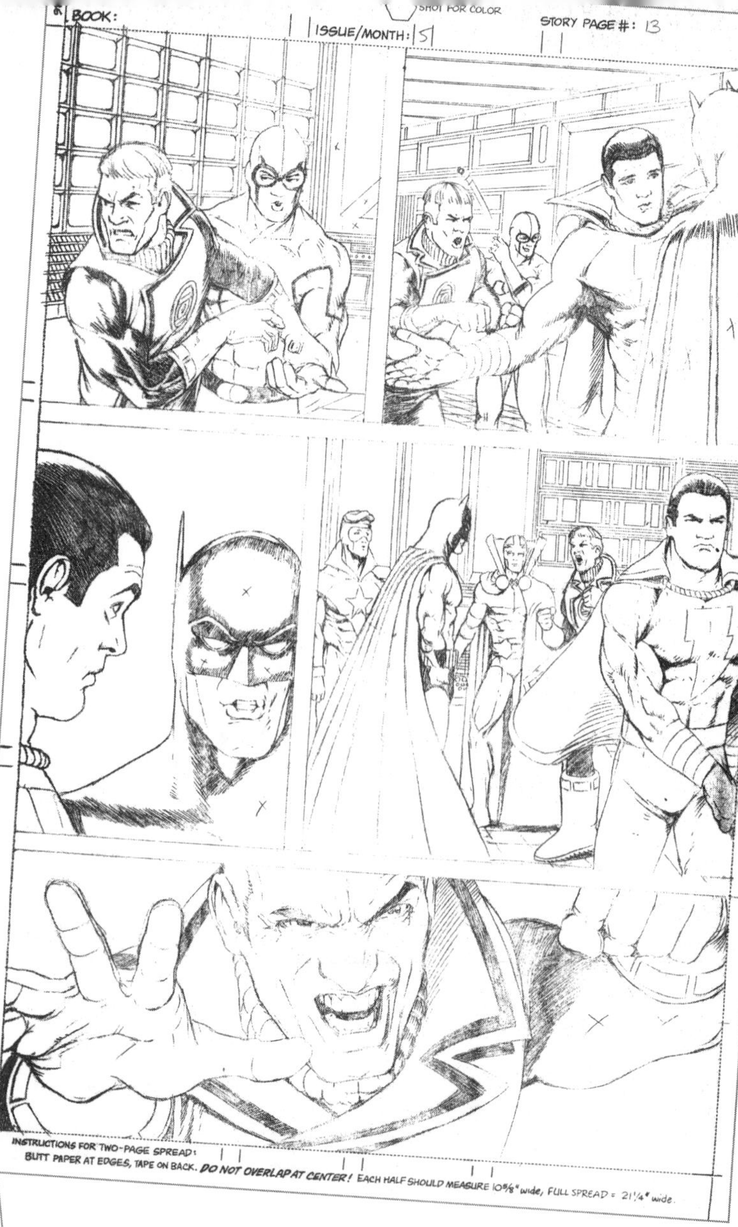
BOOK:
ISSUE/MONTH: 5
STORY PAGE #: 13
INSTRUCTIONS FOR TWO-PAGE SPREAD:
BUTT PAPER AT EDGES, TAPE ON BACK. DO NOT OVERLAP AT CENTER! EACH HALF SHOULD MEASURE 10⅝" wide, FULL SPREAD = 21¼" wide.

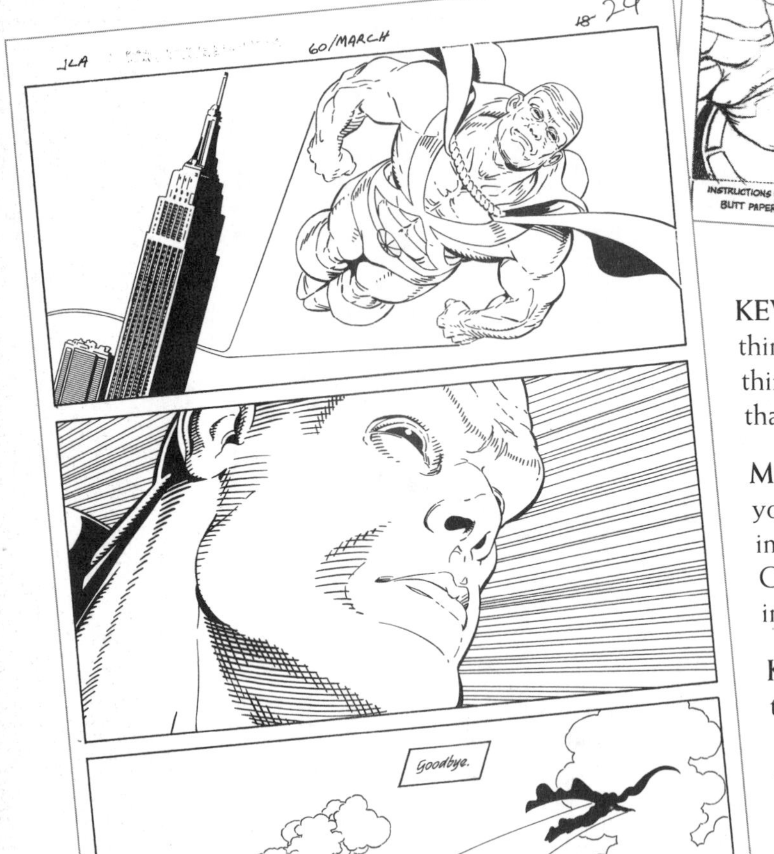
JLA
60/MARCH
18-24
Goodbye.
COLOR - THE SUN IS BEHIND CLOUD JOHN IS APPROACHING - K.

Right and Next Page: This sequence really made an impact around the comics world—and not just on Guy's face! Pages 13 and 14 from *Justice League* #5. **Below:** The end of an era... for several years, at least. *JLA* #60, page 18.

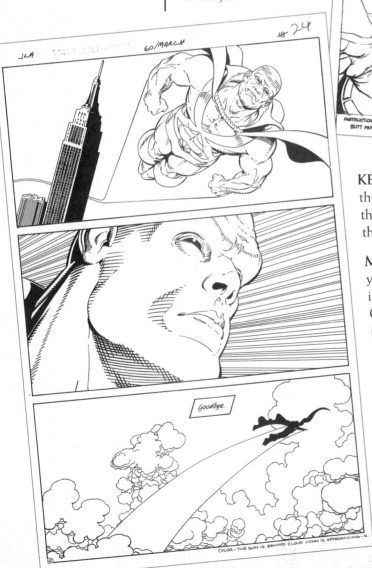

KEVIN: Yeah, it's just doing that moment the way you think that moment ought to be, and, again, you just don't think that, "Wow, somebody might rethink comics based on that."

MM: You didn't think this was groundbreaking work when you were doing it? You can see a lot of this kind of subtlety in a lot of the art out there today. In someone like John Cassaday and some other guys, you can see your influence in their work.

KEVIN: No, I didn't think it was groundbreaking at all. I thought it was going to be a flop. [*laughter*]

MM: How did they lure you back for issue #60, the last DeMatteis/Giffen issue?

KEVIN: They just asked. It's not like they backed up a Brinks truck to my house or anything like that.

MM: So you didn't think of it as closure for you?

KEVIN: No, it was just a healthy rest.

8/86

DC Comics, Inc. ×

SHOT FOR COLOR

STORY PAGE #: 14

BOOK: ISSUE/MONTH: 5

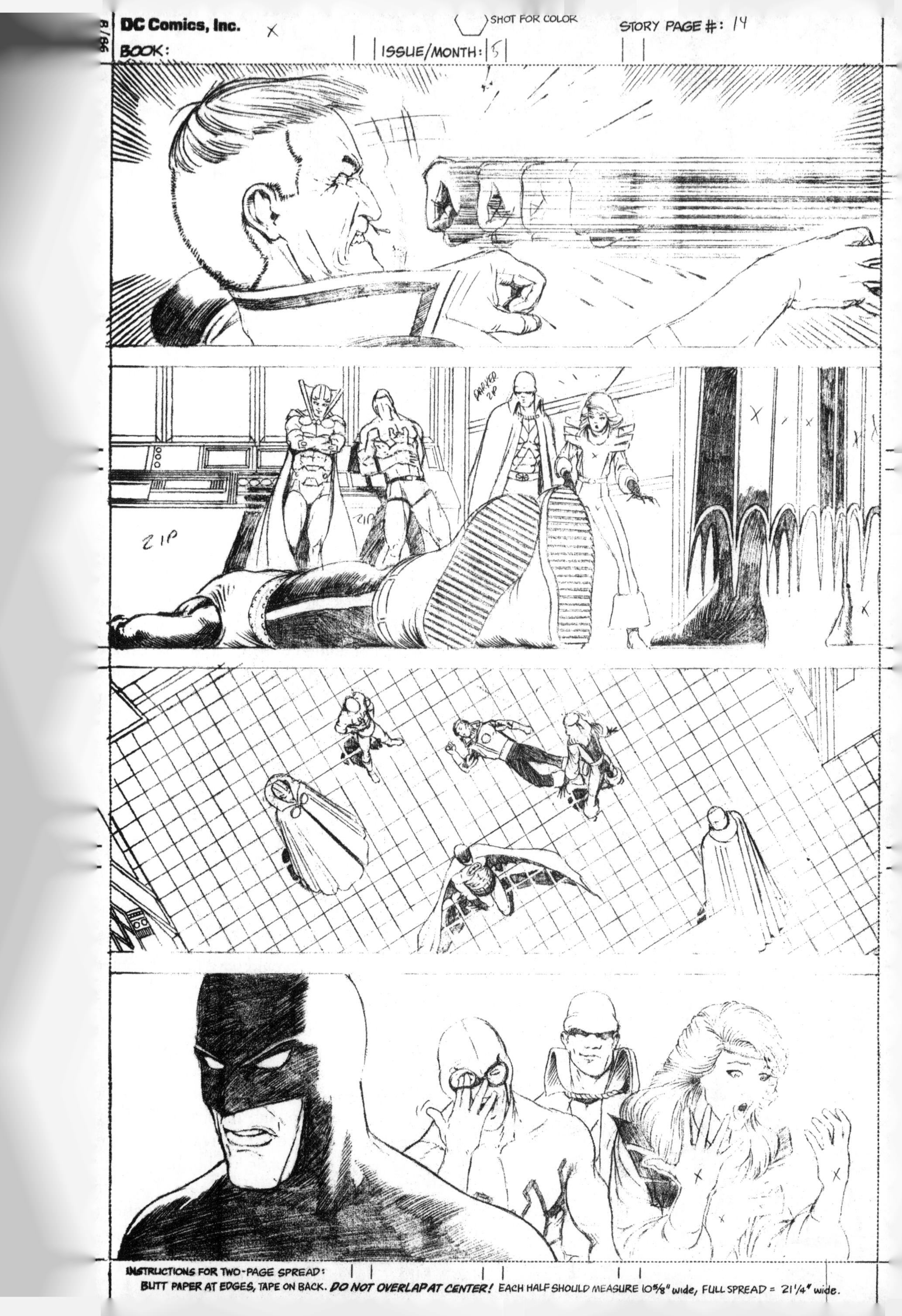
ZIP
ZIP

INSTRUCTIONS FOR TWO-PAGE SPREAD:
BUTT PAPER AT EDGES, TAPE ON BACK. ***DO NOT OVERLAP AT CENTER!*** EACH HALF SHOULD MEASURE 10 5/8" wide, FULL SPREAD = 21 1/4" wide.

Part 3: The Man Who Would Be Captain America

MM: When you left the Justice League, were you looking to go back to Marvel?

KEVIN: No, except my friend, Fabian Nicieza, said that Tom DeFalco wanted me to do work over there. Fabian proposed doing a Captain America thing, and that's what got that ball rolling.

MM: You helped get that started, because Fabian, I think, was still starting his writing career at that time.

KEVIN: Yeah, yeah.

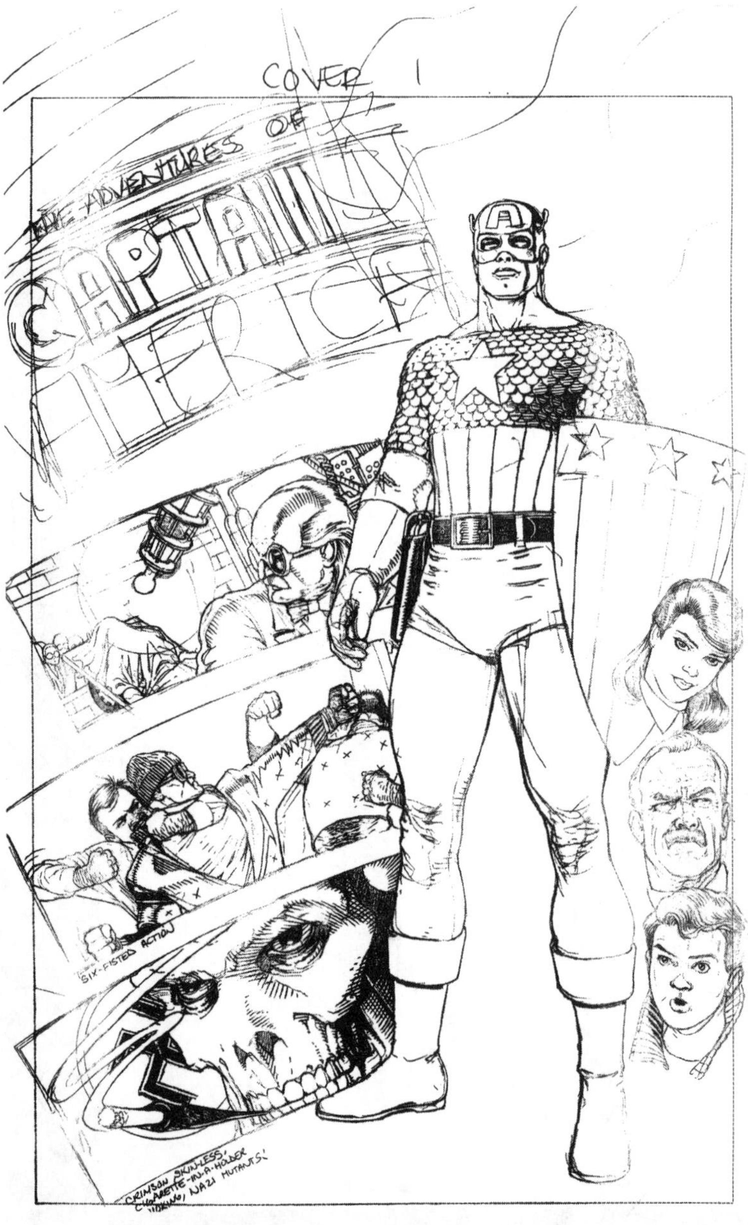
COVER 1
THE ADVENTURES OF
CAPTAIN
SIX-FISTED ACTION
CRIMSON SKIN-LESS,
CIGARETTE-IN-A-HOLDER
NAZI MUTANTS!

MM: It must have been a good feeling, to feel wanted by Marvel?

KEVIN: Oh, yeah. I mean, it's nice to feel wanted.

MM: Did DC try to counter that offer once they found out you were going to go do the series?

KEVIN: I don't recall anything specifically being offered, but I had a lot of friends up at DC. I don't think it was "our side/their side" at that point. There was a lot more camaraderie between the two companies.

MM: Who originally had the gist of the idea? Did it come from you or Fabian?

KEVIN: Well, it was Fabian's idea to do *The Adventures of Captain America*. Originally, he had this idea for a story that involved illegal immigration, which I guess has come full circle and topical. But I was like, "Ennnh, I don't want to do that. I want something like *Raiders of the Lost Ark*. Let's do something like a movie serial." I think Captain America works best in the '40s, because there is much more of that patriotic feeling around that time. Now it's a little more cynical, so Captain America has this kind of a mixed imagery. I mean, the character's still Captain America, but the whole point of the illegal immigration thing in *Captain America* was to contrast with what America stands for and that kind of thing.

MM: And if Fabian had done his story that way, it would have been in a modern setting?

KEVIN: Yeah, it would have been a contemporary setting.

MM: That's what appealed to you, doing it in the '40s and having to do the research?

KEVIN: Well, yeah. I thought that was the most fun period for Captain America, and I don't think at that point there had been a real comprehensive origin. It was a really basic kind of beginning.

At first Fabian was like, "I don't know, the '40s? I don't know." Then he called me back after thinking about it, "That's going to be cool!" [*laughter*]

MM: He wrote a treatment?

KEVIN: I don't know. I'm sure he had to write something up. I don't know if he had to write something up or just talk to someone verbally.

MM: In terms of the schedule, did they give you a great amount of time for preparation?

KEVIN: They were as patient as they could be. [*laughter*] Until they lost their patience.

MM: Let's see... you left *Justice League* in '89. So from '89 to '90 you had time to work on this, right?

KEVIN: Yeah.

MM: What type of research did you do?

KEVIN: I got a bunch of books on the '40s, World War II, all that.

MM: Did it psych you up, doing that kind of research? Did you feel like now you were a real artist?

KEVIN: No, no. I'm not a big research maven. Research is not my strong suit.

MM: But you had something here that could have been great. I'm sure you were excited about it and wanted to put a lot of detail into it.

KEVIN: Oh, yeah. I wanted it to be my masterpiece, which is why it took so long. And why it was eventually yanked.

MM: Fabian said you were living in a basement in New York and that you had the walls full of notes and drawings.

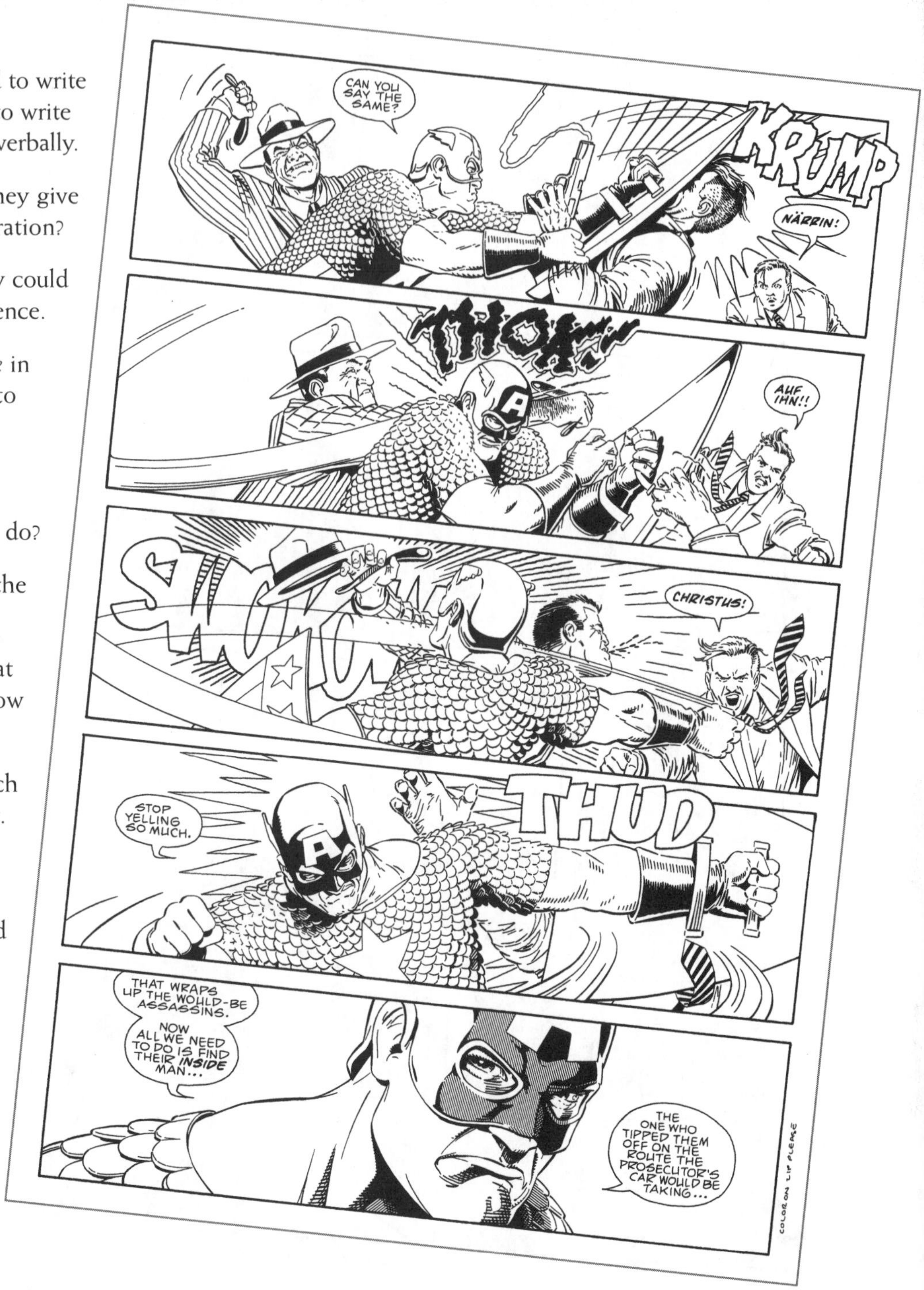

CAN YOU SAY THE SAME?
KRUMP
NÄRRIN!
AUF IHN!!
CHRISTUS!
STOP YELLING SO MUCH.
THUD
THAT WRAPS UP THE WOULD-BE ASSASSINS.
NOW ALL WE NEED TO DO IS FIND THEIR *INSIDE* MAN...
THE ONE WHO TIPPED THEM OFF ON THE ROUTE THE PROSECUTOR'S CAR WOULD BE TAKING...

KEVIN: Well, that's why I got credited as "storyteller" on the fourth issue even though I didn't pencil it. Fabe and I wrote it together. He came to my apartment and we—I read that this is how John Cleese had written *Fawlty Towers*—just took big sheets of paper and put them on the board, and then just started writing down what we wanted to see in the story. Then we had them on the wall, so could just stand there and point to do this over here, or, y'know, "We can't do this because this competes with that back there." We wrote out the whole story that way.

MM: Did Fabian write a script right from the beginning, or did you guys just have a plot?

KEVIN: Yeah, initially we had a plot, and then I imagine he wrote it out in script form. But we had obviously run it past the editor.

MM: But when you were working with him, did you feel comfortable? That if you didn't like something, some dialogue he wrote, that you could change it?

KEVIN: Oh, yeah, yeah. He and I worked very well together.

Previous Page: Kevin's pencils for the cover of *The Adventures of Captain America* #1.
Above: Cap gets in a workout. Page 23 of *The Adventures of Captain America* #2.

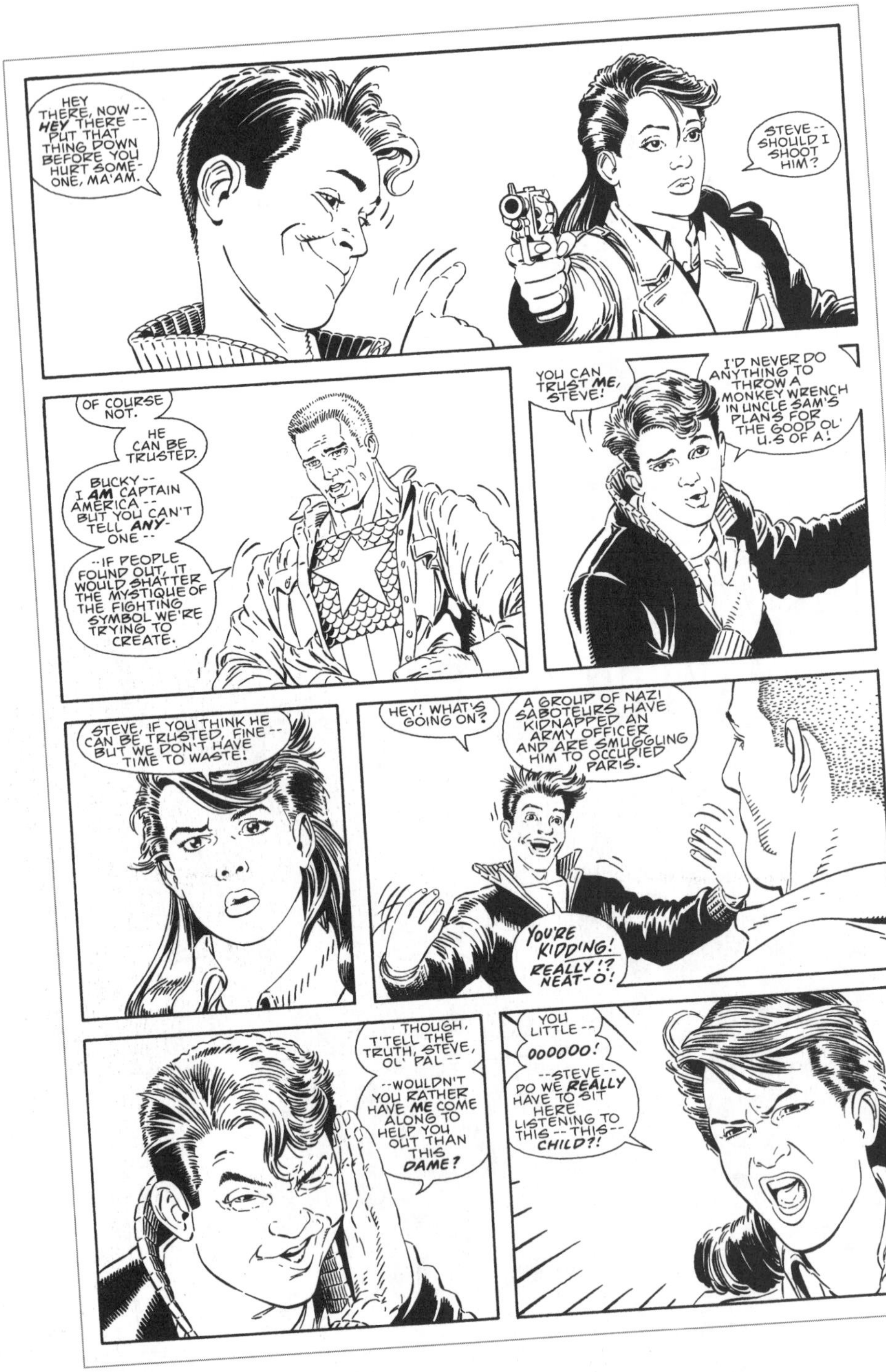
HEY THERE, NOW -- HEY THERE -- PUT THAT THING DOWN BEFORE YOU HURT SOME-ONE, MA'AM.
STEVE -- SHOULD I SHOOT HIM?
OF COURSE NOT.
HE CAN BE TRUSTED.
BUCKY -- I AM CAPTAIN AMERICA -- BUT YOU CAN'T TELL ANY-ONE --
--IF PEOPLE FOUND OUT, IT WOULD SHATTER THE MYSTIQUE OF THE FIGHTING SYMBOL WE'RE TRYING TO CREATE.
YOU CAN TRUST ME, STEVE!
I'D NEVER DO ANYTHING TO THROW A MONKEY WRENCH IN UNCLE SAM'S PLANS FOR THE GOOD OL' U.S OF A!
STEVE, IF YOU THINK HE CAN BE TRUSTED, FINE -- BUT WE DON'T HAVE TIME TO WASTE!
HEY! WHAT'S GOING ON?
A GROUP OF NAZI SABOTEURS HAVE KIDNAPPED AN ARMY OFFICER AND ARE SMUGGLING HIM TO OCCUPIED PARIS.
YOU'RE KIDDING! REALLY!? NEAT-O!
THOUGH, T'TELL THE TRUTH, STEVE, OL' PAL --
--WOULDN'T YOU RATHER HAVE ME COME ALONG TO HELP YOU OUT THAN THIS DAME?
YOU LITTLE --
OOOOOO!
--STEVE-- DO WE REALLY HAVE TO SIT HERE LISTENING TO THIS -- THIS -- CHILD?!

Above: Bucky works his way onto the team. Page 9 of *The Adventures of Captain America* #3.
Next Page: A Dark Knight, indeed. A Batman commission piece.

MM: Out of all the work that Fabian and you have worked on together, was this series the most difficult?

KEVIN: No, actually, it wasn't, because a lot of it was already predetermined. Captain America has to do this, he has to do this, and he has to meet Bucky. There were a lot of things we couldn't change, so that kind of made it easier. It was kind of like refinishing a car or rebuilding a car. We already knew what's it was supposed to kind of look like, as opposed to coming up with something fresh and new where there aren't the borders you can't cross.

MM: This series didn't test your friendship with him, did it?

KEVIN: No, not at all.

MM: There was never any point where you would get angry with him that, "You know, I could do this on my own!" [*laughs*]

KEVIN: I don't recall anything like that. I mean, we've worked on other projects where we've just not seen eye-to-eye on how it's supposed to go, but that's how any two creative people will work. Y'know, Lennon and McCartney didn't always see eye-to-eye, either.

MM: That's true. When you undertook this series, did you set yourself in a different sort of mindset? Like, "I have to think differently. I've got to get this done differently. I've really gotta push myself"?

KEVIN: I did two years on a monthly book, so I was used to having to produce a certain amount of pages every week, and with this I saw it as more.... It's like going from a TV series to a movie or a play. You have to churn out a TV series because you think you have more time, so you can languish sometimes. But I took a little too much time.

MM: So you didn't reorganize yourself? Did you just approach this like a monthly book when you started it?

KEVIN: Well, I took my time with it.

MM: And when did you start getting worried that you were falling behind? Was this right from the beginning?

KEVIN: I don't remember at exactly which part, but obviously it had gotten to the point where people were starting to get antsy and nervous, and part of it was that, I think it was in the summer of '89, I had moved to Florida for two years. So I wasn't popping into the office every week. I wasn't a New Yorker any more.

MM: You were living in Florida when you did this?

KEVIN: When I did the bulk of it, yeah.

MM: I thought Fabian said you were living in New York.

KEVIN: During the plotting sessions, yeah.

MM: Oh, okay. When you guys plotted this, did you plot all four books together?

KEVIN: Yeah, as just one long story.

MM: In the course of a week or so?

KEVIN: I'm sure it took longer than that.

MM: Fabian would stay over in your apartment and you guys would just talk about this endlessly?

KEVIN: He didn't sleep over, but he would come over and we'd just have these work sessions.

MM: So you would talk about this thing 24-7, or what? Were you really living it at that point?

KEVIN: I don't know that I was completely "living it." It was my focus at the time, work-wise, but I don't know that it was all-consuming. It was the summer that *Batman* came out, I remember that. [*laughs*] That was very big back then. You know, it was my job, I guess.

MM: Was Mike Rockwitz, the editor of the book, staying on top of you?

KEVIN: Yeah. Not every day, but, y'know, every few days.

MM: You also said that Mark Gruenwald served as an editor on this thing, too. How did you work with him on it?

KEVIN: Well, he was the executive editor working with the day-to-day editor, but Gruenwald was writing *Captain America*—the regular book—and I remember Fabian telling me he was very, very pleased. I don't know whether it was after it came out or when he first read the script, but he was very pleased that Gruenwald was like, "Yeah, yeah. I know this character"—that we had gotten it right.

MM: But at the same time, you guys had kind of done something that hadn't been done. Remember, Gruenwald had a different sense of adventure. He never

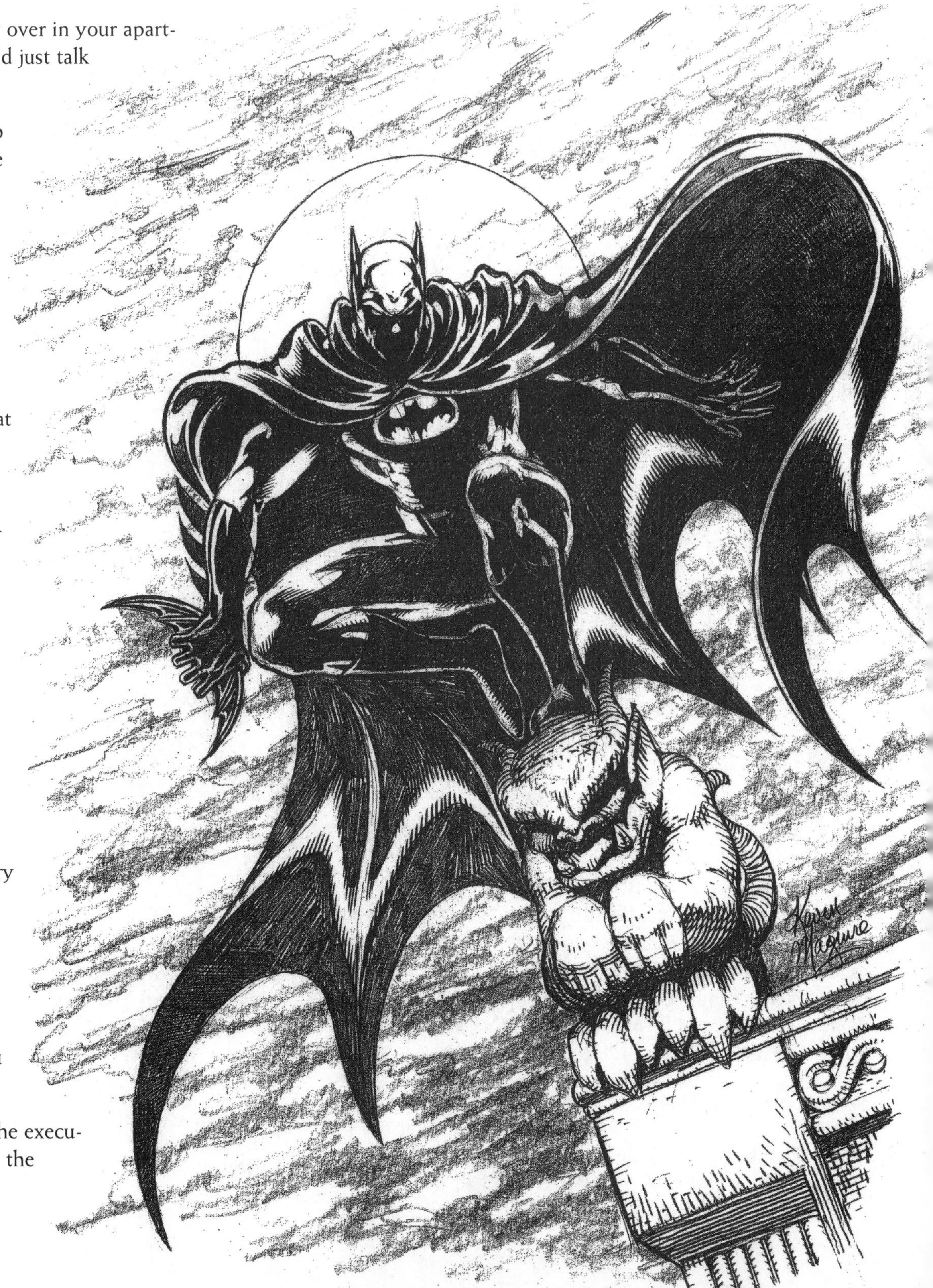

gave it that real classic spin. Was that something that you became conscious of? Did you want your story to be a little different from what he was doing?

KEVIN: Since I've gotten into the business, I've never really read a lot of other books, so I wasn't really conscious of what—I'm sure Fabian was, because he reads everything—but I wasn't really conscious of what the other books were like. Again, I was just looking at it as a movie serial, and that's how I wanted to go with it.

MM: But you also saw a lot of potential in the character?

KEVIN: Yeah, yeah. And, again, for a movie serial feeling, but also because it's the most important chapter in Steve Rogers' life—him first becoming Captain America. So you have the opportunity to have this guy—this skinny, enthusiastic guy—become Captain America, and you have that character change that was very appealing. And it's not going to happen, but it's always been a little dream in the back of my head to do a trilogy of mini-series, with Captain America close to the end of World War II with the Invaders, and then doing a third one with him waking up in the '60s. Those are two real critical moments in that character's life. Being in the '40s and then waking up in the '60s, I mean, that's got to be a little culture shock.

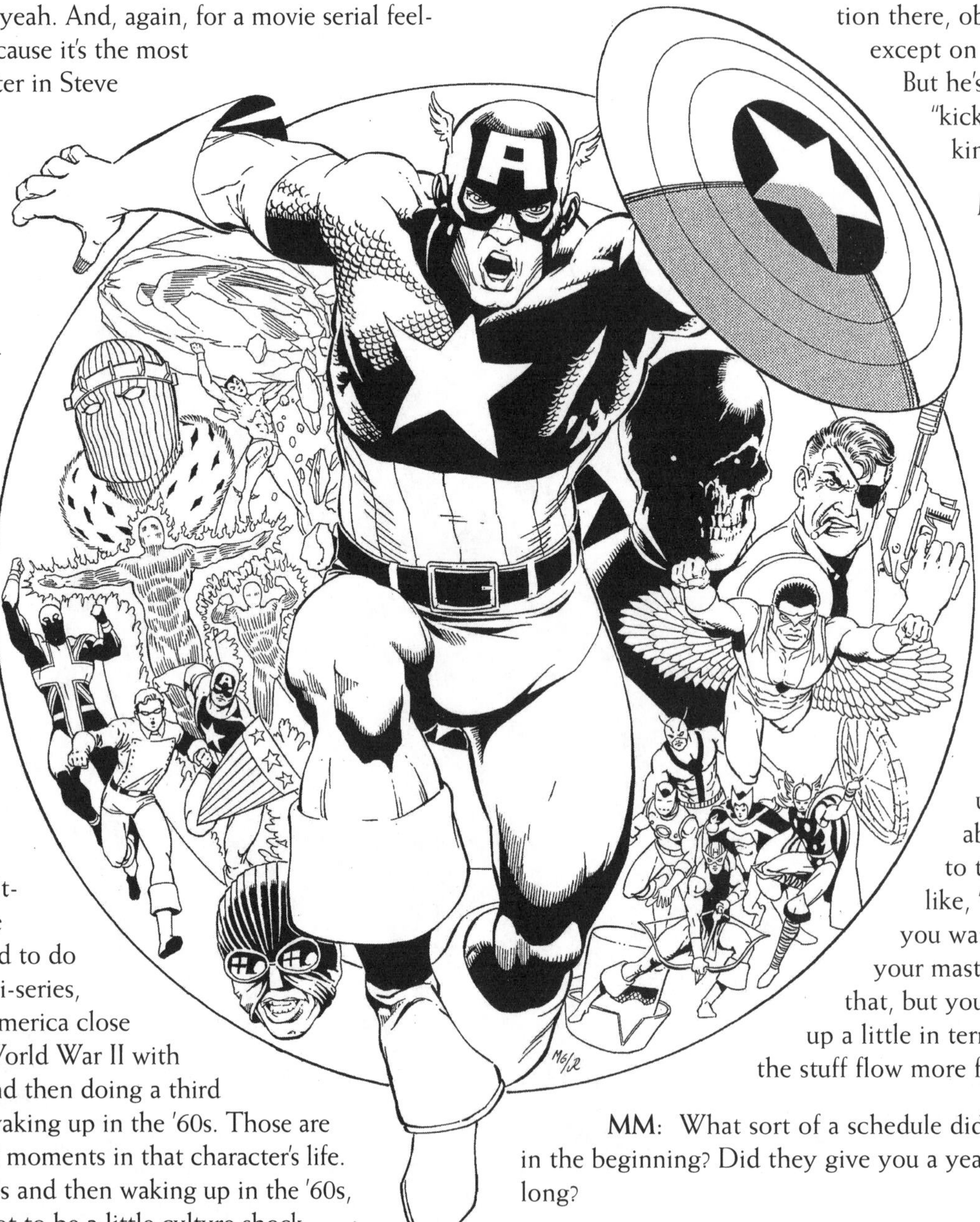

MM: I always thought that if they were to make a *Captain America* movie that would be the perfect starting point, just the reawakening, the culture shock you go through, the withdrawal from society, and all that stuff. Was that something you and Fabian were planning if this worked as it should have?

KEVIN: We were more concerned about me getting through the first arc. [*laughter*]

MM: Did Fabian motivate you? Would you guys drive each other? Like, when you were down or he was down, could you get each other going? Did he try?

KEVIN: Oh, I'm sure he tried. But by this point I was doing the bulk of the penciling and I was in Florida. There was no personal interaction there, obviously, except on the phone. But he's always been a "kick me in the ass" kind of guy.

MM: So that's the sort of discussions he would have with you toward the end? Like, "You gotta do this, come on!"

KEVIN: Yeah, yeah. Everyone would. Even Tom DeFalco—he was extremely understanding about it. Closer to the end he was like, "Look, I know you want this to be your masterpiece, I get that, but you gotta loosen up a little in terms of having the stuff flow more frequently."

MM: What sort of a schedule did they give you in the beginning? Did they give you a year? Was it that long?

KEVIN: No, I doubt it.

MM: They wanted this thing to come out real quick?

KEVIN: Yeah, they wanted it for the 50th anniversary.

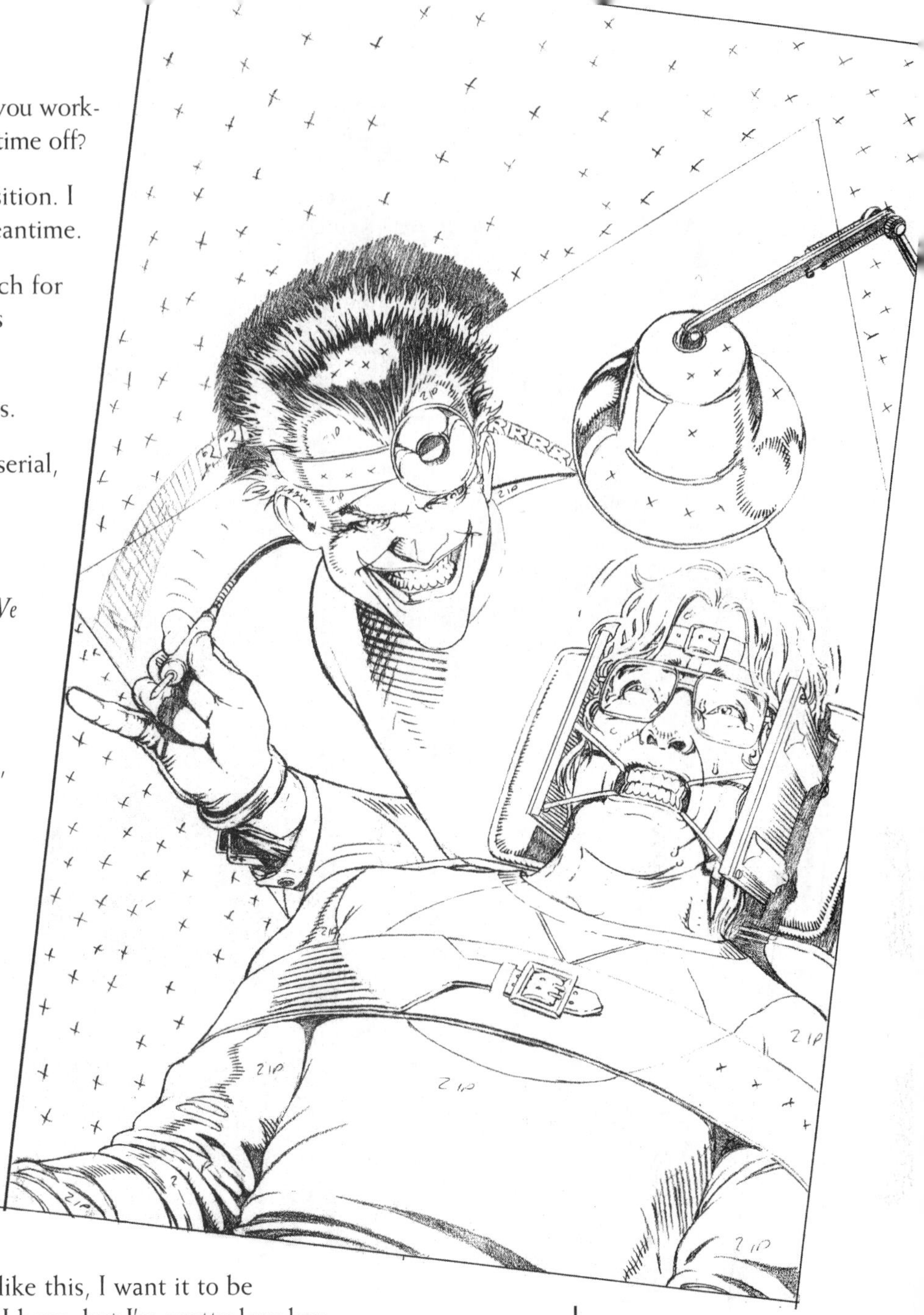

MM: After you dropped *Justice League*, were you working on this right away or did you take some time off?

KEVIN: I think probably there was a transition. I might have done covers and stuff in the meantime.

MM: What sort of movies would you watch for inspiration when you were working on this thing? Would you listen to '40s era music?

KEVIN: I'd watch movie serials and videos.

MM: You didn't watch the *Captain America* serial, did you?

KEVIN: No, no.

MM: Did you watch Frank Capra's *Why We Fight*?

KEVIN: Well.... I do remember, though, that at that time the *Captain America* movie was being made, and people would ask me, "Is this an adaptation?" I'm like, "No. No, no, no. Nothing to do with that, please. No." I'd heard how bad the script was.

MM: The rubber ears.

KEVIN: Rubber ears. And there was the Italian Red Skull. [*laughter*]

MM: When you were working on this, were you very controlling of your art? Did you want to be involved in all facets of production: coloring and the lettering?

KEVIN: I've never been known to throw my weight around saying, "I want it to be like this, I want it to be like that." I'm sure there were times where I have, but I'm pretty low-key.

MM: Yeah, but this was your baby.

KEVIN: Yeah, but I also understand that—actually, you know what? It isn't my baby, because it's Marvel's baby. I'm playing in their yard, so I don't have final say on anything, and I recognize that. I can have input on what I think, what I'd like, but it wasn't my baby.

MM: Were you happy with the production values, the way the book was presented? Did it come out sort of like you wanted to see it?

KEVIN: Really unhappy with the coloring. And he [*Paul Mounts*] actually colored me on something later on, and the stuff he did later on was really good. But I was disappointed with the coloring, because I remember some page being really red. I don't remember which page specifically off the top of my head.

MM: There are a lot of things in there that are kind of dark.

KEVIN: Yeah. I never understood why they were colored the way they were.

Previous Page: Cap and his friends and foes through the crucial moments of his history. **Above:** Kevin actually penciled a few covers in between his time on *Justice League* and *Captain America*, such as this cover to *Robin II* #2.

The comic panels contain:

"AT THAT MOMENT, IN A HOLDING CELL IN THE DISTRICT OF COLUMBRIA MILITARY BRIG..."

"HODGE... I WANT SOME ANSWERS..."

"...WHO HIRED YOU TO TURN TRAITOR TO YOUR COUNTRY..."

"...AND WHERE CAN I FIND THEM..."

Above: An intense Captain America. *The Adventures of Captain America #2*, page 36. **Next Page:** Talk about your bombshells! Cap gets a little flustered in this commission sketch.

Captain America ™ and ©2007 Marvel Characters, Inc.

MM: Did you lay out the whole story on those sheets of paper that you had on the wall? Did you have thumbnails for the four issues?

KEVIN: No.

MM: You just went issue by issue?

KEVIN: Yeah.

MM: In terms of scope, how did you go about that? You had more scope here than you ever had in *Justice League*. It gave the story a bit more of an epic sense. What was the inspiration? Were there certain movies that you were thinking of besides *Indiana Jones*? Did you watch a lot of David Lean films?

KEVIN: Not really, no. I just thought whatever was appropriate that shows the story.

MM: You didn't want to look through a lot of movies and a lot of books to get it—

KEVIN: I'm not that kind of guy. No, I'm not. I'm really not. I'm not a learned person as much as a kind of instinctive person.

MM: Weren't there certain times where, you wanted to make sure you get it right just in case you had somebody from that time reading the book— what kind of pants they wore, or what sort of shoes they would have used in that era?

MM: But it was still different from what the norm was back then.

KEVIN: Yeah, I was coming off of the monthly *Justice League*, which was just the regular printing process of the time, to the prestige format thing.

MM: Was this a big deal for you when you saw the first issue? "Wow, finally a book!"

KEVIN: Yeah, yeah. Well, y'know, more of a relief for Marvel, to a degree.

KEVIN: Yeah, I mean, I referenced that way. Like I said, I had a lot of books, and I had a few *Life* magazines from that time period. So, yeah, I researched in terms of making it look like the '40s, but that's pretty much it.

MM: And did you have to look at a lot of the old *Captain America* issues from the '40s to see what they had done?

KEVIN: Not really, no. I remember that I

didn't like that half-mask thing. I just thought it was a dopey look.

MM: The way you did it, it came out very nice.

KEVIN: I wanted to do the hood, the regular mask. But they were like, "No, no, he started out this way." Which is what I meant about parameters that we had to follow. "It's not a circular shield, it's the other one."

MM: That first issue took you a long time to draw. Are we talking about months or...?

KEVIN: Oh, clearly months.

MM: Pages would take a week or so?

KEVIN: Some of them, yeah.

MM: When did you start getting concerned?

KEVIN: Wow, I don't remember when I got concerned. Once the people at Marvel started getting concerned, I suppose.

MM: When you did the skinny Steve Rogers, did you have anyone in mind when you were drawing that? The skinny guy in those Charles Atlas ads who gets the sand kicked in his eyes?

KEVIN: No one in particular, just was working backwards from Captain America. You know, what would Captain America look like if he was really skinny?

MM: And the girl—was there any sort of vintage starlet you were thinking of?

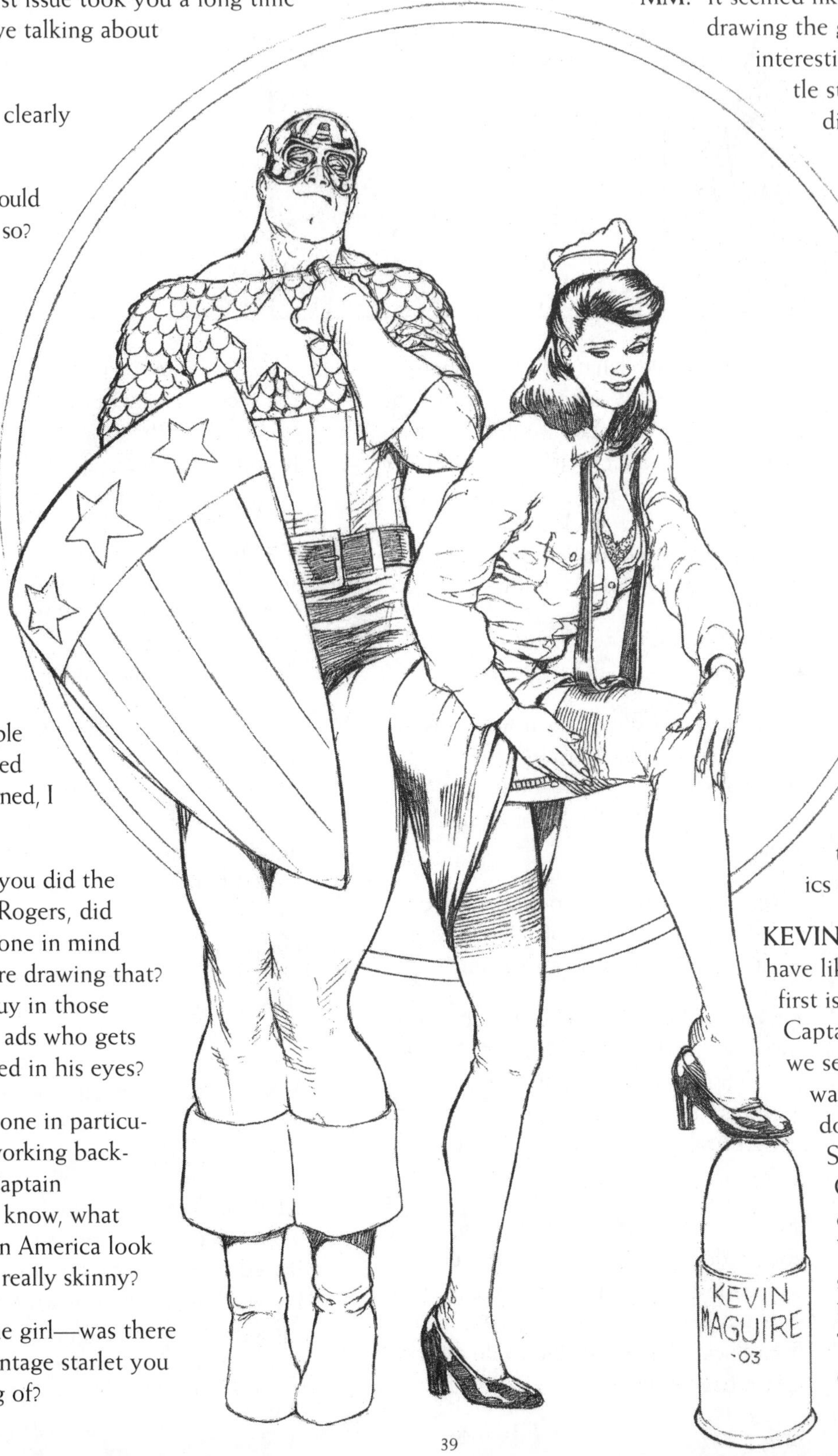
KEVIN
MAGUIRE
-03

KEVIN: There were a couple of actresses current for that time we looked on as far as the sort of type we were looking for. Cynthia Gibb was one of them; she was a contemporary. Paulette Goddard. I'd gotten a book about '40s movies, looking at a lot of different looks and stuff like that.

MM: Was that the most fun in the series, drawing her?

KEVIN: I don't know. She was fun.

MM: It seemed like you had a lot of fun drawing the girls. There's some interesting panel work and little stylistic things that you did with her in some of her panels that came out really nice.

KEVIN: Yeah.

MM: Was it a problem not having Captain America in the first issue? That first issue is basically all drama and set-up. I think you're still very good in it; it is a good example of storytelling seeing how you told the story without having to show any super-heroics or a ton of action.

KEVIN: We probably would have liked to have ended the first issue with him being Captain America, but once we set out the whole story, it was just breaking his story down into quarters. And Steve Rogers becoming Captain America doesn't end at the first quarter. We still had too much story to tell beforehand, before getting to it. There was a lot of interesting questions that

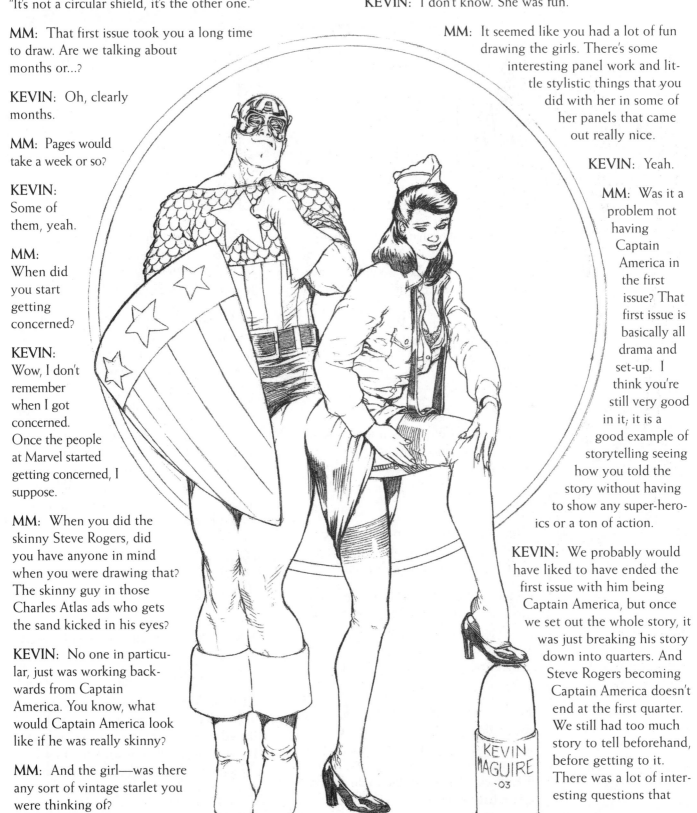

NOT LIKE ME, CINDY.

NO -- YOU'RE RIGHT -- YOU'RE A GOOD MAN -- I THOUGHT I'D NEVER SEE YOU AGAIN --

uhm -- uh -- WE --

WE HAVE TO FIND THE COLONEL -- QUICKLY!

Above: Cindy plays the hapless damsel in distress and reels in Cap. From *Adventures of Captain America #3*. Inks by Terry Austin.

Next Page: A nice use of an inset panel makes for both an interesting layout and a nostalgic feel. Page 5 of *Adventures of Captain America #3*. Inks by Terry Austin.

were asked, like, what was this Super Soldier Project? Was he the only one that was found for it? Who else did they consider for it? And all that kind of stuff. So once we got to play around with that, there was so much backstory that we needed to cover before he put the costume on. That's just how it worked out.

MM: Was the first issue the most challenging of the three that you did?

KEVIN: Probably, yeah. It was dense. I'm trying to remember certain panels or pages that had so many panels. I had to make sure that there was background in all of them.

MM: And in the first couple of pages, you could see you put a lot of references to whatever was going on at the time.

KEVIN: The first panel of the first page there's an establishing shot, and there are two people walking across the street. That's me and Fabe. [*laughter*] So we did a lot of Hitchcock things right off the bat.

MM: Was the second issue a more agreeable experience, then? Because you were able to do a lot more of your trademarks, and I think there was even one page where you only had a series of facial expressions from Bucky. You were able to do a lot of splash pages and—

KEVIN: I guess I opened up a little after the second issue. I probably should have looked at all these books before we talked. It probably would have helped.

MM: I think that the artist is more like the mother hen in that the writer—in this case, Fabian—has to write it but you're the one who has to execute it, y'know? Did you feel a lot of pressure in terms of that? "We're a team and I'm letting him down."

KEVIN: Well, yeah, sure. I felt that disappointment. I mean I knew it was just brutal. It was a disappointment by the end. But, it was my fault. I took too long. In my mind I had created this mountain for myself that it had to be at this level, and my self-esteem was saying, "You're never going to get it to that level." And that's what causes the creative blocks that make things take longer to finish than they should.

MM: And how would you describe Steve Rogers? What do you think? Was he a lot more fun to draw once takes the serum?

KEVIN: Yeah, because he wasn't the "super soldier" yet. He wasn't the well-honed veteran—the steely professional. He was clumsy; he was working his way through it. He was figuring things out. I just thought that was more interesting.

MM: In the second issue, you did a lot more of the stylistic things that I mentioned before. I'm looking at some of the panel work. You did the page with Bucky, then you've got a great two-page splash with Cap just jumping around, and you can see a montage with all the headlines and stuff.

KEVIN: [*laughs*] Are you looking at that double-page spread?

MM: Yeah, why? What's wrong with it?

KEVIN: Okay. You see there's a picture of Captain America shaking hands with someone?

MM: Yeah.

KEVIN: Who does that guy look like? It was supposed to be John Wayne.

MM: Oh, it does looks like him.

KEVIN: I wrote a little note to Fabe saying, "Captain America shaking hands with the Duke." So didn't he write something like "Captain America meets the Duke of..."?

MM: "...of Windsor," yeah. The Duke of Windsor.

KEVIN: Yeah. It's supposed to say "John Wayne." [*laughter*]

PHROUMPH
CINDY?!
STEVE! HELP ME!
SHKVM
SHKVM
SHKVM
SHKVM

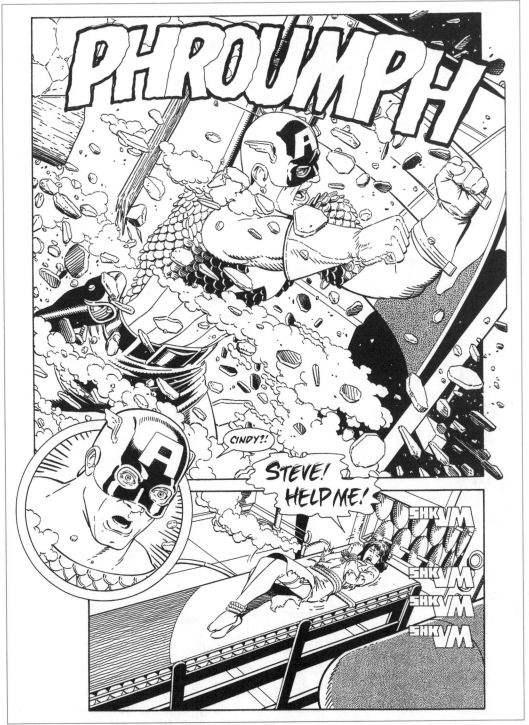

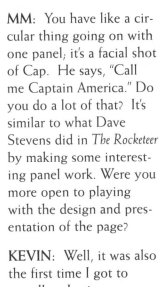

MM: You have like a circular thing going on with one panel; it's a facial shot of Cap. He says, "Call me Captain America." Do you do a lot of that? It's similar to what Dave Stevens did in *The Rocketeer* by making some interesting panel work. Were you more open to playing with the design and presentation of the page?

KEVIN: Well, it was also the first time I got to actually—Justice League—with Keith's layouts—was a fairly committee process, and this was the first time I actually got to say, "I can try this, and I can try this, and I can do that."

MM: When was it that they decided to get the fill-in artists, when they got Kevin West? What happened there? They just called you one day and said, "We can't wait for you anymore"?

KEVIN: Well, yeah, but it's not like I didn't see it coming. There were plenty of warnings, but I think that they had decided that, "It has to come out; it has to come out now, we just can't wait anymore."

Below: The covers for the series were designed to feel like a movie serial one-sheet, adding to the overall experience of the comic. Cover art for *Adventures of Captain America* #4. Inks by Terry Austin.
Next Page: A romantic interlude with Superman and Lois.

MM: But couldn't they have gotten somebody that at least drew a little bit like you?

KEVIN: I don't know. It had to be someone who could finish it quickly.

MM: Did you break down the fourth issue?

KEVIN: No, whatever he did, he did. I didn't do layouts for him.

MM: You didn't tighten it or try to fix it, try to get—

KEVIN: No.

MM: What happened? Did you just want to remove yourself completely once they got the new artist?

KEVIN: No, no, but they were looking to get it done, so I'm pretty sure they didn't want me, y'know, "fixing" things. [*laughter*] That kind of defeats the purpose.

MM: You could see that Terry Austin was making a real conscious effort to make it look like your stuff.

KEVIN: Well, that's what they want. They didn't want to go from me to Jae Lee or something. They did want to keep some sort of consistency to it.

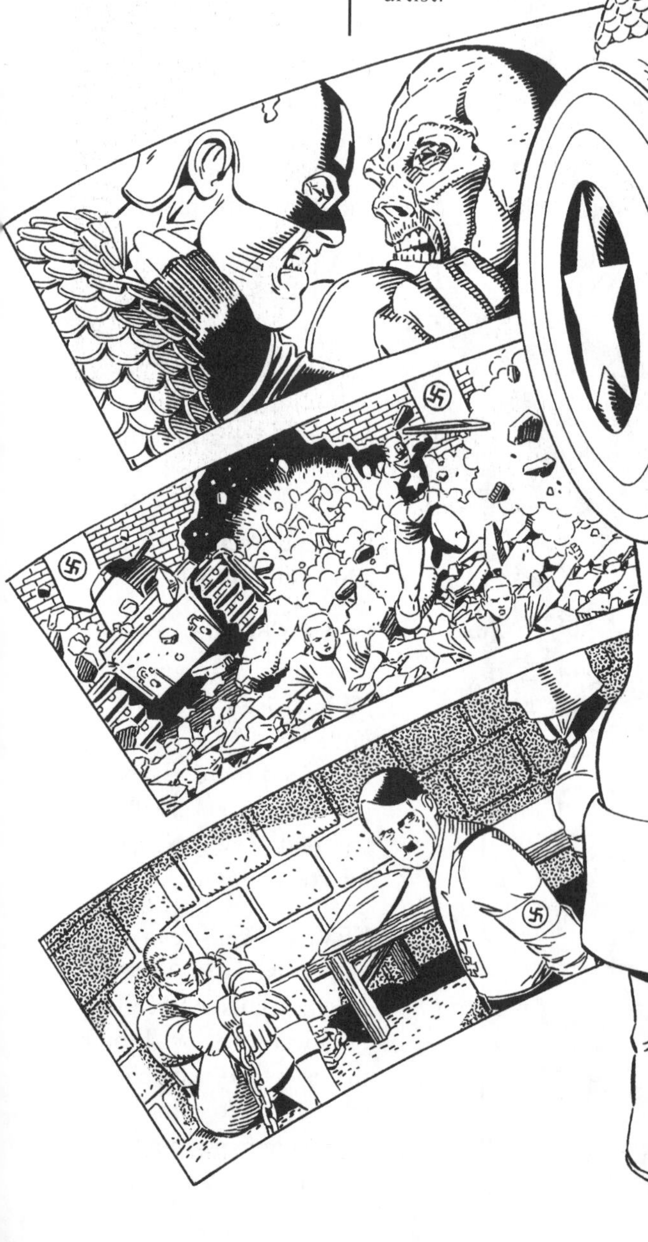

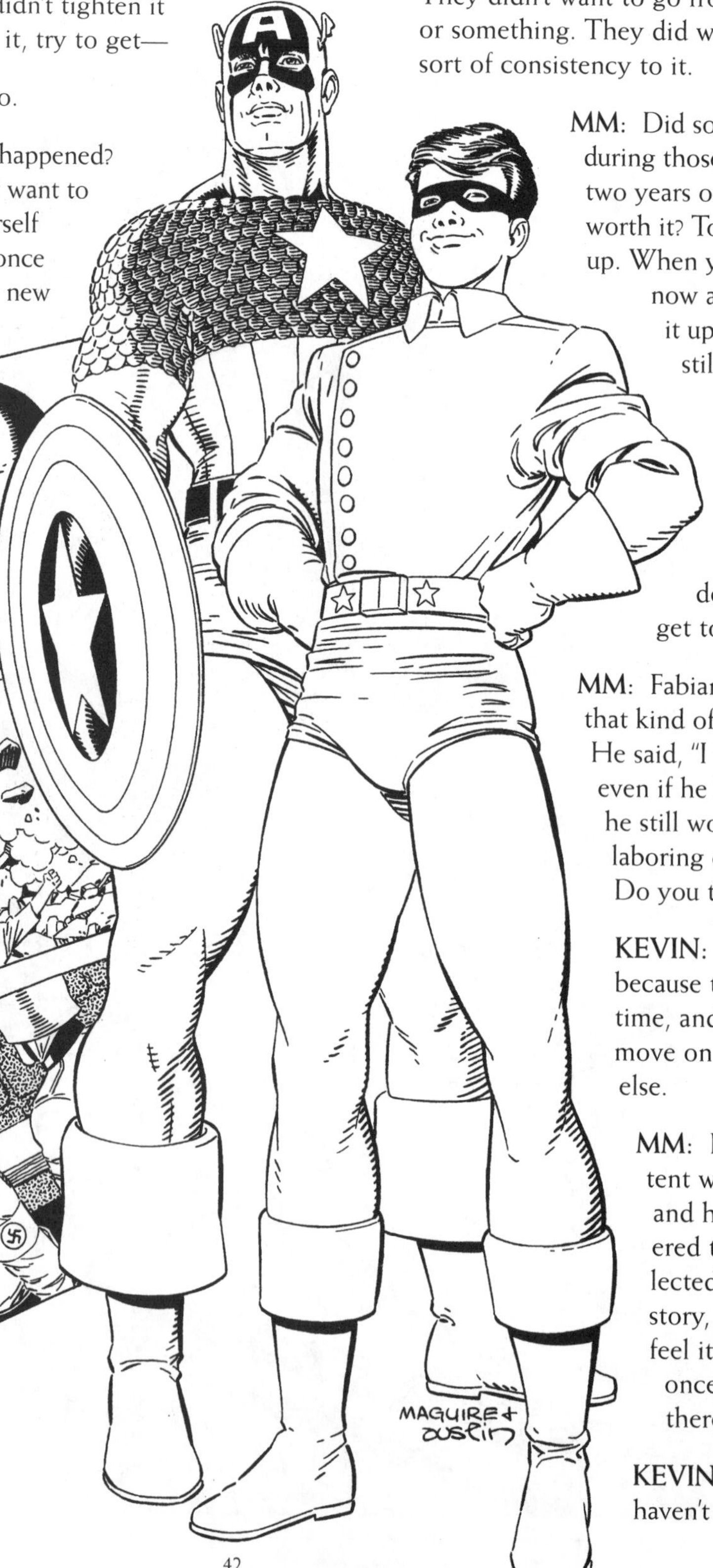
MAGUIRE+
austin

MM: Did something happen during those two years? The two years on *Cap*—was it worth it? To me it still holds up. When you look at it now and the fans bring it up to you, are you still proud of it?

KEVIN: It's that mixed feeling of I'm proud of what I got to do, but I didn't get to do it all.

MM: Fabian said something that kind of bothered me. He said, "I think if Kevin, even if he had five years, he still would have been laboring on that book." Do you think that's true?

KEVIN: Probably not, because that was of its time, and I'd rather just move on to something else.

MM: Fabian feels content with what's here, and he's a little bothered that it's not collected. It's a good story, but don't you feel it veered off a bit once you weren't there?

KEVIN: I don't know, I haven't read it. [*laughter*]

MM: I was so disappointed when I saw that you only did half of the third issue.

KEVIN: Honestly, we sort of failed, because the whole point of it is that you get wrapped up in the characters, you want to see what happens next to the characters.

MM: It's like if Coppola only directed 2/3 of *The Godfather* and then you had some Joe Schmoe directing the last third. Not to belittle the other guy.

KEVIN: Yeah, I understand.

MM: It did lose a lot when you left.

KEVIN: Yeah, it's like *Superman II*. There's a weird little symmetry, too. You had [*Superman II* director] *Richard* Donner replaced by *Richard* Lester, and *Kevin* Maguire replaced by *Kevin* West.

MM: How much of the third issue is you? It looks like there's a lot there.

KEVIN: There's a decent amount. I don't know what the exact page count is, but it was a decent amount.

MM: Because Fabian was telling me, "Those beats are there. Granted, it's not what it should have been, but the beats are still there." I don't know. It's still a great series. The first issue even stands up all by itself; you don't need to see any more. I think the series is still the best Captain America story I've ever read.

KEVIN: Oh, cool. We have done well.

MM: Yeah! Because you've given the character some respect. It's kind of serious, but fun. I don't know if you still consider it your masterpiece or anything, but there's enough there to get you wanting more, and hopefully one day you'd finish it, but....

KEVIN: Hey, I don't think they're going to pay me to finish it. [*laughs*]

MM: But it's the only way I could see it collected. I'm sure you could collect it like this, but it would be so much better if it worked the other way around, if they did it—

KEVIN: Again, I don't think Marvel is going to fork up money to have me finish it.

MM: Did you lose a lot of work at Marvel?

KEVIN: Well, I'm sure it strained things.

MM: Did it strain your relationship with DeFalco?

KEVIN: No, not really. He understood what my block was about.

MM: In your career, was this the worst block you ever had?

KEVIN: It's up there.

MM: Did you feel at this point you were ready to write?

Right: Marvel must not have held any hard feelings, because before long Kevin was back drawing a Spider-Man story for the '95 *Marvel Holiday Special*. **Below:** Right after being dismissed from *Captain America* Kevin found himself drawing a parody of the character in *Justice League America* #60. **Next Page:** Kevin's layouts and inks for *Superman/Batman* #27, page 2.

KEVIN: Yeah. I was enjoying the storytelling process. Actually, one of the things I was very happy about was how we approached Bucky. I've never been a fan of the child sidekick because it's so stupid. [*laughter*] Why would you bring a kid into these sort of dangerous situations? And I'm thinking of him as, all right, if Cap is this straight-laced, law-abiding guy, then Bucky should be the "Ferris Bueller." That was really the inspiration—*Ferris Bueller*. He would be the guy who knew how to grease the wheels. He could be the sly one, the con man as a kid.

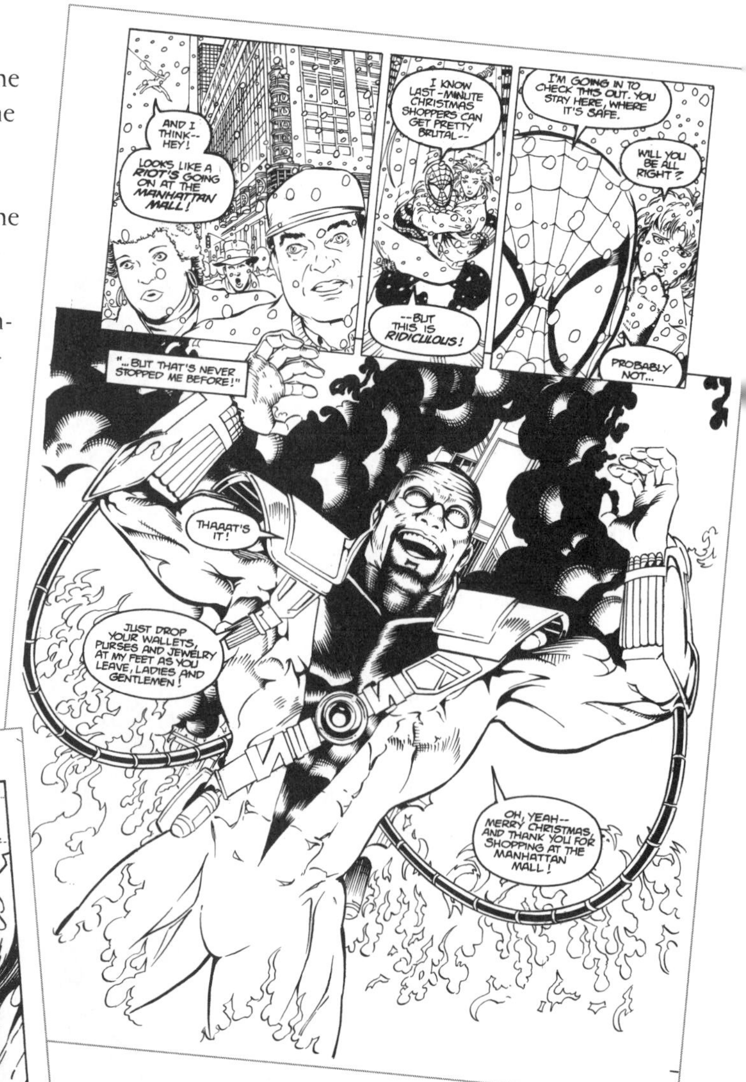
AND I THINK-- HEY!
LOOKS LIKE A RIOT'S GOING ON AT THE MANHATTAN MALL!
I KNOW LAST-MINUTE CHRISTMAS SHOPPERS CAN GET PRETTY BRUTAL--
--BUT THIS IS RIDICULOUS!
I'M GOING IN TO CHECK THIS OUT. YOU STAY HERE, WHERE IT'S SAFE.
WILL YOU BE ALL RIGHT?
PROBABLY NOT...
"...BUT THAT'S NEVER STOPPED ME BEFORE!"
THAAAT'S IT!
JUST DROP YOUR WALLETS, PURSES AND JEWELRY AT MY FEET AS YOU LEAVE, LADIES AND GENTLEMEN!
OH, YEAH-- MERRY CHRISTMAS, AND THANK YOU FOR SHOPPING AT THE MANHATTAN MALL!

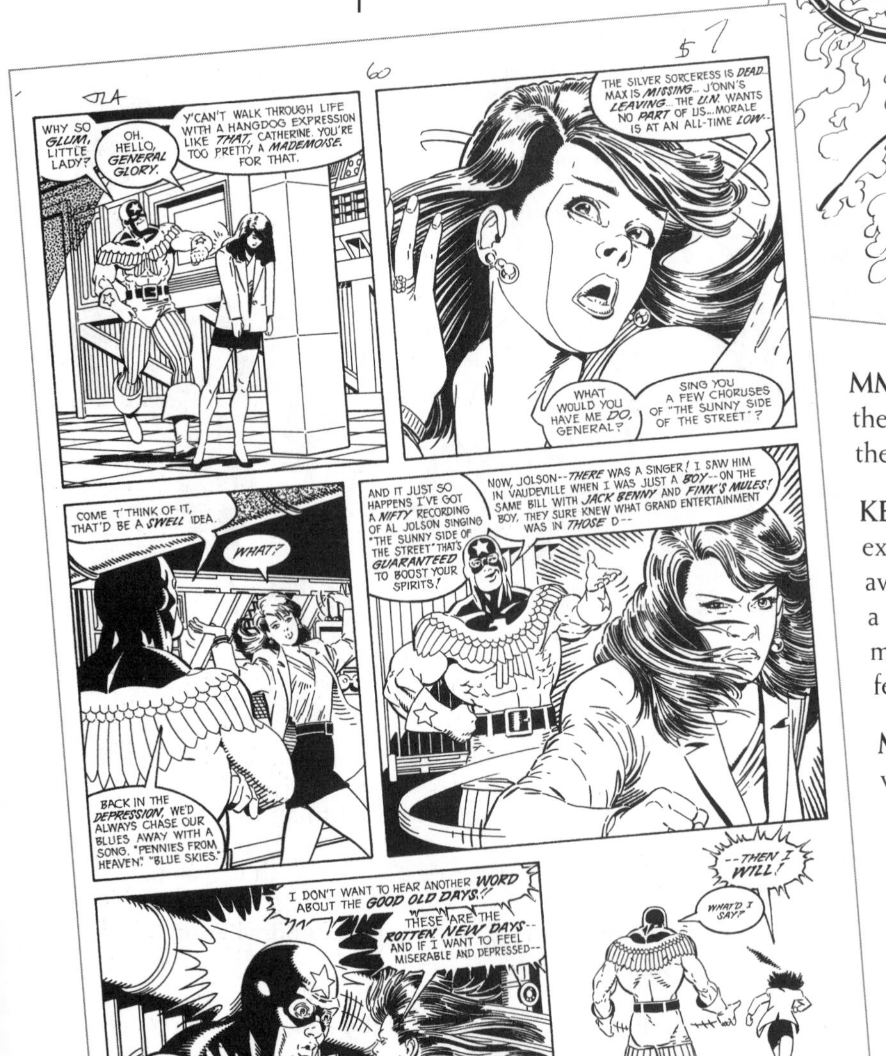
WHY SO GLUM, LITTLE LADY?
OH. HELLO, GENERAL GLORY.
Y'CAN'T WALK THROUGH LIFE WITH A HANGDOG EXPRESSION LIKE THAT, CATHERINE. YOU'RE TOO PRETTY A MADEMOISE. FOR THAT.
THE SILVER SORCERESS IS DEAD... MAX IS MISSING... J'ONN'S LEAVING... THE U.N. WANTS NO PART OF US... MORALE IS AT AN ALL-TIME LOW--
WHAT WOULD YOU HAVE ME DO, GENERAL?
SING YOU A FEW CHORUSES OF "THE SUNNY SIDE OF THE STREET"?
COME T'THINK OF IT, THAT'D BE A SWELL IDEA.
WHAT?
BACK IN THE DEPRESSION, WE'D ALWAYS CHASE OUR BLUES AWAY WITH A SONG. "PENNIES FROM HEAVEN." "BLUE SKIES."
AND IT JUST SO HAPPENS I'VE GOT A NIFTY RECORDING OF AL JOLSON SINGING "THE SUNNY SIDE OF THE STREET" THAT'S GUARANTEED TO BOOST YOUR SPIRITS!
NOW, JOLSON--THERE WAS A SINGER! I SAW HIM IN VAUDEVILLE WHEN I WAS JUST A BOY--ON THE SAME BILL WITH JACK BENNY AND FINK'S MULES! BOY, THEY SURE KNEW WHAT GRAND ENTERTAINMENT WAS IN THOSE D--
I DON'T WANT TO HEAR ANOTHER WORD ABOUT THE GOOD OLD DAYS!!
THESE ARE THE ROTTEN NEW DAYS-- AND IF I WANT TO FEEL MISERABLE AND DEPRESSED--
--THEN I WILL!
WHAT'D I SAY?

MM: And right from the start you guys wanted to make the girl, Cindy, the traitor of this story?

KEVIN: Well, we figured that would be the least expected. And it's the kind of thing you can get away with in a comic, because having someone in a hood talking in a comic is not the same as in a movie, because you couldn't tell there was a female voice. [*laughter*]

MM: And the Red Skull, you did change his visuals. You didn't like that big forehead he had?

KEVIN: I don't know. I was probably given a lot of different reference, a lot of different versions of him. I don't remember whether it was settled whether he was wearing a mask or whether it was his face.

MM: It looks like his face. It looks pretty good.

KEVIN: If it's a mask, then I want it to *look* like it's a mask. If it's his face, then I want it to look like it's his face.

MM: Other than the costume things, what sort of other problems did you run into?

KEVIN: Oh, the frickin' uniform. But that was my own fault, too. [*laughter*] Why did I decide to draw every scale? [*laughter*]

MM: Did you want to ink this book? Would you have been comfortable inking it back then?

KEVIN: No. I'd done very little inking, and I wasn't very happy with it. Actually, I was just asked that question yesterday at DC. They were like, "Why don't you ink your own stuff?"

MM: They wanted you to ink the pages that you were going to do digitally [for *Superman/Batman* #27]?

KEVIN: Well, they just asked me why I don't. I've never been very adept at using a brush, because there's definitely a skill to that. I'm never really happy with stuff that I ink of my own.

MM: Do you use a brush or a pen?

KEVIN: I use both, but I mostly use a pen. And it eventually just became a marker because I hated dipping that damned crow quill.

MM: When you were with Romita's Raiders, did they teach you how to ink-correct?

KEVIN: I'm sure there were tips thrown around there, but they hired people for penciling and they hired people for inking. My strong suit wasn't the inking.

MM: When you left *Captain America*, what was your mindset like? Did you want to go back to DC? Did you get as far away from Marvel—

KEVIN: Yeah, there didn't seem to be much choice out there. [*laughs*] "I guess I'll go to DC again."

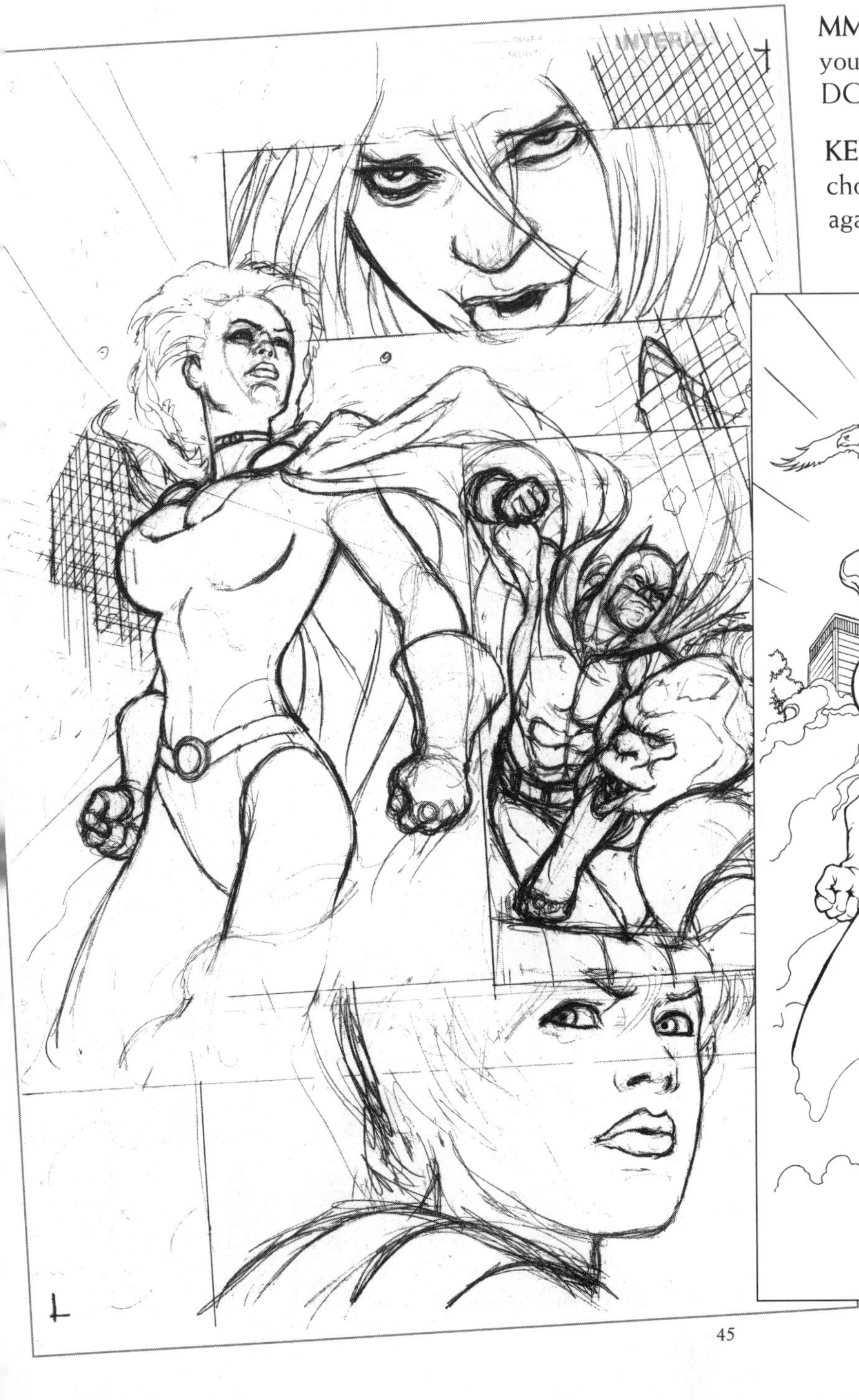

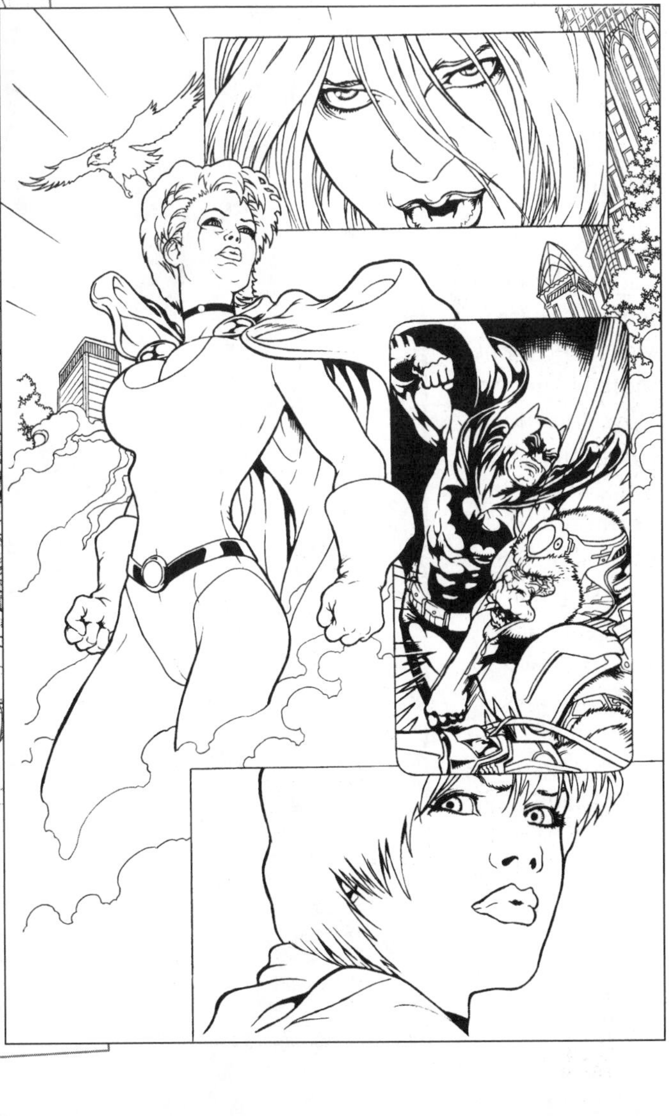

Part 4: Comic Story: First Strikeback!

MM: The Image thing was starting to happen. I don't know if they ever approached you at the beginning.

KEVIN: Not at the very beginning, but the intention was to do *Strikeback!* at Image.

MM: Then you ended up at Bravura.

KEVIN: Yeah. It was originally intended to be an Image thing.

MM: Did you get to pitch the book to Image?

KEVIN: Yeah.

MM: And they didn't want it? What happened?

KEVIN: I think part of the problem was there was no up-front money. You own it, you pay for everything yourself. I wasn't in a position to do that. Which is why originally Savage Dragon was supposed to be in the first issue, and then it got changed to the Savage Spinster. [*laughter*]

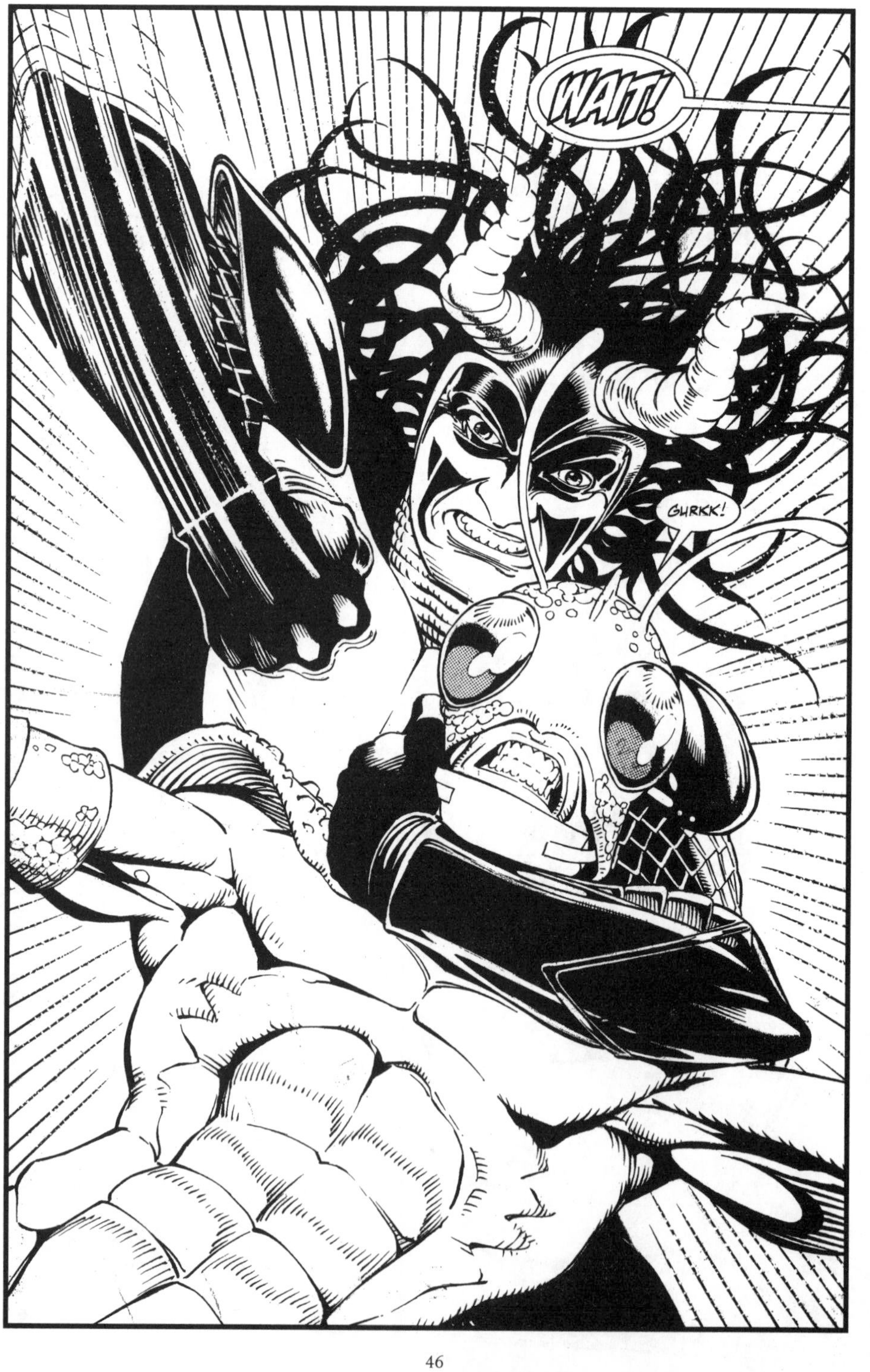

WAIT!
GURKK!

MM: You won the Russ Manning Award? Did you get a good feeling from it, since a lot of good guys had won it in the past, like Art Adams?

KEVIN: Yeah, oh, of course. Any time you win awards, you feel it. Although I'm not always a big fan of awards for artistic things, because how do you really say one person's better than another when it's so subjective? One person can like a certain style, another can like a different style. Who's better?

MM: You must have felt you were on a roll. Finally things were starting to go your way.

KEVIN: At that point, yeah, I think so.

MM: You started to become a cover artist. You were doing a lot of covers for *The Adventures of Superboy* and *L.E.G.I.O.N.* You have had some long stretches on those titles. Do you remember how you got those gigs?

KEVIN: Hanging around in the DC offices.

MM: Did you have to commit yourself to a run of *Superboy* and *L.E.G.I.O.N.*, like two years or something?

KEVIN: It just seemed like fun pages to do, as well as you got paid a little better, and there was something different every month. I don't remember actually having to write down or verbally commit to it, because I was always happy to do covers.

MM: Did you ever worry you were doing too many covers for DC? There were months when you had two or three covers on the stand in the same week.

KEVIN: I don't think I really sweated that.

MM: How long does it take you to do a cover?

KEVIN: It really varies, because it depends on what's on it, but you can safely say it's probably 50%

longer than it would take most people. [*laughter*]

MM: Do you ask them for a script? What would be the essential thing you need to get started?

KEVIN: Just to talk it over with the editor, what happens in the issue. It's all to see what the editor wants, because he's the one who's selling the book, so he sometimes has a vision of what he sees on the cover. I'll do a few thumbnail sketches and then go over it with the cover editor.

MM: Did the cover work ever get in the way of your regular books?

KEVIN: At that point I probably wasn't on any regular books.

MM: This started happening after you left *Justice League*, right?

KEVIN: Yeah.

MM: When you did *Captain America*, were you doing a lot of covers on the side? I made a timeline of your work and I noticed you did a lot of covers during that period. All of this might have been right after you left *Captain America*, though.

KEVIN: Or it might have been during *Captain America*, which might be why I ran late.

MM: You were doing covers, card art, and all sorts of merchandising, too. I think when you were doing *Cap* you only did *that*.

Previous Page: Midnight Devil puts a hurting on Rock Lobster. *Strikeback!* #4, page 1.
Above: For the cover of *Superboy* #18, Kevin was able to indulge his love for giant monsters of the Godzilla variety.
Left: Kevin drew the covers for the 3-issue adaptation of *Demolition Man* shortly after his time on *Captain America*.

Midnight Devil, Rock Lobster ™ and ©2007 Jonathan Peterson & Kevin Maguire. Superboy ™ and ©2007 DC Comics. Demolition Man ™ and ©2007 Warner Bros.

KEVIN: No, I did other things as well, as I recall.

MM: Is there anything you want to stand out with your covers? Something your fans can identify right away as being a Kevin Maguire book?

KEVIN: I don't approach it that way, no. Especially not the cover for a book I'm not penciling.

MM: But one of the reasons you were doing those covers was because they were using your name to sell whatever was inside.

KEVIN: Well, yeah. That's fine.

MM: You've never worried about, "Maybe I should do that issue just to give fans sort of a taste of what I can do on *L.E.G.I.O.N.* or *Superboy*?"

KEVIN: Mmm, no, not really. I mean, covers just seemed like bonus checks, y'know? You get to do a cool pin-up sort of page and you get paid a little bit more.

MM: I want to ask you a little bit about the *Hawk and Dove* issue [#20] you did. Do you remember how that came about?

KEVIN: I was good friends with Jonathan Peterson, who was the editor, who asked me if I would do it.

MM: Were you happy how Giordano made your pencils look? I thought he was a lot better on this than he was on the *Secret Origins* story that you did with him.

KEVIN: It's been so long since I've actually seen that issue.

MM: I think he stuck truer to what you put down on the page, rather than change it like he did on the "Deadman" story in *Secret Origins*. That had a stronger Giordano feel to it.

KEVIN: Well, y'know, he was editor-in-chief; I was just a new boy. [*laughter*]

MM: Was that issue written specifically for you? It has romance and lighthearted scenes.

KEVIN: It probably was, but Jonathan thought of me.

MM: How did you get the *Hulk Annual* [#18]? Because that's sort of your return to Marvel after the *Captain America* thing. Were you looking forward to working with Peter David?

KEVIN: Well, I was a Defenders fan. When I was a kid, *Defenders* was one of my favorite books, so that's why I did that annual. I don't remember who approached me or how it was approached, but I liked the Defenders.

MM: You said in the past that you weren't too happy with the art.

KEVIN: A lot of the stuff I did back then I just haven't seen in a long, long time.

MM: You didn't look at it when you started working on the new *Defenders* mini-series?

KEVIN: No.

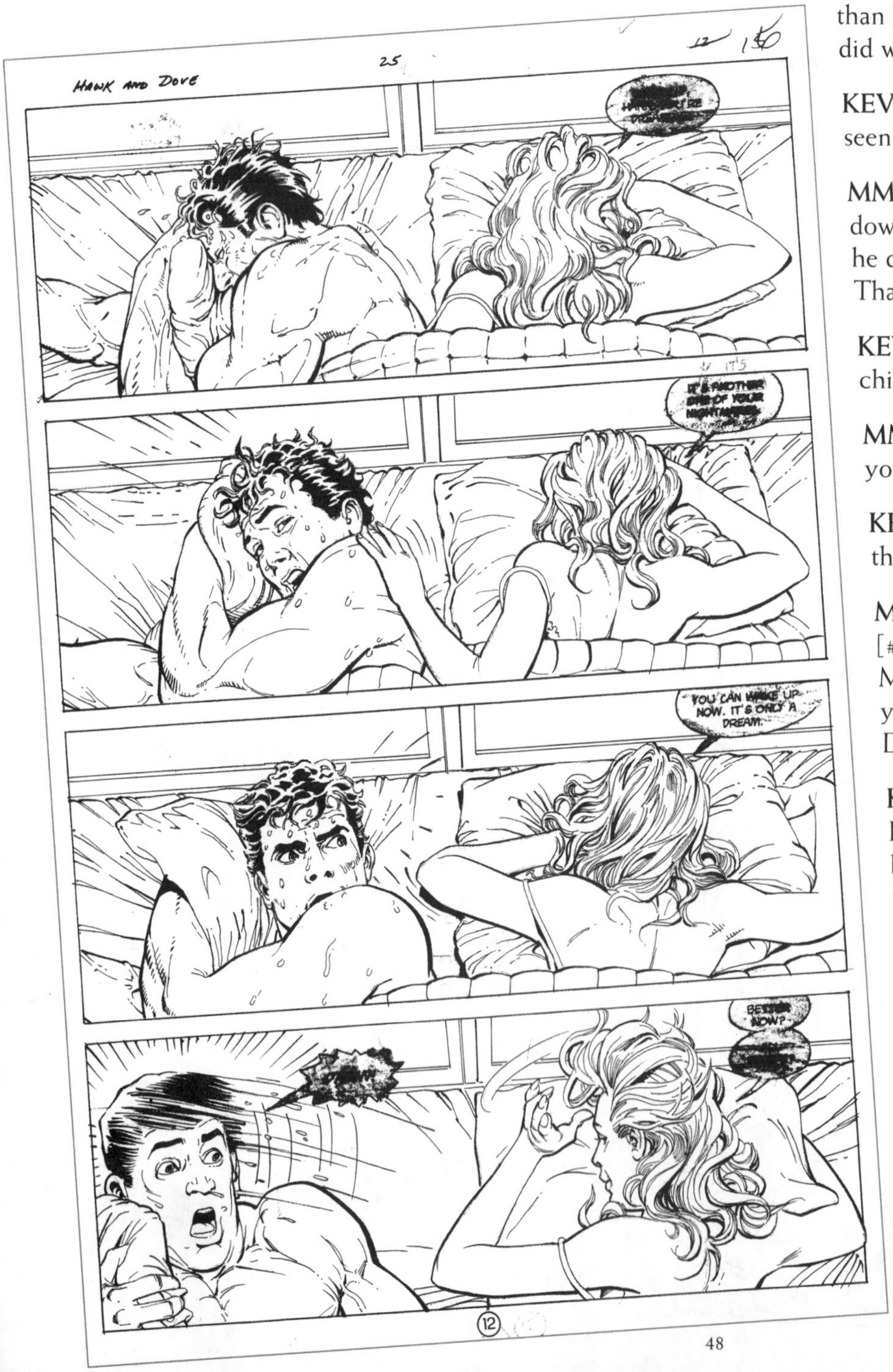

HAWK AND DOVE
YOU CAN WAKE UP NOW. IT'S ONLY A DREAM.

MM: The only thing that seemed the same between the two was your visualizations of Sub-Mariner were kind of similar.

KEVIN: I have Bill Everett's original Sub-Mariner in mind. The original triangle head—you know, the head seems a little bigger than the rest of the body.

MM: Well, he looks a little like Spock sometimes, when he's raising his eyebrows and making—

KEVIN: Well, they're similar characters, you know, in terms of the—not the arrogance, but the.... It seemed appropriate to the character. I wasn't basing him on Leonard Nimoy.

MM: You're not a closet Trekkie?

KEVIN: I don't want to see Leonard Nimoy in a green Speedo—that's all I've got to say about that. [laughter]

MM: What lured you back to DC to do *Team Titans*? That was your return back to penciling a regular series.

KEVIN: Yeah, for three issues. [laughter] Jonathan Peterson.

MM: Were you looking for a series, or did you just commit to only three issues?

KEVIN: Well, the intention was to go farther than three issues into it, but that's really around the time all the Image stuff started taking off, and the opportunity to do creator-owned stuff popped up.

MM: I was just looking at the first issue, and it's very different from anything you'd done in the past—a lot more violent, and with more action. And it's all extreme action, and babies being born, and all that kind of stuff.

KEVIN: Action and childbirth—that sells comics. [laughter] I liked doing teen books.

MM: And working with Wolfman had an appeal to it?

KEVIN: I didn't really have too much real interaction with him. It really was more with Jonathan.

MM: How'd you find the scripts to be? Was there a lot of room for you to do your thing?

Previous Page: Besides penciling *Hawk & Dove* #20, Kevin also pitched in as part of the "Tag-Team Art Squad" for issue #25, as shown here.
Above: Donna Troy comes face to face with her future son... Lord Chaos!
Below: Kevin's layouts for pages 10 and 11 of *Defenders* #1.

Donna Troy, Hawk & Dove, Lord Chaos ™ and ©2007 DC Comics. Dr. Strange, Namor ™ and ©2007 Marvel Characters, Inc.

KEVIN: I don't think so. I mean, I generally stick to one of two modes. Either I just follow the script—whatever's on the written page—or, if I'm getting involved, I'm the biggest pain in the ass in terms of story and "This doesn't make any sense. Why is he doing that?" I'm either in or I'm out. So, generally, I tend to say, "Just give me the strip and I'll draw it." I mean, that's how the *Justice League* stuff was.

MM: And this was like that, too?

KEVIN: Yeah, I had no input on the story. Whatever the script was, okay, boom.

MM: You can draw something without having your heart into it.

KEVIN: Well, most of the stuff is like that.

MM: If it's a decent book, by the time you're halfway through the first issue, do you become a little more involved, especially with something like the launch of *Team Titans*?

KEVIN: Well, yeah. You have a sense of, not ownership, but stewardship over the characters. Of course, that's there. But you also realize that you're playing with someone else's toys and you're playing in someone else's yard, so it's not yours. You can't go home with it.

MM: Do you remember any of these characters being particularly fun to draw?

KEVIN: I don't even remember the names of them anymore. [*laughter*]

MM: Okay, Kilowatt, Mirage, Redwing....

KEVIN: That electrical guy?

MM: That's Kilowatt.

KEVIN: That was a pain in the ass to draw. The whole process was just—you would have to draw him twice because you had to do the overlay.

MM: What about the girl? I assume you had a fun time drawing—

KEVIN: Oh, probably. I like the flying girl.

MM: That's Redwing.

KEVIN: Yeah. There was the vampire guy, and there was Terra.

MM: And that huge guy that looks like Darkseid's son—I just forgot his name.

KEVIN: Oh, Battalion.

MM: Did this book seem like typical DC stuff to you? Maybe that's why you don't have that attachment to these characters like you do the Marvel ones.

KEVIN: I don't know, because they all fall around the same time I was percolating on *Strikeback!*, when that was something that I had a proprietary interest in. That's something

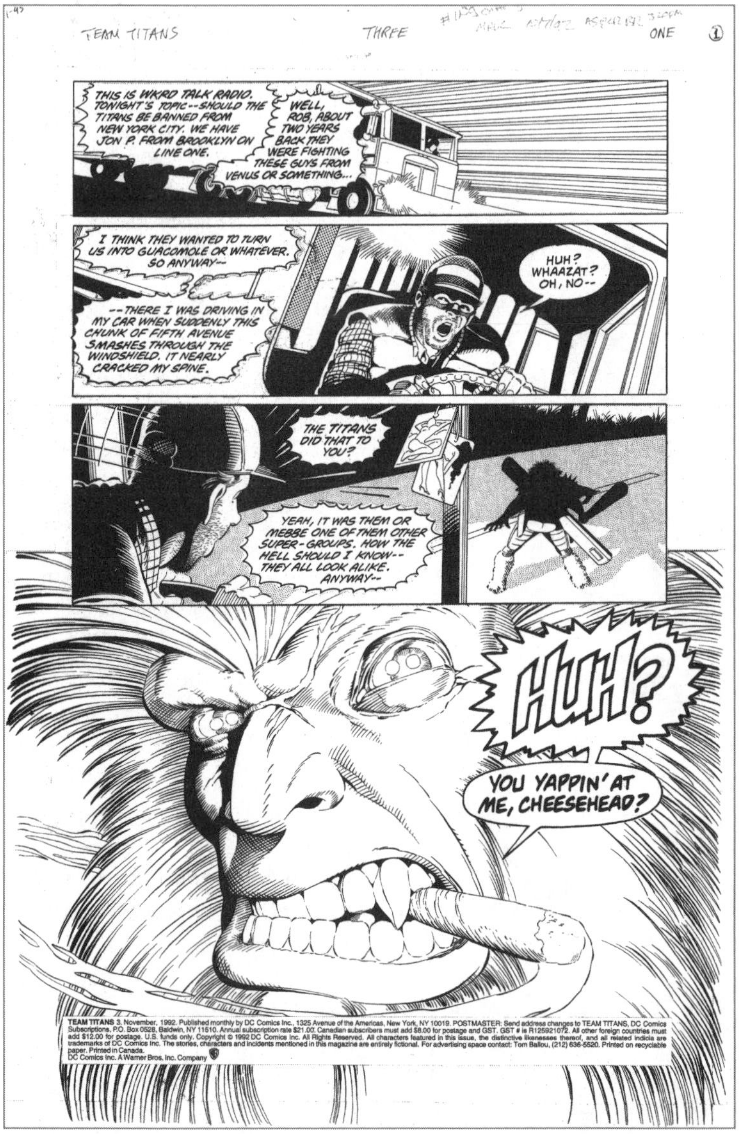
TEAM TITANS
THREE
ONE
THIS IS WKRD TALK RADIO. TONIGHT'S TOPIC--SHOULD THE TITANS BE BANNED FROM NEW YORK CITY. WE HAVE JON P. FROM BROOKLYN ON LINE ONE.
WELL, ROB, ABOUT TWO YEARS BACK THEY WERE FIGHTING THESE GUYS FROM VENUS OR SOMETHING...
I THINK THEY WANTED TO TURN US INTO GUACOMOLE OR WHATEVER. SO ANYWAY--
--THERE I WAS DRIVING IN MY CAR WHEN SUDDENLY THIS CHUNK OF FIFTH AVENUE SMASHES THROUGH THE WINDSHIELD. IT NEARLY CRACKED MY SPINE.
HUH? WHAAZAT? OH, NO--
THE TITANS DID THAT TO YOU?
YEAH, IT WAS THEM OR MEBBE ONE OF THEM OTHER SUPER-GROUPS. HOW THE HELL SHOULD I KNOW-- THEY ALL LOOK ALIKE. ANYWAY--
HUH?
YOU YAPPIN' AT ME, CHEESEHEAD?
TEAM TITANS 3. November, 1992. Published monthly by DC Comics Inc., 1325 Avenue of the Americas, New York, NY 10019. POSTMASTER: Send address changes to TEAM TITANS, DC Comics Subscriptions, P.O. Box 0528, Baldwin, NY 11510. Annual subscription rate $21.00. Canadian subscribers must add $8.00 for postage and GST. GST # is R125921072. All other foreign countries must add $12.00 for postage. U.S. funds only. Copyright © 1992 DC Comics Inc. All Rights Reserved. All characters featured in this issue, the distinctive likenesses thereof, and all related indicia are trademarks of DC Comics Inc. The stories, characters and incidents mentioned in this magazine are entirely fictional. For advertising space contact: Tom Ballou, (212) 636-5520. Printed on recyclable paper. Printed in Canada.
DC Comics Inc. A Warner Bros. Inc. Company

that came out of my own head. That meant more to me than these characters that I had no.... Back then, you didn't have creatorship stake, as you do now.

MM: But you seemed re-energized, that's why I ask, because I'd seen the *Hulk Annual* and I thought it looked kind of bland compared to the stuff you could do. Then you did this thing and you had these huge panels going on, and detail—

KEVIN: I liked the script, too. If you're given a script with, "Page one, a big explosion," then that's what it calls for, but it's not something that I came up with in terms of this is how the story will go, it'll be open, it'll be tight.

MM: In terms of your figure work, it looks a lot better.

KEVIN: Well, thank you. [*laughs*] I must have been happy at the time.

MM: But looking at the *Hulk Annual*, there're no backgrounds.

KEVIN: I've always hated backgrounds. But *Team Titans* was probably my best book in terms of the royalties for a single issue, because I had the five or six separate covers and five or six separate back-up stories.

MM: Tell me a little bit about Jonathan Peterson. You two became friends when you were working in the DC offices, I guess?

KEVIN: We liked a lot of the same things.

MM: Who approached who about doing *Strikeback!*?

KEVIN: I had the idea for the characters. We talked about it, and he knew the Image guys. I'd heard of them, but I didn't know them personally. At that point Jonathan was also deciding that maybe it was time to expand and... it was a mutual thing.

MM: Were you ready to move on at this point from doing work-for-hire?

KEVIN: Well, yeah. This is the first time I actually got to completely steer something.

MM: You were saying that you were very insecure about Image, because they didn't pay up front.

KEVIN: I think that's why we didn't actually go to Image, as opposed to Bravura, who paid up front.

Previous Page: Introducing the Team Titans: Nightrider, Terra, Killowatt, Mirage, and Redwing. Cornerbox art for the various *Team Titans* #1 covers.
Left: Enter Battalion. *Team Titans* #3, page 1. Inks by Will Blyberg.
Below: It starts with a dance. The opening panel to *Strikeback!* #1.

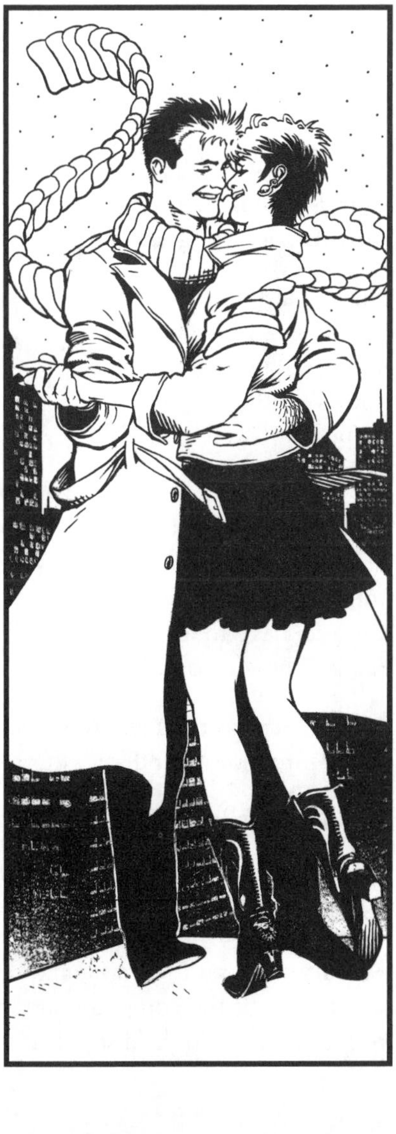

MM: What are the influences on *Strikeback!*? Was it supposed to be a satire on the kind of comics that were coming out at that time?

KEVIN: No, because in general I'm not really that plugged into what's going on in the comic book universes. I don't know what's going on in *Spider-Man* now; I don't know what's going on in *X-Men* now. I have a vague idea of DC because they send me all these comps every month.

MM: But you never take a look at the competition?

KEVIN: Sometimes I'll look through them when there are artists whose work I like, and the stuff that's good, but in general, no. So *Strikeback!* wasn't really a reflection of what was going on as much as just what I wanted to do.

MM: It feels like those crazy Image comic books, those Rob Liefeld Extreme comic books—wall-to-wall action, y'know?

KEVIN: Well, I like that. I like fast-paced, moving forward stuff.

MM: I also like the characters. I love how when each one first shows up they say their name: "Rottweiler," and "Doberman."

KEVIN: That was probably Jonathan's input, his influence. Being an editor, you have to let the reader know who's who.

MM: But who talks like this? [*laughter*] It's not like you come into a room and say your name.

KEVIN: Well, it's a comic book. [*laughter*]

MM: Was this more yours? Was this your idea, and Jonathan just scripted it?

KEVIN: We sat in a room and scripted it together. He was typing at the computer and I was pacing around the room saying, "No, he'd say this," or "How about this,"

and we were bouncing things back and forth.

MM: Did he quit his job at DC around this time?

KEVIN: Yes.

MM: How were you invited to Bravura?

KEVIN: Again, that was probably Jonathan's connections.

MM: Do you remember the deal? Could he have gone to Image right away, or could he have gone to Dark Horse Legends?

KEVIN: I don't know. I'll tell you what, Jonathan was something like the editor/business guy. He covered all that stuff—the legalities and the contracts and who had a better deal and all that stuff—and I just sat back and made stuff up.

MM: You had a lot of faith in him to do that.

KEVIN: Oh, yeah, yeah, yeah.

MM: Because you were trusting your career a little bit, and your finances.

KEVIN: Yeah, well.

MM: How quickly did Bravura pick up this book?

KEVIN: I'm sure it was very quickly once discussions—I mean, they were looking to start their own Image thing. They wanted us to be part of their first wave of titles.

MM: I always thought that Bravura was more of a response to Dark Horse's Legends line, considering the names that were involved, like Starlin and Chaykin and Simonson. You were happy to be part of that company, to be associated with those sorts of names?

KEVIN: Sure. Again, it really didn't have anything to do with that. I mean, I was just more focused on what I was doing other than what names I was a part of. I don't

STRIKEBACK #1
3
NIKKI, ARE YOU ALL RIGHT?
HUH? OH--
--YEAH. SORRY MY MIND WAS SOMEPLACE ELSE.
SOMEWHERE NICER?
THERE'S NO PLACE NICER THAN HERE WITH YOU.
OH GOD, SHE'S GETTING SAPPY ON ME.
C'MERE YOU BIG LUG.
UH-OH I'M GETTIN' GREASED FOR SOMETHING.
AM-SCRAY, AT-CAY.
ALONE AT LAST.
SO..HOW ABOUT A KISS THAT'LL LAST YOU ANOTHER 25 YEARS?
WHY? YOU GOING SOMEPLACE?
THERE'S NO PLACE NICER THAN HERE WITH YOU.
OH GOD, HE'S GETTING SAPPY ON ME.
OOH--!
BONG! BONG! BONG! BONG! BONG!

think people who bought *Man Called A•X* were necessarily going to buy *Strikeback!*.

MM: As soon as you guys started work, you encountered problems with Malibu?

KEVIN: Not as soon as we started, no, but later on. It was actually when Marvel bought out Malibu.

MM: You guys were still working when Marvel bought out Malibu?

KEVIN: Yeah, yeah.

MM: Because the first issue said "one of six," and by the second issue that number had changed to "two of *five*." Were the sales pretty bad?

KEVIN: Well, yeah. It was always intended to be a six-issue thing, and by the time we got finished with—I don't know if it was #3 or #4—that was when Marvel bought Malibu out, and they felt like Malibu overpaid the people in Bravura. I guess, obviously, ourselves included. I don't think we were paid substantially more than most regular comics, but I have a feeling that Chaykin and Starlin probably got more than we did. They're probably savvier business people.

So Marvel was trying to cut it down. I remember having a conversation with a lawyer from Marvel who was just nasty. And I know he lied about things, because then he also talked to Jonathan Peterson, and Jonathan would say, "He said you said this." "Well, I never said that, I never...." Basically the bottom line was they said they weren't going to pay us for finishing unless we agreed to do the last two issues for free. I was like, "I can't afford to do that! I can't do two issues for free." Could these lawyers go unpaid for the time it would take for me to do two penciled books for free? I mean, how many people could? So that's where it all fell apart.

A LOVE THAT WILL LAST--
--TIL THE STARS GROW COLD.

MM: Did you get to wrap up the story the way you wanted? Did things have to change?

KEVIN: We never got to wrap it up the way I wanted, no.

MM: The minute you got that phone call, you immediately stopped working on the book?

KEVIN: Yeah, until that stuff got settled.

MM: Was that one of the first times you had a lawyer call you about anything?

KEVIN: Yeah.

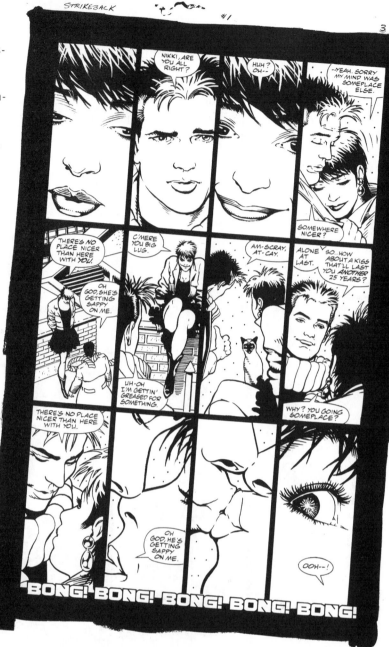

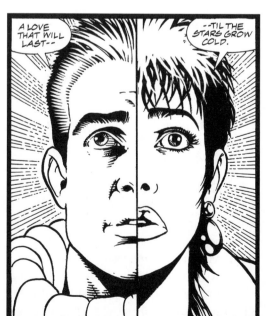

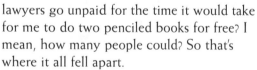

Previous Page: Cover art for Bravura's *Strikeback!* #1. When Image reprinted the issue, a new cover was used.
Above: A romantic interaction between the two principle characters, Rascal and Nikki, to establish why Rascal goes through so much trouble to get her back after she is kidnapped. Page 3 of *Strikeback!* #1.
Left: Panel from *Strikeback!* #1, page 16.

MM: Was it intimidating?

KEVIN: Well, yeah. Not intimidating so much in the sense that the guy could stop my paychecks. I just told the guy he was being an ass. Maybe that's his job, I don't know.

When we landed it at Image, we have to thank Jim Lee for that, because it was very kind of him to allow us to do that at Wildstorm. Even then sales weren't what we were hoping for. We had to have the fifth and sixth issue combined and just be a fifth issue. The original plan in the story is that we were going to have these two giant monsters fighting in Hong Kong. I just wanted to have all these kickass giant monster fight scenes. Well, all of a sudden, we can't do that, because we have to wrap up the story.

MM: I was amazed that Wildstorm reprinted the first two issues so quickly.

KEVIN: Except that Savage Dragon is back in issue #1.

MM: Were you able to finish the story like you wanted?

KEVIN: No, in the fifth issue I was definitely like, "I don't care anymore." I was so disgusted with the whole thing. So the fifth issue was done really quickly. The fifth issue's just like, "All right, just get it done."

MM: The timing was a little bit off, even when Bravura started, it was already a little too late. The book came out a little past that prime Image era.

KEVIN: Yeah, I'm known for catching the wave after it has already crashed....

MM: Did Bravura promote the book at all?

KEVIN: They promoted it a decent amount, it was just a mixed experience. The high point was being able to create something and going with that, and that was fine, I enjoyed that, but then all the legalities were just a pain in the ass.

MM: How did you keep together while you were working on the series? How did you stay focused for this book?

KEVIN: Well, I don't know how focused I stayed, in general, but partially it was something that reflected my sensibilities, it was something that I was coming up with, so I was enjoying it more.

MM: What was the deal with the scarf your hero wore in the book? Where'd you get that idea from?

KEVIN: I don't remember. I just had this idea that this guy had something that he could create into anything. I don't remember exactly where the whole scarf—it's funny you mentioning that. I guess it's going to happen because we're interviewing about my career, but in this apartment complex I lived I was part of a group of people

Below: No, it's not Godzilla vs. King Ghidorah—it's X vs. Dragon! Too bad their battle had to be scaled back to make room for a condensed ending. Inks by Joe Rubinstein.
Next Page: Cover for the Image reprint of *Strikeback!* #2.

Strikeback! ™ and ©2007 Jonathan Peterson & Kevin Maguire.

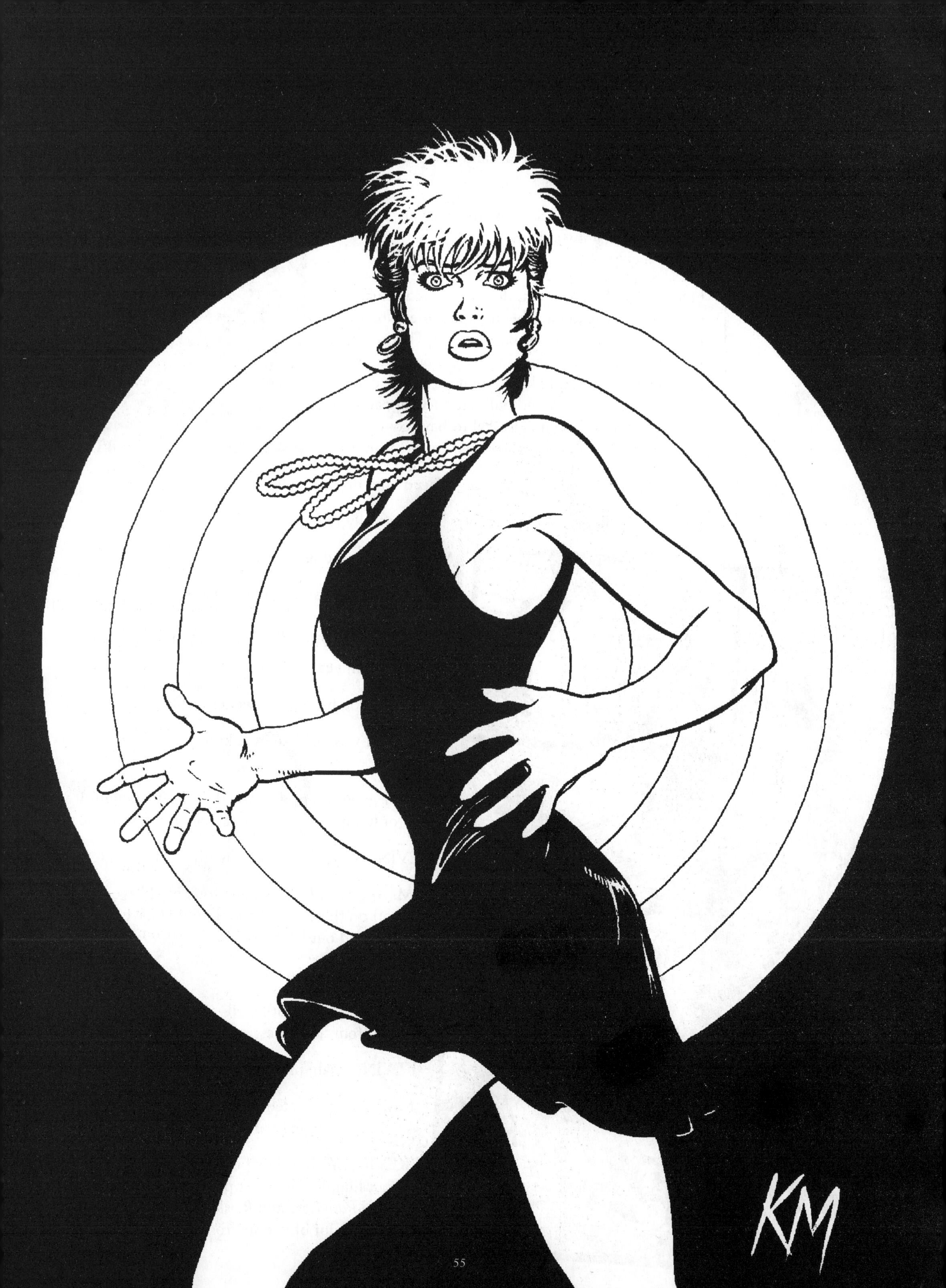
KM

Right: Kevin's dog, Jack. **Below:** Midnight Devil lends Nikita a hand. Page 20 of *Strikeback!* #4. Inks by Joe Rubinstein. **Next Page:** Midnight Devil feels the wrath of... Doberman! Cover art for Image's reprint of issue #3.

who would go on a dog run. Someone I became friends with in the dog run got a couple of comics from eBay or something, and one of them was an issue of *Strikeback!*. So they were circulating it amongst themselves, and they just constantly made fun of me about "the guy with the scarf."

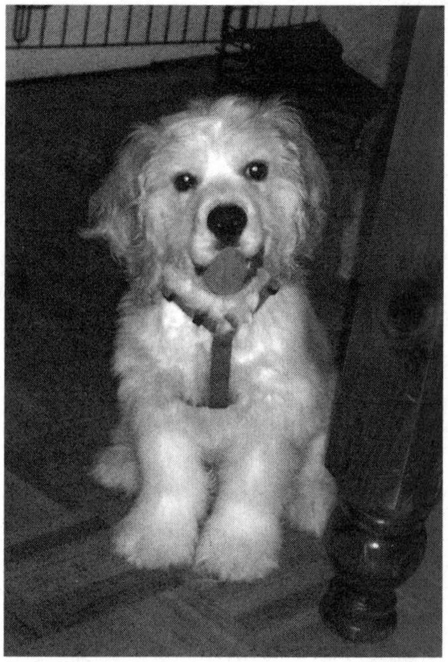

MM: Was that supposed to be funny or just something you thought was kind of cool?

KEVIN: I thought it was kind of cool. This was before CGI. At that point, doing that as a visual movie effect would have been impossible. No, you know what it was? It was Bugs Bunny. That was the inspiration. I wanted Rascal to have a Bugs Bunny kind of attitude, and I liked how Bugs Bunny could reach behind his back and pull out a frying pan or a giant camera, so I wanted Rascal to have something that would give him access to whatever he wanted.

MM: Rascal started out as a straightlaced kind of super-hero, didn't he?

KEVIN: Yeah. And again, rascally. Like a rascally rabbit.

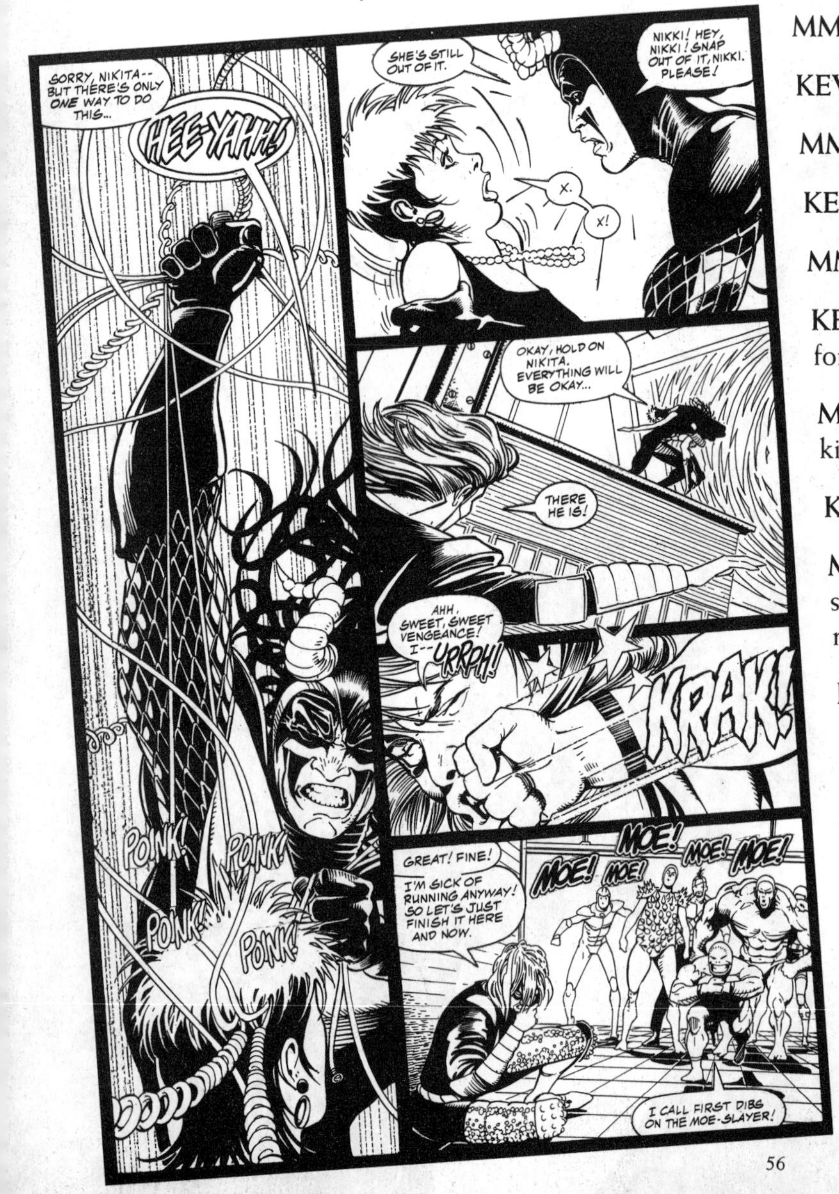

SORRY, NIKITA-- BUT THERE'S ONLY ONE WAY TO DO THIS...
HEE-YAHH!
SHE'S STILL OUT OF IT.
NIKKI! HEY, NIKKI! SNAP OUT OF IT, NIKKI. PLEASE!
X.
X!
OKAY, HOLD ON NIKITA. EVERYTHING WILL BE OKAY...
THERE HE IS!
AHH, SWEET, SWEET VENGEANCE! I--URRPH!
KRAK!
PONK! PONK!
PONK! PONK!
GREAT! FINE! I'M SICK OF RUNNING ANYWAY! SO LET'S JUST FINISH IT HERE AND NOW.
MOE! MOE! MOE! MOE! MOE! MOE!
I CALL FIRST DIBS ON THE MOE-SLAYER!

MM: Are you a dog person?

KEVIN: Oh, I'm a huge dog person.

MM: Oh, you are? You have a dog right now?

KEVIN: Oh, yeah.

MM: Do you have a Rottweiler or Doberman?

KEVIN: I was just like, you know, it seemed to work for me.

MM: I've got no problem with it, I just thought it was kind of funny. Two dog characters in the same book?

KEVIN: Well, they work together; they're a team.

MM: If this had succeeded, you could have done a spin-off on these characters. Did you have more stories planned out for them?

KEVIN: Oh, yeah.

MM: And Midnight Devil—is that your favorite design from this series?

KEVIN: Yeah, probably. That was Jackie Chan.

MM: You dedicated the third issue to Jackie Chan, so you're a big martial arts fan?

KEVIN: Yeah. It was before most people knew about him, for the most part, over here. This was before *Rush Hour* and *Rumble in the Bronx* came out. Me and a lot of people from DC would scramble

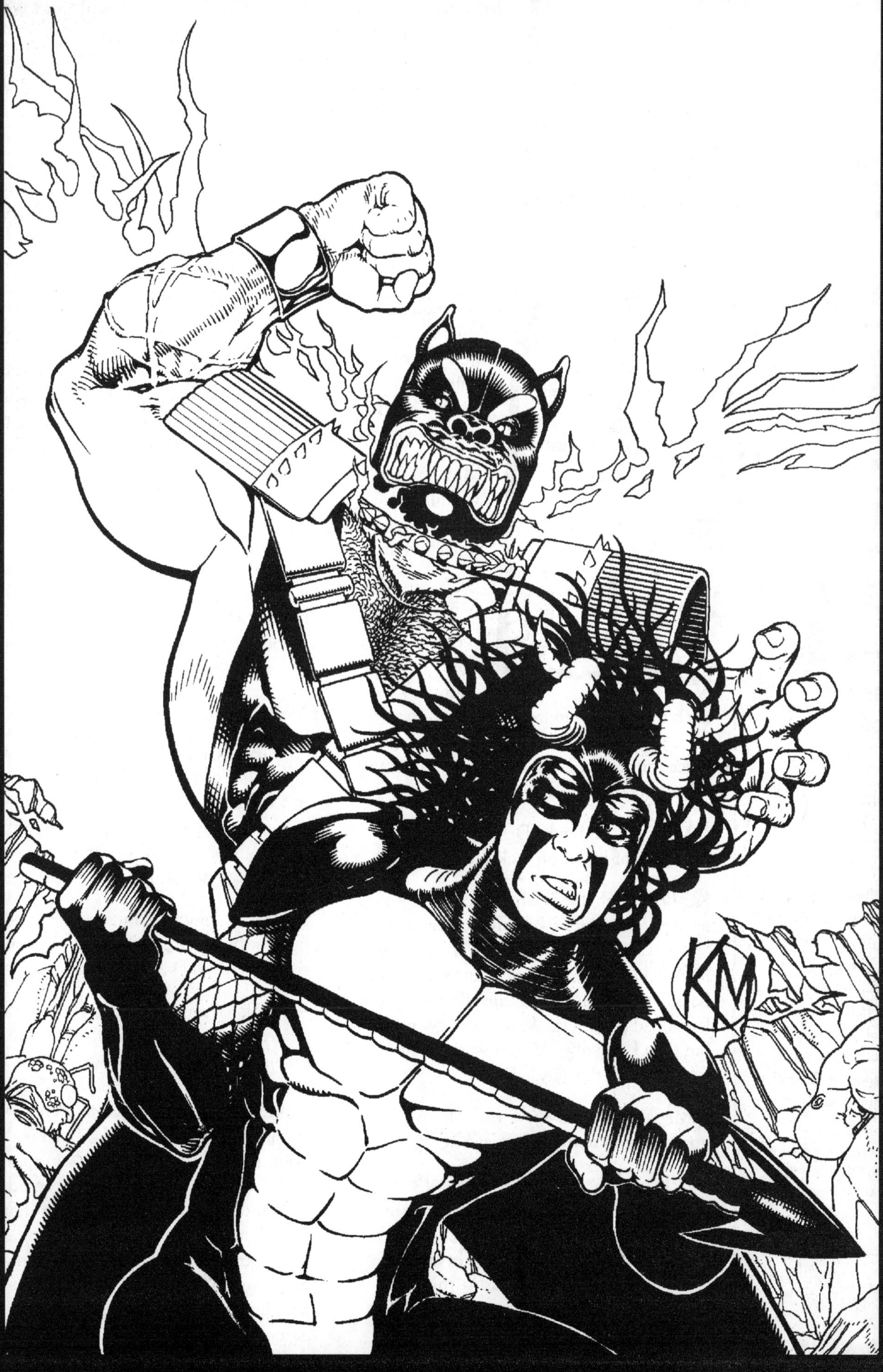

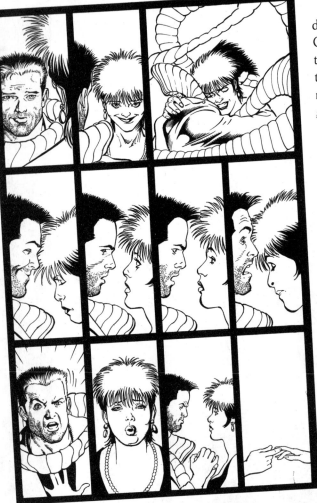

Above: Rascal and Nikki bid each other adieu. Will they ever get back together? Not likely at this point. Inks by Joe Rubinstein.

Right: Godzilla may be down, but he's never out. Inks by another Godzilla fan, Arthur Adams.

down to Chinatown every time we heard that one of his new movies was going to be playing. We just had this great find. "Yeah, new movie opening!" It was called *Dragons Forever*. We would go down into these horrible Chinatown theaters with wooden chairs.

MM: You wouldn't buy the bootlegs? That's what I did.

KEVIN: Oh, yeah, we'd get the bootlegs. Back then I was buying videotapes that were very poor quality, and then I found a place there selling laser discs, so I was buying a bunch of those instead.

MM: Even Midnight Devil's movements were sort of based on Jackie Chan.

KEVIN: Yeah, that's why he's not wearing a mask. That's why he has his face painted. There was a movie called *Painted Faces* about how Jackie Chan grew up. I just wanted to be able to see his face. Originally, Midnight Devil had a black mask, just a scary mask, but then I thought, "Well, I want Jackie Chan to play this guy." [*laughter*]

MM: That's good. Were the sales pretty good throughout the time at Bravura?

KEVIN: Well, I don't think any of the Bravura stuff was selling very well. If the rest of Bravura's stuff was selling well but ours wasn't, it might not have been as much of a problem, but I don't think any of them were doing all that well, which is why Marvel's axeman came in to cut stuff.

MM: Were you happy with how your inking reproduced?

KEVIN: That first issue was the first time I inked a whole issue, and inking is not my strong suit.

MM: What did you do wrong?

KEVIN: I'm not that good with a brush. There's a skill to that which, if I applied myself I could do it, but I just got bored....

MM: When you wrote *Godzilla* you didn't draw it? What happened?

KEVIN: It was supposed to be a twelve-issue thing and I was going to draw the last three issues. I just wasn't seeing eye-to-eye with the—not the editor, the editor and I got along really well. The problem was from higher up. And I think—this is what's been related to me, not to spread rumors, but this had come at a time when editors weren't allowed to write anymore. This was a rule that came down at Dark Horse, which is why Randy Stradley hadn't been writing the *Godzilla* series. So he was kind of taking a very hands-on—

MM: Taking it out on you?

KEVIN: It was all, "No, we don't want to go in that direction. No, I don't want to go in that direction." I just felt hamstrung, and it just became frustrating. It got to the point where it was just, "You know what? This just is not worth it to me."

MM: But they had agreed to a direction before they started changing their minds, right? Had you sent in a proposal?

KEVIN: Yeah, I had several proposals. There were times where things were changed after the book was printed and the dialogue that was mentioned didn't make sense anymore. [*laughs*] There were things that I wanted to do. I can really understand you don't do certain things with Godzilla, because it's a licensed property and Toho is very anal about that. So it was all about the characters.

I wanted to make the G-Force more of an army than just the Fantastic Four for the simple reason that I wanted to create characters you get to know, and then kill them off during the course of the adventures. I just don't buy these people getting into these life-and-death situations and always walking away unscathed. But they were like, "No, it has to be the four characters and that's that," and, "The last time I saw Godzilla he was poisoned, so deal with that," and stuff like that. There were ideas for things I wanted to do later on that were shot down. I don't know if they were terrible ideas, it just seemed like they wanted it to be something else. Not the actual editor I was working with, he was getting really frustrated too. That's just my recollection of how it went; it was just a very frustrating situation.

MM: I remember being so disappointed with that series, because there was your name on it, and then it was Art Adams—two really good artists—and the interiors suck. [*laughter*] Did you type it yourself on a computer?

KEVIN: Actually, in fact, it was a typewriter. Back then it was typewriters and faxes. [*laughter*]

MM: So this is the first time you actually sat down and wrote something, right?

KEVIN: Yeah.

MM: Did it take you a long time to do it?

KEVIN: I don't recall. A lot of it was working out the back-and-forth with editorial. I mean, that was probably more time-consuming than anything else.

MM: Did you have any doubts? "I'm not a writer." I mean did you have that type of self-doubt when you were writing it?

KEVIN: Actually, I'm not polished as a writer, but I've been a rabid Godzilla fan.

MM: When you looked at the artwork, were you happy with it? Did it match what you wrote? Was it weird seeing something that you've created—

KEVIN: It is kind of odd seeing, just "I would have done this differently," or, "I would have done that differently." But, that's me.

MM: So you didn't ask for drawing revisions?

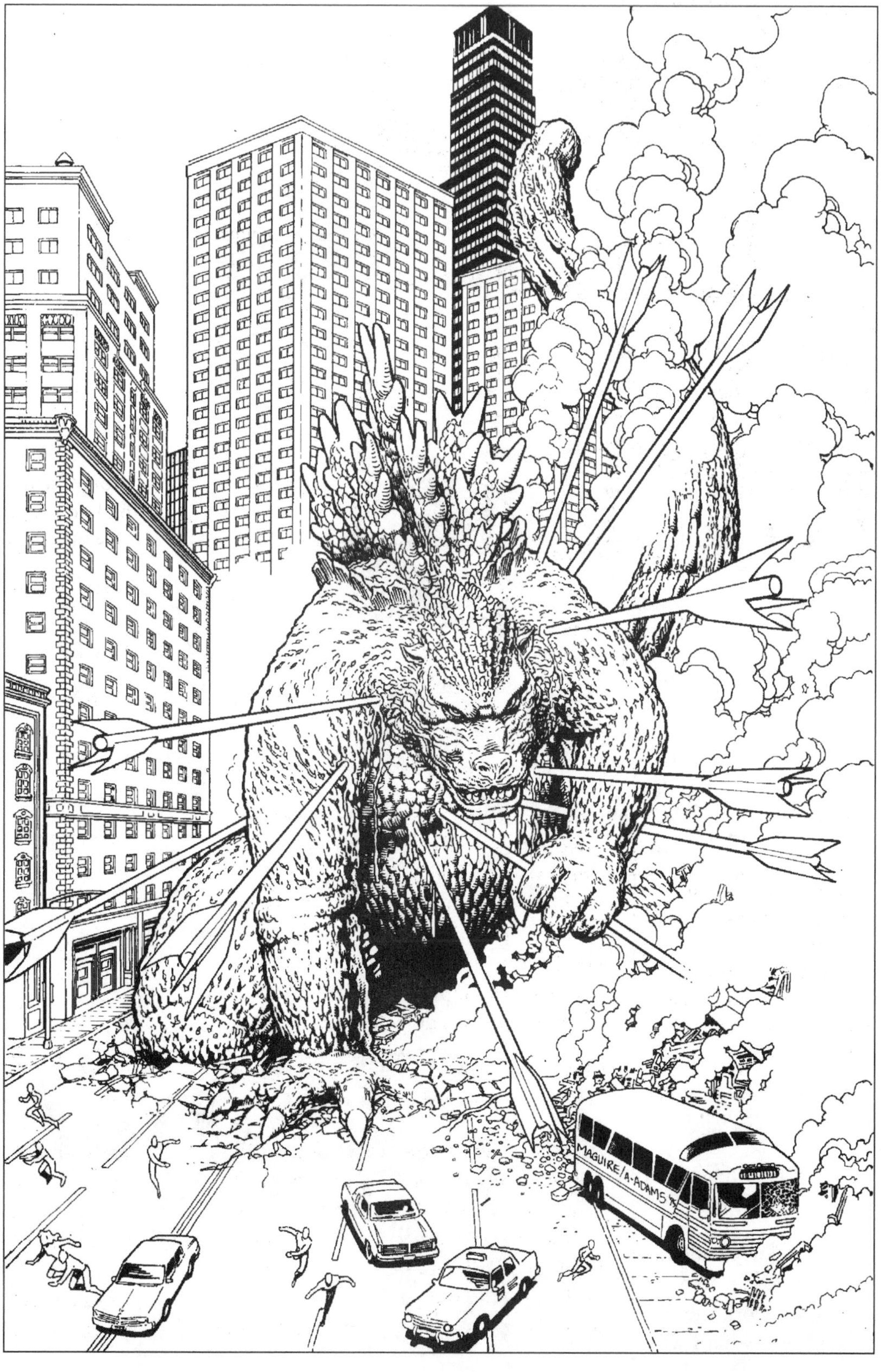
MAGUIRE/A-ADAMS

KEVIN: Not at all. No, no. I mean, you have respect for the artist, because obviously I've been there, and I hoped to treat him with the same respect that I would like to be treated myself in terms of latitude about what you should or shouldn't do on a page.

MM: You didn't make a conscious effort to tell yourself, "If I'm going to make it in comics, I need to work for more companies besides DC"?

KEVIN: No.

MM: Well, it seemed like you got all over the place.

KEVIN: That's where opportunities presented themselves.

MM: Did you create those monsters, like Bagorah and Cybersaur?

KEVIN: Those weren't my names; somebody else named them. I had different names for them and then they changed them. I think they insisted on one of them being a robot. Was there a robot in there?

MM: I think Cybersaur was, yeah.

KEVIN: Why would they build a robot to look like Godzilla? I mean, what's the function?

MM: I guess it's because once he's beaten all the monsters, he has to beat the machines.

KEVIN: Yeah, but this is my gripe: Why are you creating robots to look like Godzilla? How does that function better than just a big, freakin' tank, y'know?

MM: So you grew up watching Godzilla on Channel 9 [WOR in New York]?

KEVIN: Yeah, some of them. I wasn't really into the goofier ones. It's not like any of them are *Citizen Kane* or *The Godfather*.

MM: How did you start working for *Penthouse Comix*?

KEVIN: They called me. It was probably Rubinstein. Rubinstein was doing work there. I guess the editor knew what I was doing.

MM: But you had no reservations about doing that kind of material?

KEVIN: I felt a little odd about it. I was engaged at the time. [*laughs*] So it was, "It's reference, honey. It's reference." [*laughter*] It paid very well. The stories are just kind of weird.

MM: Did you work on any of George Caragonne's scripts? I think you did, right?

KEVIN: Oh, yeah.

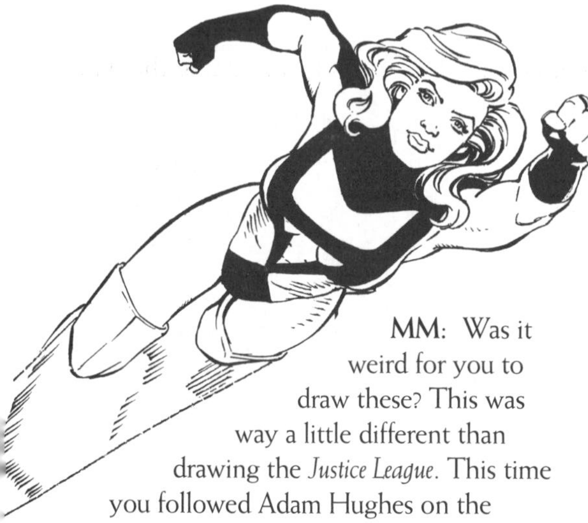

MM: Was it weird for you to draw these? This was way a little different than drawing the *Justice League*. This time you followed Adam Hughes on the "Hericane" strip.

KEVIN: I didn't think of it that way. I don't usually put myself in that position thinking about that. I was just thinking about, what do I need on the page?

MM: I think their page rate was astronomical at the time, it was huge.

KEVIN: Yeah. Obviously that was the big appeal.

MM: But it's not like you're very proud of it?

KEVIN: I don't want to say proud or ashamed. I mean, it is what it is, and I'm not a prude or anything. It just seemed kind of silly. I would have no problem doing an overtly sexual thing if it wasn't dumb. [*laughter*]

MM: When you brought *Strikeback!* to Wildstorm, had you started doing other stuff for them?

KEVIN: I did one issue of *WildCATs* which was a fill-in... *Wildstorm Rising* or something?

MM: Was working with Alan Moore a big to-do for you?

Previous Page: Pencils for page 10 of "Old Flames"—the fourth episode of "Hericane" from *Penthouse Men's Adventure Comix* vol. 2, #7. **Left:** Panel detail of Hericane. **Below:** A 2-page spread from *Wildstorm Rising* #2. Inks by Terry Austin.

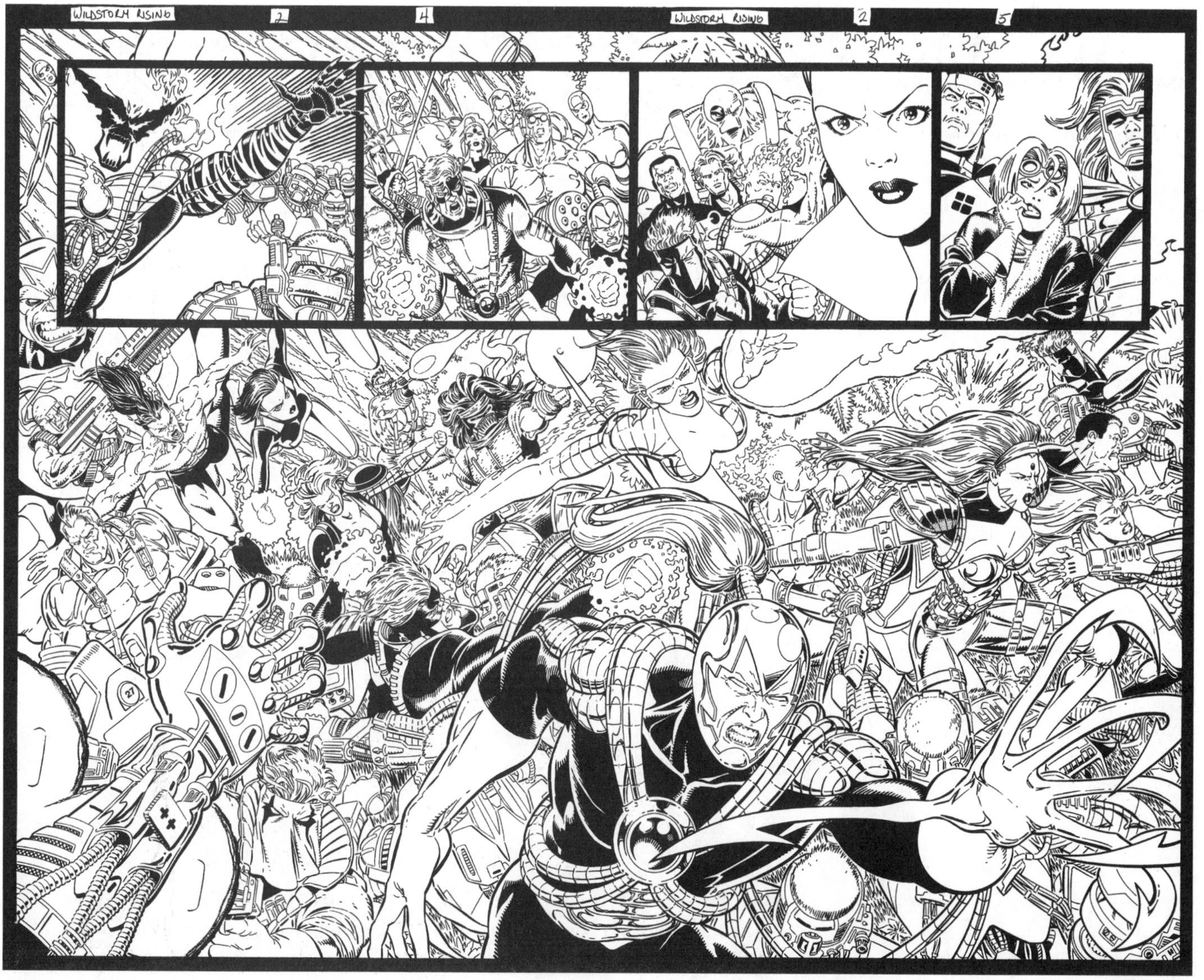

WILDSTORM RISING 2 4
WILDSTORM RISING 2 5

Right: Panel from *Wildstorm Rising* #2. **Below:** Kevin's design work for Earth Angel. **Next Page Top:** The original 99 mourn for the loss of a fallen comrade. **Next Page Bottom:** Early designs for fellow "heroes," the Rumblin' Guys.

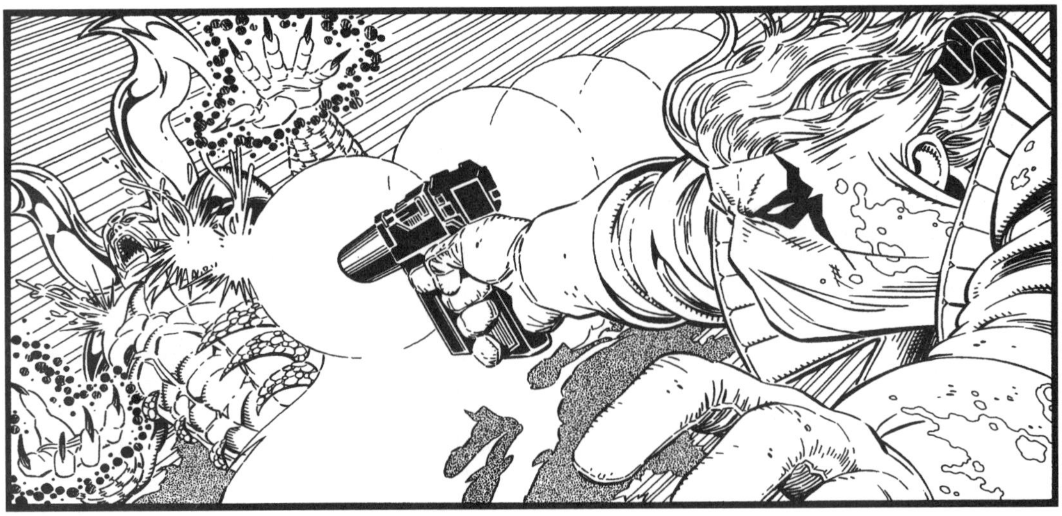

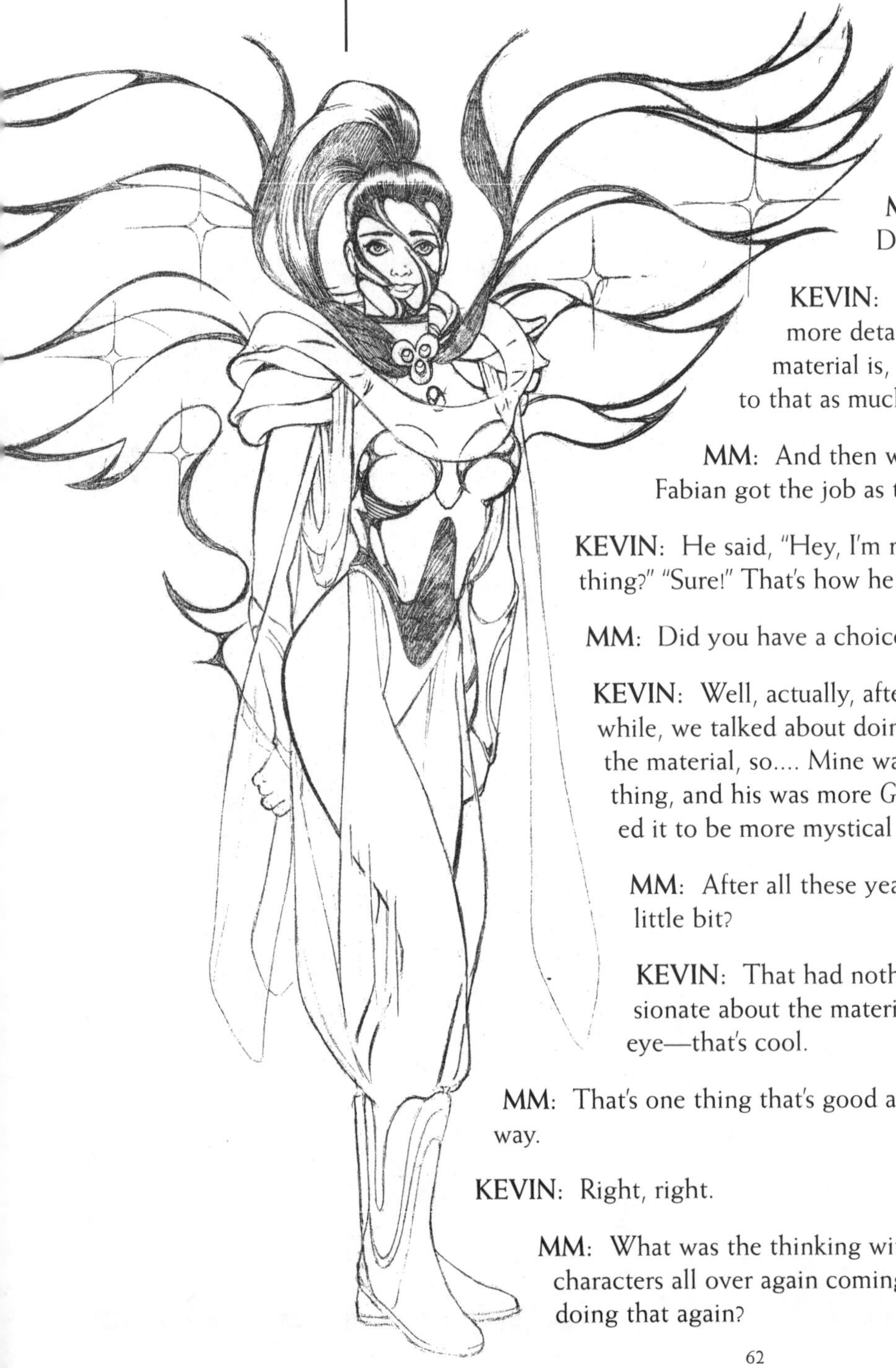

KEVIN: It was a big, thick script. I don't remember at the time schedule-wise. I just remember getting the script and just being amazed at the mountains of detail Alan Moore puts in a script.

MM: Did you feel that made it easier for you? Did it make you concentrate more on a page?

KEVIN: It was a little more daunting, because the more detail he puts in, the clearer his vision of the material is, so you just felt like you had to kind of stick to that as much as possible. Not screw that up.

MM: And then we get to *Trinity Angels*. That came about after Fabian got the job as the editor-in-chief at Valiant/Acclaim?

KEVIN: He said, "Hey, I'm running a company now. Want to write something?" "Sure!" That's how he talked me into it.

MM: Did you have a choice from any of the Valiant characters?

KEVIN: Well, actually, after '91 and working on *Trinity Angels* for a while, we talked about doing *Doctor Mirage*. We had different visions of the material, so.... Mine was more a romantic, black magic kind of thing, and his was more *Ghostbusters*—more about the tech side. I wanted it to be more mystical and he wanted it to be more scientific.

MM: After all these years he still doesn't trust your storytelling a little bit?

KEVIN: That had nothing to do with it. I mean, I wasn't that passionate about the material, so that's all right. We don't see eye to eye—that's cool.

MM: That's one thing that's good about Fabian—everybody can't think the same way.

KEVIN: Right, right.

MM: What was the thinking with *Trinity Angels*? You created a new stock of characters all over again coming off *Strikeback!*. Were you looking forward to doing that again?

KEVIN: Yeah. A lot of these things are always percolating. It's kind of ironic now, because Fabian is now doing a book called *The 99* for a Middle Eastern country, and originally the title was *99 Villains*. These people release 99 villains and the good guys have to round them up. That was the essential premise.

MM: And *Trinity Angels*—was that a spin on the bad girl books that were hot at the time?

KEVIN: Oh, a lot of people said that. I like drawing women. It was more influenced by *Heroic Trio*, the Hong Kong film about three female super-heroes.

MM: Okay, I've see that, yeah. But they weren't martial artists or anything.

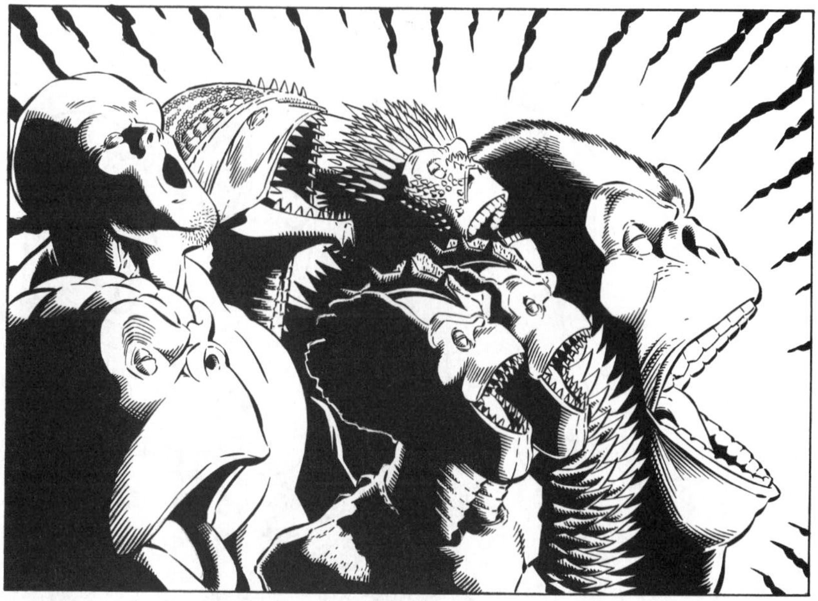

KEVIN: No, and originally they didn't even have those wings. That was Fabian's idea. Originally they were to kind of just float around like in the Hong Kong movies. Again, it was very passionately a Hong Kong influence.

MM: Was this very intense for you? You were writing and drawing it yourself.

KEVIN: Well, just for the first few issues. The first four issues, I think.

MM: So what did you do? Did you actually write a script for yourself or did you just draw it straight to the board?

KEVIN: For the purposes of the editor, you had to write out what you were doing in terms of plot, and then there was dialogue later.

MM: Was he tougher on you than the other talent at Acclaim?

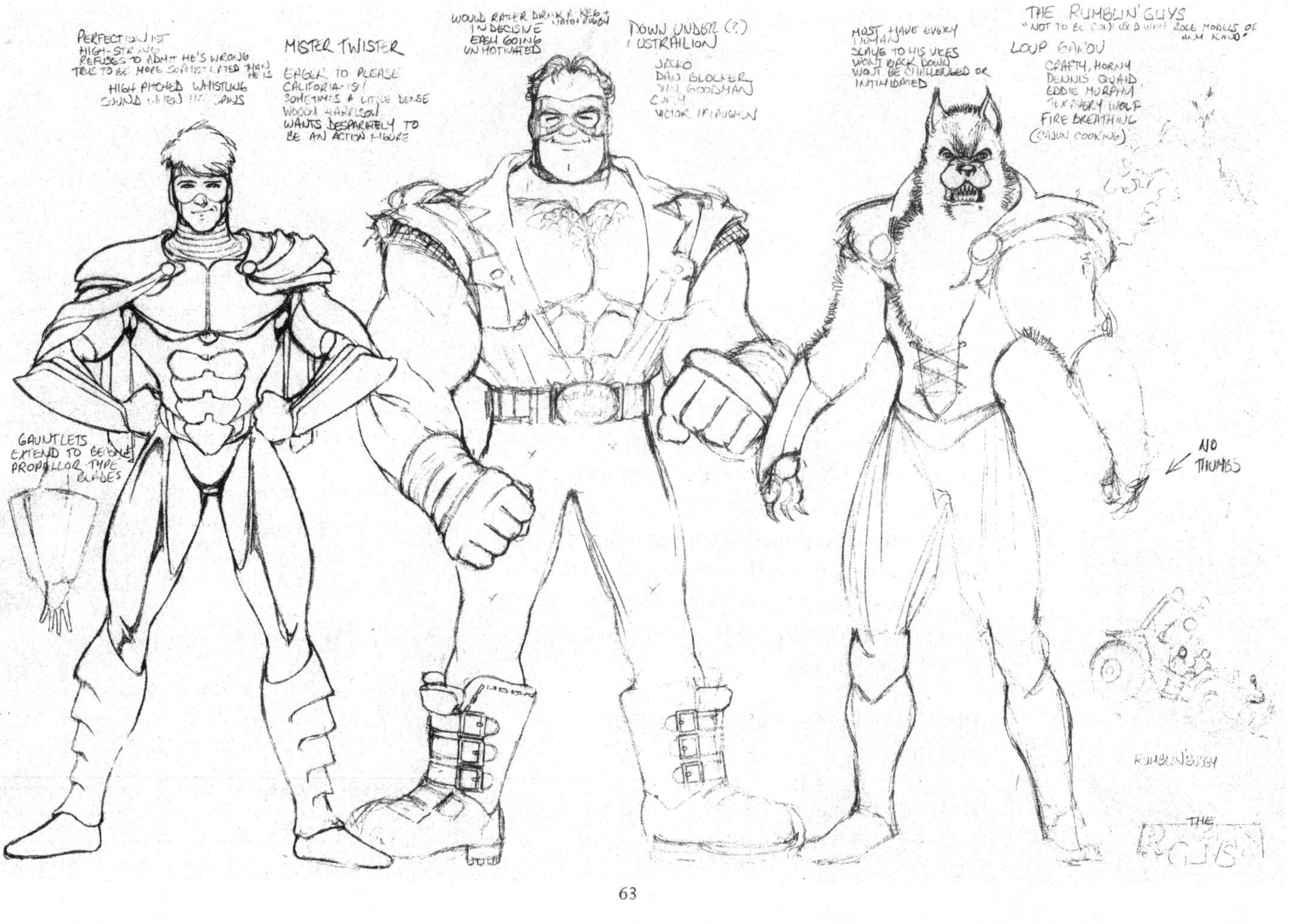
PERFECTIONIST
REFUSES TO ADMIT HE'S WRONG
HIGH PITCHED WHISTLING
MISTER TWISTER
EAGER TO PLEASE
WANTS DESPARATELY TO BE AN ACTION FIGURE
INDECISIVE
EASY GOING
UNMOTIVATED
DOWN UNDER (?)
JACKO
DAN BLOCKER
MUST HAVE EVERY
SLAVE TO HIS VICES
WON'T BACK DOWN
INTIMIDATED
THE RUMBLIN' GUYS
LOUP GAROU
CRAFTY, HORNY
DENNIS QUAID
EDDIE MURPHY
FIRE BREATHING
(CAJUN COOKING)
GAUNTLETS
EXTEND TO BECOME
PROPELLOR TYPE
BLADES
NO
THUMBS

Above: Page 4 pencils from *Trinity Angels* #1.
Next Page: Pencils for page 12 of *Trinity Angels* #1.

KEVIN: No, not really. He gave me latitude. I remember we had this sort of summit meeting of all the people who were creating the new Acclaim books, and everybody would be discussing the physics of their characters—the science of it, how does it work—and every time they'd come to me, I'd go, "Magic. My characters can do that with magic."

MM: Would everyone laugh when you said this?

KEVIN: It's magic. I don't have to scientifically explain what happens. It's magic.

MM: Were you excited about this new relaunch? This was during a really bad time in comics. Marvel had fired a whole bunch of people.

KEVIN: Yup.

MM: As hard as you guys tried at Acclaim, you didn't succeed.

KEVIN: Well, you do what you do, and you can only hope that people will respond to your work.

MM: You fared a lot better than the other guys did.

KEVIN: We did okay, and we certainly weren't their number one for them, but we did all right.

MM: Did you feel you were going to finish the series? Fabian said he made an effort of trying to get you twelve issues.

KEVIN: Well, after a certain point you realize that things aren't selling well, and you want to wrap it up. That decision was being made on the eleventh issue just to wrap it up.

MM: Why wasn't the series creator-owned, since these were brand new characters?

KEVIN: I had a stake in it as a creator. I think after Image and Bravura, a lot of companies were like, "Maybe we don't want to go that creator-owned route." It was owned by Valiant and Acclaim, and like most other publishers around that time they were looking to mine potential video game possibilities out of their books.

MM: Did they ever give you any kind of hope that this might be a video game?

KEVIN: It came very close.

MM: Did you make a demo or anything?

KEVIN: I don't know if they made a demo, but there was a lot of talk about it, and the guy who was in charge really liked it and wanted to do it, but for some reason it didn't happen.

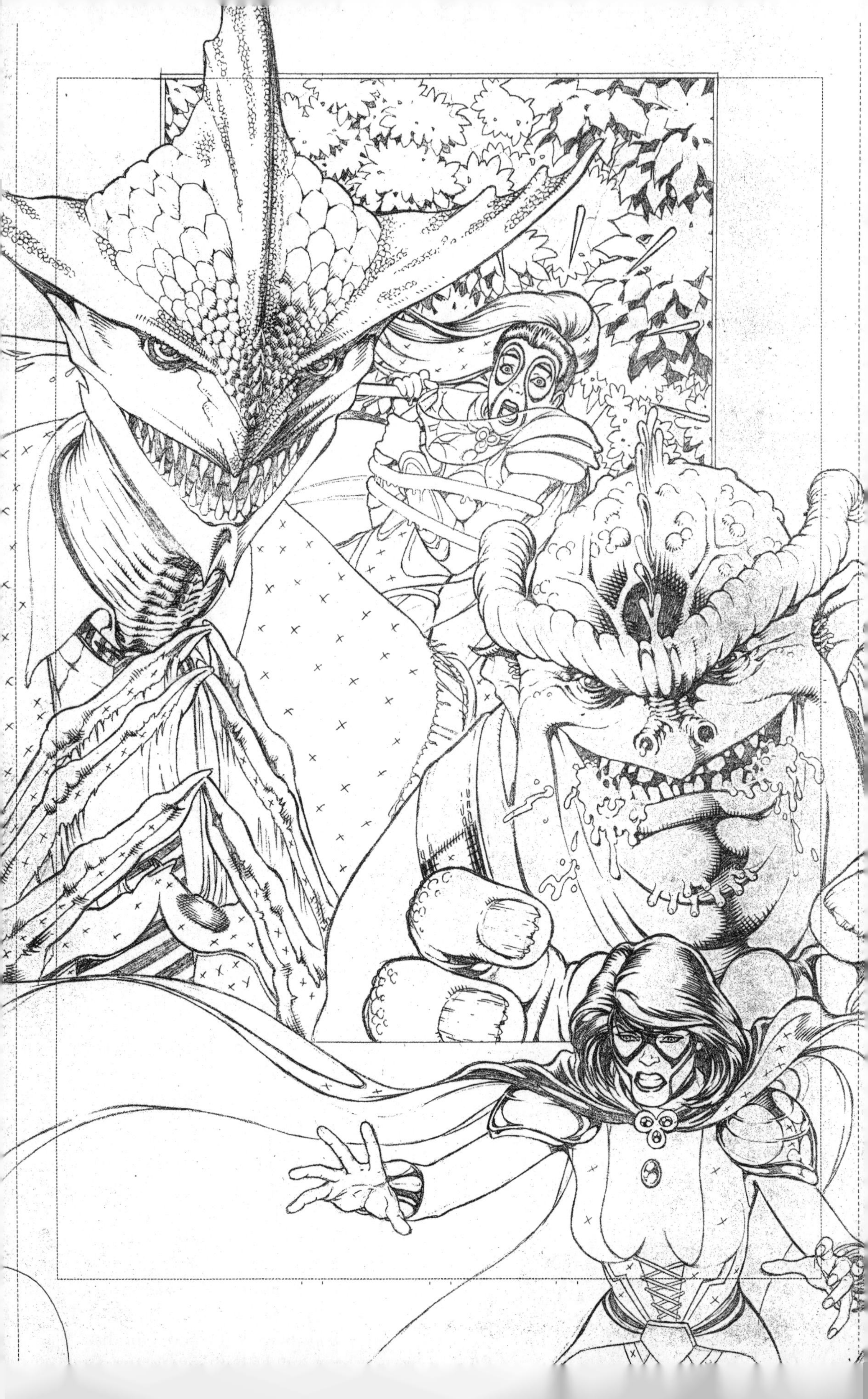

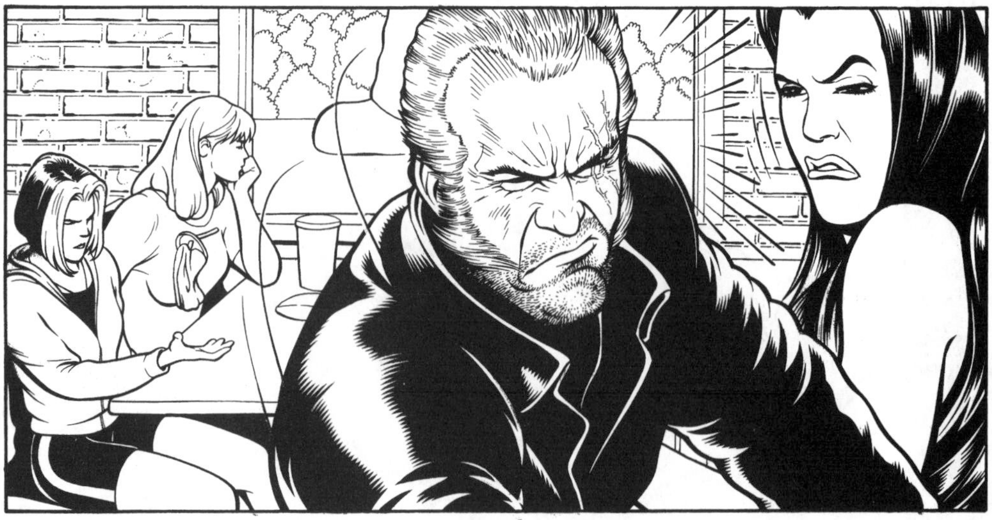

MM: So you have no copyright or anything on this thing?

KEVIN: That sounds really nutty now. Apparently, there was something in the contract that says you can buy the copyright back from the company for a certain price based on sales or profits or something like that, and after a certain time it reverts. Just about a year or so ago I was told that there was stuff going on. A company had bought all the copyrights and it was legally murky. But I had a lot of fun with that series.

MM: What was the appeal about doing the *Gen13/Fantastic Four* crossover?

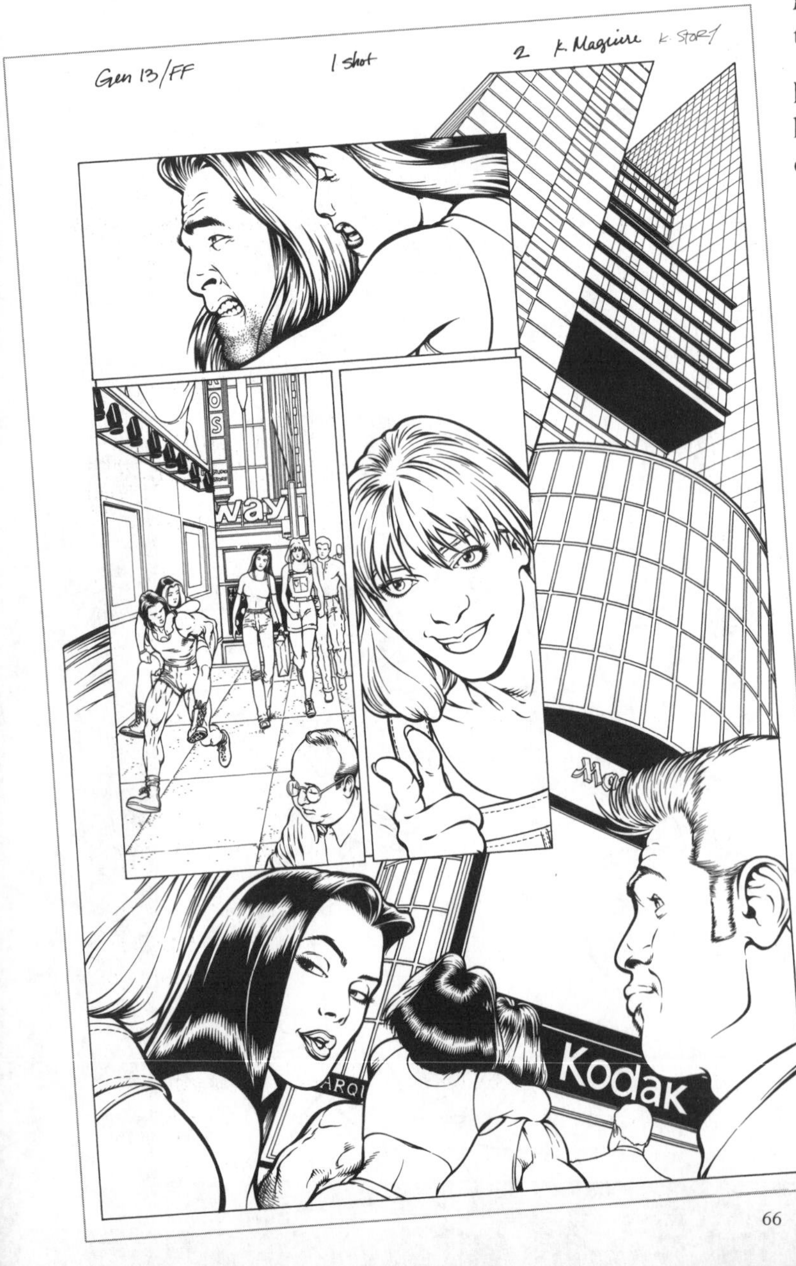
Gen 13/FF
1 shot
2
K. Maguire
K. Story
Kodak

KEVIN: I don't know. It was just something fun to do. I mean, I always liked the Fantastic Four. I really wasn't all that familiar with the *Gen13* characters, but I boned up on it. Yeah, it was just a fun little gig to do.

MM: Did they offer you that chance, or were they thinking of getting somebody else to write it?

KEVIN: There's always those sorts of discussions you have with editors. I talked to Wildstorm about doing a crossover, and we just settled on those characters.

MM: Do you remember having to write the script first, since you'd like to get it approved?

KEVIN: Yeah.

MM: How long did it take you to write? How did you figure out where you were going to go with this story?

KEVIN: Well, I really wanted to do something that had to do with giant monsters, because I just love doing giant monster stories. I think for a while we were all actually toying around with the idea of Grunge becoming a giant. I had this picture of Grunge like King Kong on the top of the Empire State Building, but we ended up settling on a little silly character, Queelocker.

MM: Do you remember, the whole mating thing? Was that something you were planning all the way, that the creatures were going to meet and mate in Central Park?

KEVIN: Actually, I remember having a conversation with somebody at Acclaim in the bathroom and they were talking about Godzilla movies. He said something like, "You know, Japan must have been some big mating ground for giant monsters way back in the day or something, which is why they always go there," and I guess that little thing stuck in my head. And the whole thing of how violence is okay, but sex is taboo. Not that I played it up that strongly, but that was the point to it.

MM: How did you get Spidey involved in that story? Did you just want a chance to draw him in there?

KEVIN: Not particularly.

MM: It seemed like he came out of nowhere.

KEVIN: Well, it's always good to have him in there, but he's not a favorite of mine to draw.

MM: It was one of the last crossovers, I think, between Marvel and DC, before they did the last crossover, *Justice League/Avengers*.

KEVIN: Yeah, Marvel had some sort of contractual thing and that was the last one left in the contract.

MM: Were you excited about this being that type of a book, an inter-company book?

KEVIN: Well, it was cool. I remember when I was a kid and that *Superman/Spider-Man* treasury came out. It was like, "Oh, my God! The worlds collide! I can't believe it! They're actually gonna have Superman meets Spider-Man! That's really big!"

MM: Did you gain an affinity for the Gen-13 characters? I mean, you certainly drew them very well.

KEVIN: I can't really say I had a major league affinity for the characters. They were okay, but I've had this discussion with Fabian, amongst others. I'm just not really all that interested in "teen angst" stories. I'm so past that teen stuff that it holds no interest for me whatsoever.

MM: How were you chosen to do the *Silver Age: The Brave and the Bold* story with Bob Haney a few years back?

KEVIN: I don't know how I was picked. I just got the call from, I think it was [Dan] Raspler who edited it. Yeah. It was some sort of big crossover thing, with a whole bunch of different Silver Age stuff being done. Dan Raspler was the editor and Mark Waid was sort of coordinating it all. And I always wanted to do *Metal Men*. In fact, I'd still like to do *Metal Men*. I think that's right

up my alley—the comedic team thing. I remember reading the script and thinking, "Well, this sucks," because the Metal Men are tanks for pretty much the entire book. So you're not drawing the Metal Men, you're just drawing a tank with eyes on it.

MM: I thought the point of it was to make these nostalgia-driven books.

KEVIN: Yeah, and he actually wrote it on an old typewriter, so I got these typewritten pages. Y'know, the one letter just lighter than the rest.... It was—I don't

Previous Page Top:
Before the Gen 13/FF crossover, Kevin got a feel for the characters with *Gen 13* #42. Inks by Cam Smith.
Previous Page Bottom and Above:
Artwork from *Gen 13/ Fantastic Four* #1. Inks by Karl Story.

Gen 13 ™ and ©2007 Wildstorm Productions. Fantastic Four ™ and ©2007 Marvel Characters, Inc.

want to say terrible, scriptwise, but it was like, "Oh, you just draw a tank." I was hoping for all this other stuff, and then saying this to Dan Raspler and he's like, "It's fine. It's great. It's exactly like that old '60s style we're looking for." I was about 3/4 of the way done when I got a call from Mark Waid saying, "I just read the script. Change whatever you want." "It's too late, now!"

MM: And did you change the rest of the script?

KEVIN: Oh no, I followed the script. I don't like to change things unless—I'm either a co-storyteller or I'm just a penciler.

MM: That was the point, to make it feel like those old stories, kind of dry?

KEVIN: Yeah.

MM: So you didn't really feel any type of nostalgia working with Haney?

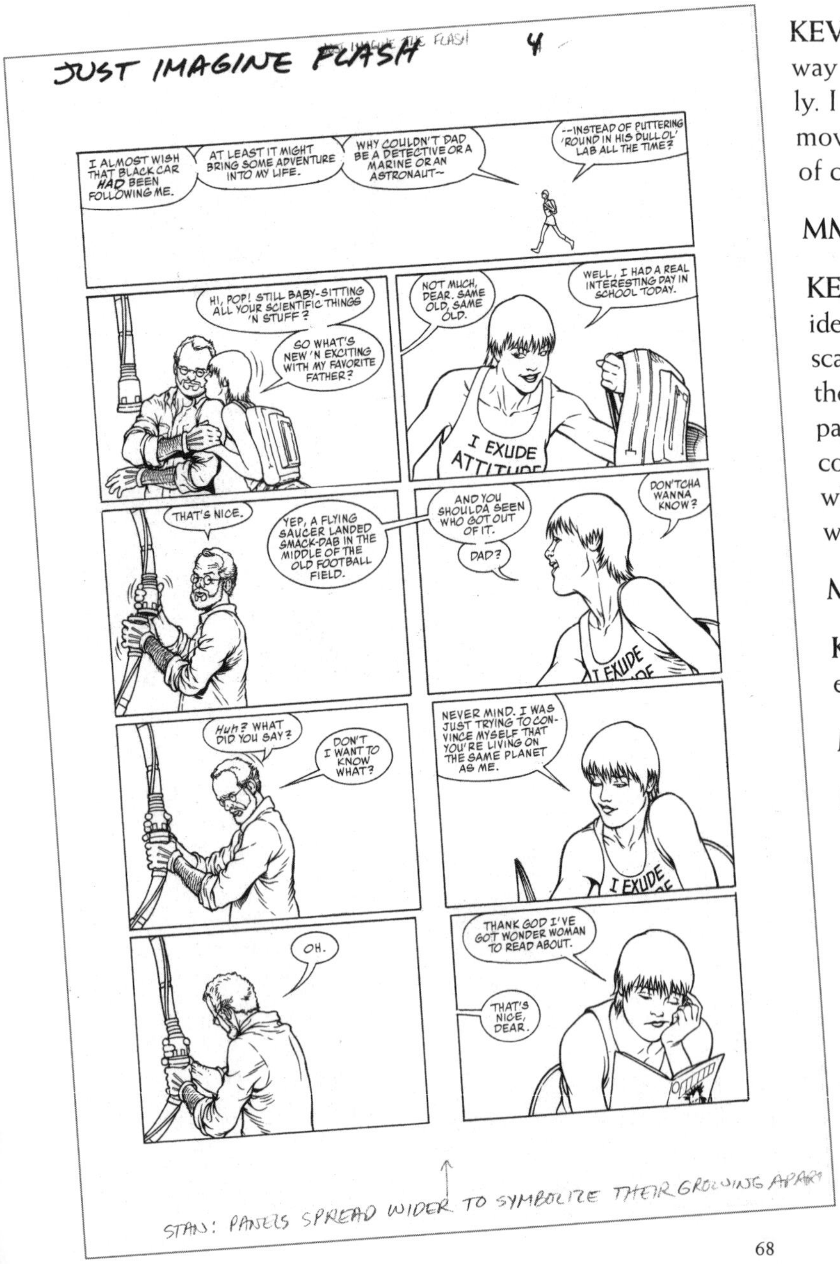

JUST IMAGINE FLASH
4
I ALMOST WISH THAT BLACK CAR HAD BEEN FOLLOWING ME.
AT LEAST IT MIGHT BRING SOME ADVENTURE INTO MY LIFE.
WHY COULDN'T DAD BE A DETECTIVE OR A MARINE OR AN ASTRONAUT--
--INSTEAD OF PUTTERING 'ROUND IN HIS DULL OL' LAB ALL THE TIME?
HI, POP! STILL BABY-SITTING ALL YOUR SCIENTIFIC THINGS 'N STUFF?
SO WHAT'S NEW 'N EXCITING WITH MY FAVORITE FATHER?
NOT MUCH, DEAR. SAME OLD, SAME OLD.
WELL, I HAD A REAL INTERESTING DAY IN SCHOOL TODAY.
I EXUDE ATTITUDE
THAT'S NICE.
YEP, A FLYING SAUCER LANDED SMACK-DAB IN THE MIDDLE OF THE OLD FOOTBALL FIELD.
AND YOU SHOULDA SEEN WHO GOT OUT OF IT.
DAD?
DON'TCHA WANNA KNOW?
HUH? WHAT DID YOU SAY?
DON'T I WANT TO KNOW WHAT?
NEVER MIND. I WAS JUST TRYING TO CONVINCE MYSELF THAT YOU'RE LIVING ON THE SAME PLANET AS ME.
OH.
THANK GOD I'VE GOT WONDER WOMAN TO READ ABOUT.
THAT'S NICE, DEAR.
STAN: PANELS SPREAD WIDER TO SYMBOLIZE THEIR GROWING APART

KEVIN: No, I'm not really a comics historian, so I wasn't really.... I mean, I remember seeing the name when I was a kid, but I wasn't like.... Like working with Stan Lee—well, obviously, that was a treat. But I'd enjoyed the possibility of working on another one.

MM: The *Just Imagine: Stan Lee* thing sort of popped up around the same time.

KEVIN: I remember being very flattered to be asked, because I figured the story worked around DC stuff, and there were only going to be so many of those, and just to be asked to be part of that was very flattering.

MM: It got a lot of media coverage, too.

KEVIN: Yeah.

MM: And did you redesign the Flash yourself? What's that thing in the back, sort of like lashes or something on her?

KEVIN: Yeah, well, they wanted us to come up with a way to show her moving fast that was interesting visually. I thought if she had rainbow tassels that when she moved there'd be that rainbow color, and that'd be kind of cool. And Mike Carlin and Stan liked it, so....

MM: That's kind of playful....

KEVIN: Yes, although I think I remember getting the idea from Hong Kong movies, where you have flowing scarves or whatever that they have. But it was just one of those things that you sit down with a blank piece of paper and a pencil and, "Oooh, let's see." I wanted the costume to be all white because "flash" is usually a bright white light. And then I tried to make it practical.... How would someone put something like this together?

MM: Did you work closely with Stan on this?

KEVIN: Not really. I didn't actually talk to him. We exchanged a couple of e-mails.

MM: Did he write it in full script?

KEVIN: Yeah.

MM: So you didn't get to work with him the Marvel way.

KEVIN: No, not very much. As I recall, I pretty much got the full script.

MM: Did you like the story?

KEVIN: It was okay.

MM: But you got to design the heroine in the manner you wanted to?

KEVIN: Yeah, yeah. Like I said, it was flattering to have even been asked to be part of it. It was fun to be able to create something like that. I enjoyed that. And I got paid more.

MM: And you get royalties, too, I bet.

KEVIN: Not as substantial as one would suspect, but, y'know....

MM: Were you hoping that the book would have gotten a bigger response? I don't believe the series was that warmly welcomed.

KEVIN: Was that around the time when comics were at its biggest low?

MM: No.

KEVIN: No?

MM: I just remember that the response from the fan base was that they didn't like them.

KEVIN: I looked at it to be more of a piece of history.

MM: That it is.

KEVIN: The wizard of Marvel doing the DC characters. That's a fonder memory, the finished product and all that.

MM: It is a privilege to work with these kinds of guys, Stan Lee or Bob Haney.

KEVIN: Yeah, yeah. That's true.

MM: Did you make a point of working more with Fabian around this time? You did a lot of stuff with him. You also did some covers for *Gambit*, which he was doing.

KEVIN: Yup, yup.

MM: Were you reconnected after the Acclaim stuff?

KEVIN: Well, we were always friends, so we were always talking about projects for us.

MM: And the *Justice League: Created Equal* mini-series, was that just a chance to draw more girls?

KEVIN: Primarily, yeah. That was primarily a way to do all the female characters of the DC Universe. That was a project that no one ended up being happy with.

MM: Really?

KEVIN: Because I saw it one way, Fabian saw it going the other way, and the editor, Andy Helfer, saw it going another way, so the three of us were tugging at each other and reaching all kinds of compromises, and no one was actually completely satisfied with how it ended up.

Previous Page: Page 4 of *Just Imagine Stan Lee with Kevin Maguire Creating the Flash.* Note Kevin's note to Stan on the bottom of the page. Inks by Karl Story.
Above: And the book's cover. Inks by Karl Story.

Flash ™ and ©2007 DC Comics.

This Page: Art from *JLA: Created Equal #1*. **Next Page:** Beetle even looks a little like Rick Moranis on this cover to *Justice League #29*. Kevin's note at the bottom reads, "The cover I was born to draw!" No argument here.

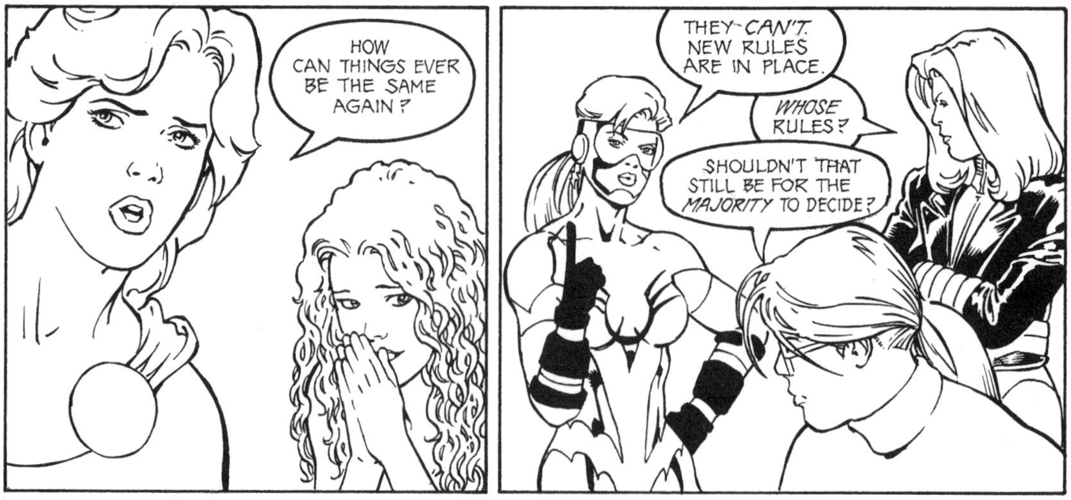
HOW CAN THINGS EVER BE THE SAME AGAIN?
THEY CAN'T. NEW RULES ARE IN PLACE.
WHOSE RULES?
SHOULDN'T THAT STILL BE FOR THE MAJORITY TO DECIDE?

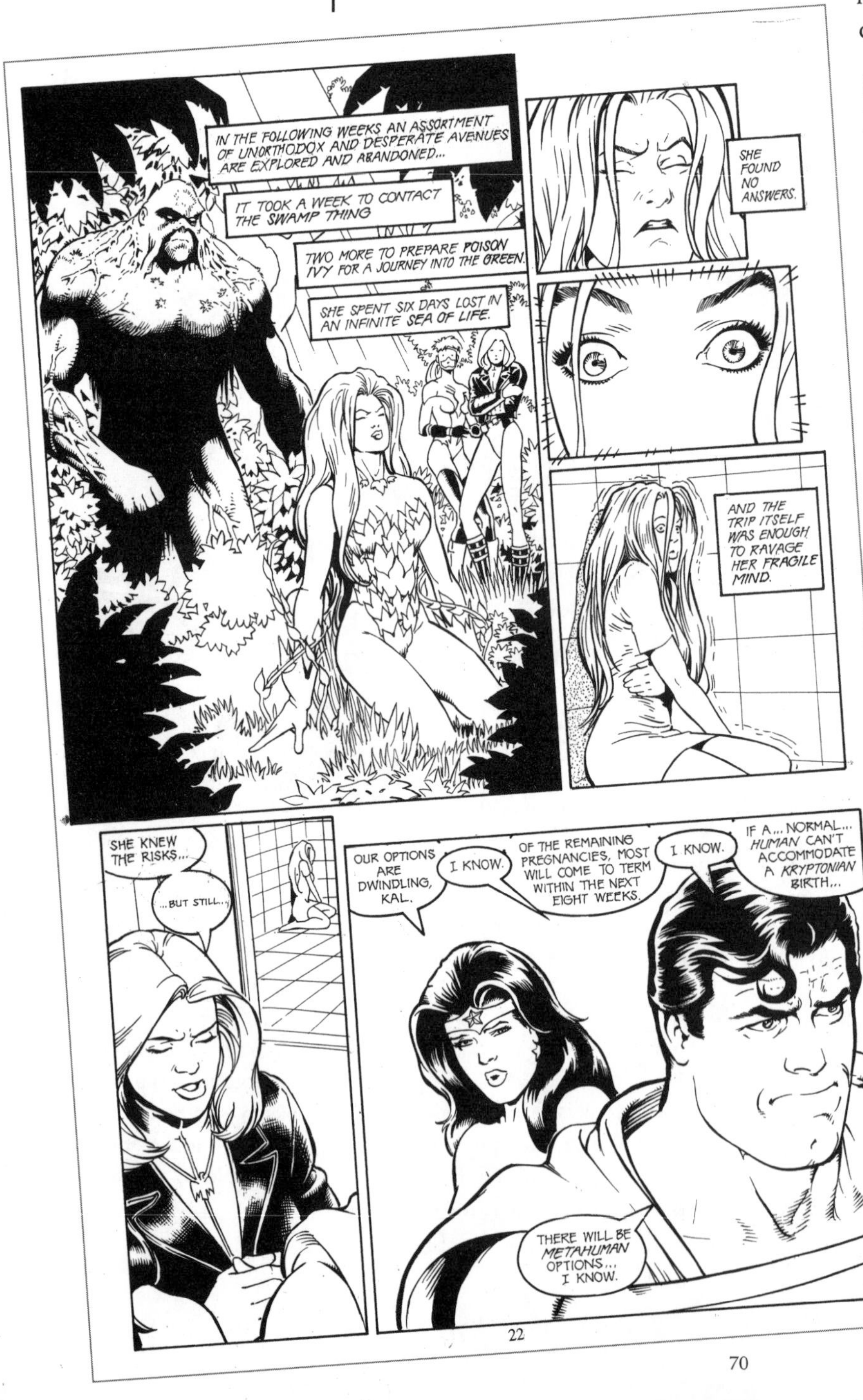
IN THE FOLLOWING WEEKS AN ASSORTMENT OF UNORTHODOX AND DESPERATE AVENUES ARE EXPLORED AND ABANDONED...
IT TOOK A WEEK TO CONTACT THE SWAMP THING
TWO MORE TO PREPARE POISON IVY FOR A JOURNEY INTO THE GREEN.
SHE SPENT SIX DAYS LOST IN AN INFINITE SEA OF LIFE.
SHE FOUND NO ANSWERS.
AND THE TRIP ITSELF WAS ENOUGH TO RAVAGE HER FRAGILE MIND.
SHE KNEW THE RISKS...
...BUT STILL...
OUR OPTIONS ARE DWINDLING, KAL.
I KNOW.
OF THE REMAINING PREGNANCIES, MOST WILL COME TO TERM WITHIN THE NEXT EIGHT WEEKS.
I KNOW.
IF A... NORMAL... HUMAN CAN'T ACCOMMODATE A KRYPTONIAN BIRTH...
THERE WILL BE METAHUMAN OPTIONS... I KNOW.
22

MM: Well, how did it get greenlit if you guys couldn't even decide where it was going?

KEVIN: Good question. [*laughter*] It got greenlit because the project obviously sounded interesting. I mean, when we're talking about different directions, it's in the little details of the story—why did they do this, why would they do that, that kind of stuff.

MM: Yeah, but those type of changes sometimes give the overall story unevenness.

KEVIN: Yeah. Everybody saw it differently.

MM: What did you see in it? What did you want it to be?

KEVIN: Geez, I don't remember. I wasn't going for it to be comedic.

MM: Yeah, because that's what it sounds like when you hear that plot: a world without men except for Superman.

KEVIN: Well, actually, Andy Helfer and I used to have debates about that. I said, "If it were comedic, what would be more funny would be for Blue Beetle to be the last man on Earth, because that's a dream come true. If you're Superman, it's like every chick in the world is into him anyway, so...."

MM: Yeah, but it wouldn't sell. It wouldn't sell as well it did with just Blue Beetle.

KEVIN: Yeah. So I remember having these debates, and Andy Helfer would say, "It would be more interesting to see if Tom Cruise is the last man on Earth." "No, it'd be more interesting if Rick Moranis was the last man on Earth."

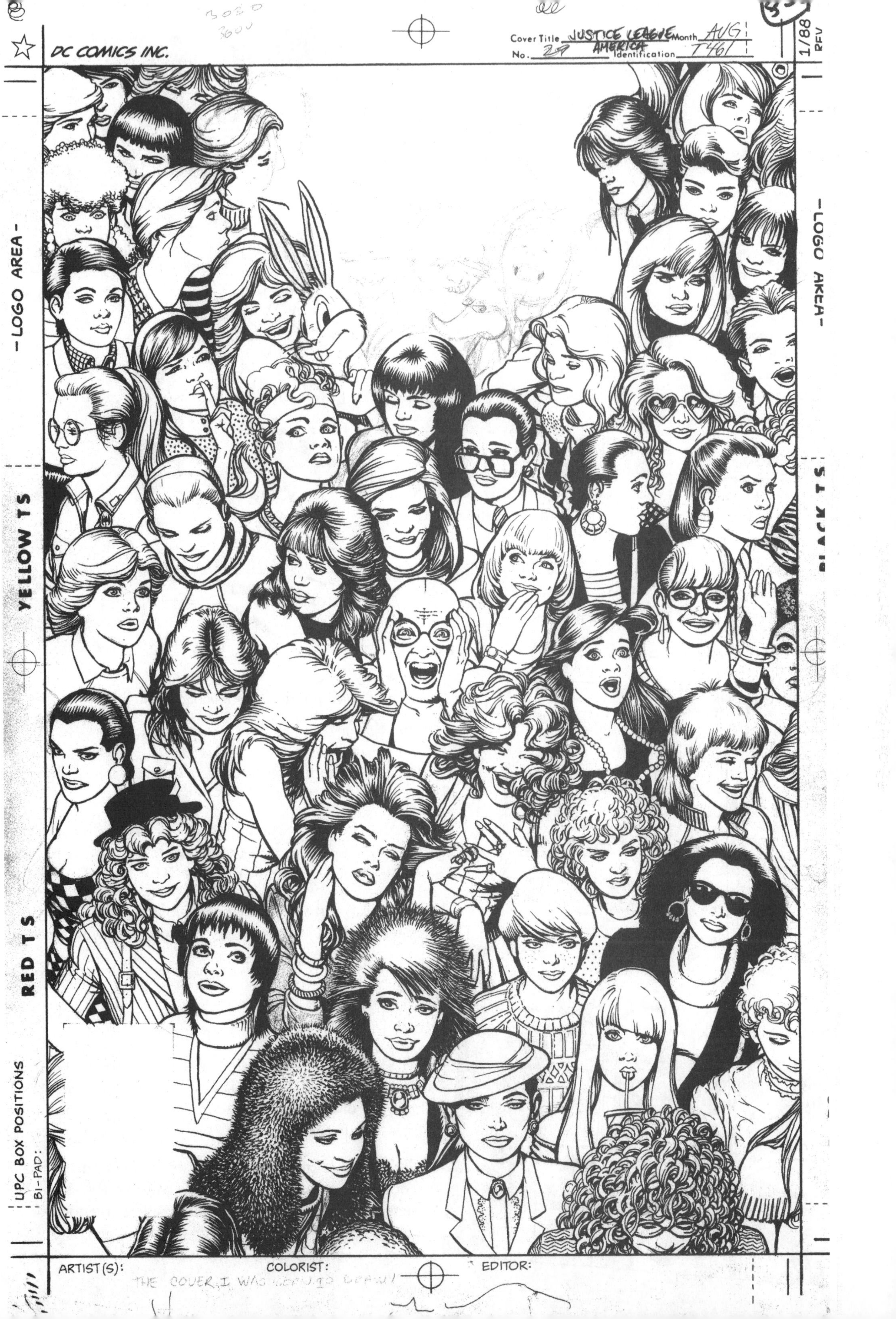
DC COMICS INC.
Cover Title JUSTICE LEAGUE AMERICA Month AUG
No. 29 Identification T461
1/88 REV
-LOGO AREA-
-LOGO AREA-
YELLOW TS
BLACK TS
RED TS
UPC BOX POSITIONS
BI-PAD:
ARTIST(S):
COLORIST:
EDITOR:
THE COVER I WAS GOING TO DRAW!

Right: Every story has a villain—in this case it's Lex Luthor. *JLA: Created Equal* #2, page 28. **Below:** Mystique relives a past tragedy. *X-Men Forever* #2, page 8. Inks by Andrew Pepoy. **Next Page:** Toad creeps around in the background in page 3 of *X-Men Forever* #4. Inks by Andrew Pepoy.

We'd have these debates about this. I mean, every girl wants to be with Tom Cruise, so having Rick Moranis as the last guy left on Earth would be a funnier story. The debates weren't even about making it a comedy, because we were arguing over all kinds of little story-telling points. I remember one thing was we wanted to have Oprah Winfrey be the president, and DC nixed that. "We can't have actual real people." "Yeah, but we're making her the *president*." It wasn't like she'd sue us for defamation.

MM: You could draw somebody that looked like her or something.

KEVIN: Yeah, I just thought that was odd. Why wouldn't they want Oprah Winfrey as president? It seems logical. If all the men in the world died, I think all the women would turn to Oprah.

MM: Are those types of prestige projects harder to work on than the regular series?

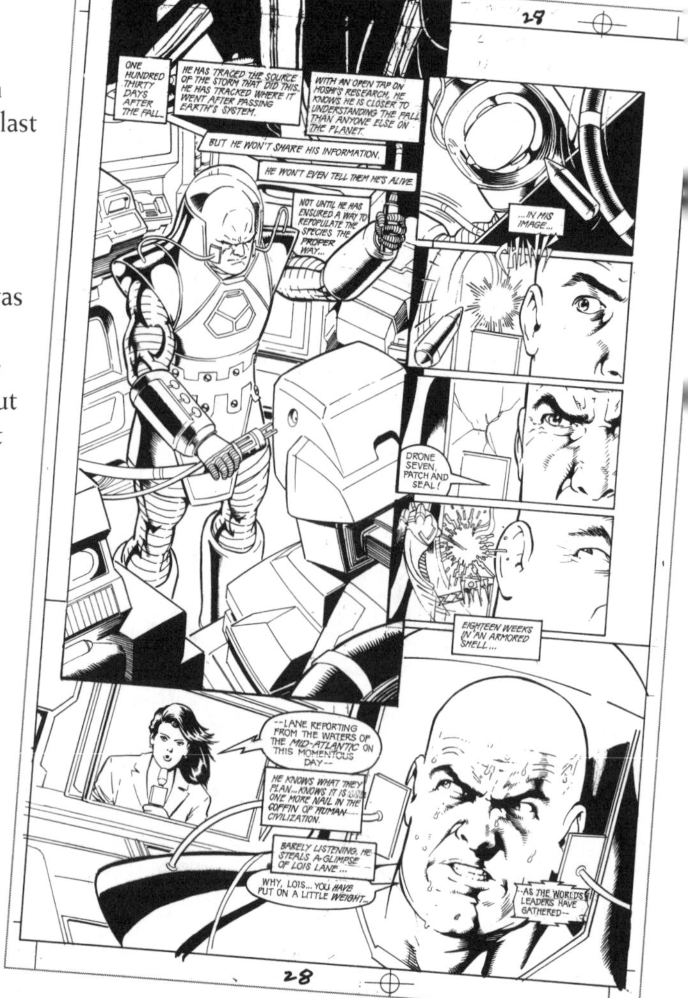
28
ONE HUNDRED THIRTY DAYS AFTER THE FALL...
HE HAS TRACED THE SOURCE OF THE STORM THAT DID THIS. HE HAS TRACKED WHERE IT WENT AFTER PASSING EARTH'S SYSTEM.
WITH AN OPEN TAP ON HOSHI'S RESEARCH, HE KNOWS HE IS CLOSER TO UNDERSTANDING THE FALL THAN ANYONE ELSE ON THE PLANET.
BUT HE WON'T SHARE HIS INFORMATION.
HE WON'T EVEN TELL THEM HE'S ALIVE.
NOT UNTIL HE HAS ENSURED A WAY TO REPOPULATE THE SPECIES THE PROPER WAY...
...IN HIS IMAGE...
DRONE SEVEN, PATCH AND SEAL!
EIGHTEEN WEEKS IN AN ARMORED SHELL...
--LANE REPORTING FROM THE WATERS OF THE MID-ATLANTIC ON THIS MOMENTOUS DAY--
HE KNOWS WHAT THEY PLAN...KNOWS IT IS ONE MORE NAIL IN THE COFFIN OF HUMAN CIVILIZATION.
BARELY LISTENING, HE STEALS A GLIMPSE OF LOIS LANE...
WHY, LOIS... YOU HAVE PUT ON A LITTLE WEIGHT...
--AS THE WORLD'S LEADERS HAVE GATHERED--
28

KEVIN: Not necessarily. They all have their good points and their bad points.

MM: But overall, did you get a lot more time to draw?

KEVIN: Well, yeah. Monthlies are a different kind of beast. It's like doing TV and movies.

MM: When you were working on the series, did you get worked up that it was a prestige series so people had to pay six bucks—"Let's give them everything we've got?" That kind of mentality?

KEVIN: Yeah, but as we were going along I was just getting more dispirited with it. I just wasn't very happy with how it turned out.

MM: I don't think Fabian was too happy with that or *X-Men Forever*.

KEVIN: [*laughs*] No.

MM: What's the story with *X-Men Forever*? You said earlier that when you got *Justice League*, you were kind of surprised at the roster of B-level super-heroes, and then you got this series and it seems like they gave you the C-level mutants.

KEVIN: You know, it's funny, I went to Fabian and I said, "Look, I've never drawn an X-Men story, so let's do an X-Men thing." At that point—and it may be true today—you couldn't pick up an X-Men book and then just figure out

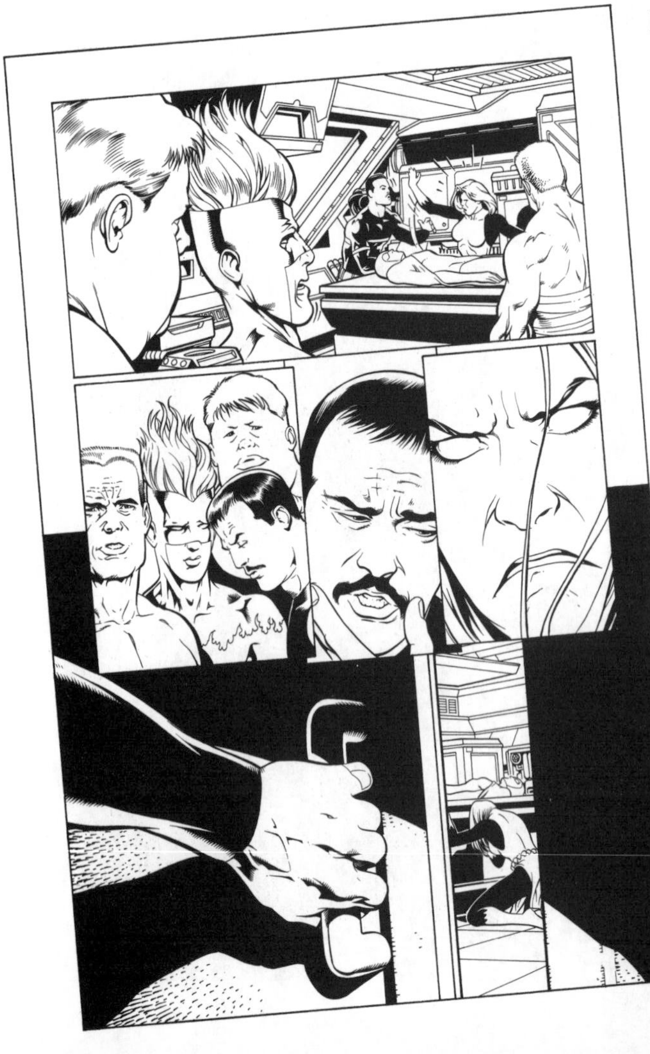

what was going on, because there was just so much dense backstory that you had to know for these things to make sense. So I said, "Let's make an X-Men story that someone who's never read an X-Men book can just pick it up and get it." And Fabian wanted the polar opposite. [*laughter*] "I have this idea for something that will tie up all the loose ends in The X-Men universe!"

MM: I'll tell you, I think it's the most convoluted X-Men story ever written.

KEVIN: And no one will 'fess to that quicker than Fabian will.

MM: It even had footnotes.

KEVIN: You should have seen the stack of notes that they were sending me. "This is what this character's wearing in this time period, and she's wearing something completely different on the next page." Really, really over-the-top convoluted.

MM: This initially sounded like an easy job to you?

KEVIN: Sort of, yeah. He actually laid that book out.

MM: Oh, he did?

KEVIN: Yeah, he wanted to try it, so I said, "Sure, go ahead."

MM: What did he do—stick figures and stuff?

KEVIN: Yeah. Yeah.

MM: And you could more or less follow it?

KEVIN: Sure. I was like, "Cook, Fabe."

MM: Did you have all the *X-Men* issues by your side when you were doing this thing?

KEVIN: Oh, yeah.

MM: Were you familiar with any of it?

KEVIN: I was. I was reading *X-Men* around the "Days of Future Past" time period.

MM: There was a lot of that in this.

KEVIN: Yeah.

MM: There's a lot of that in this book. It wasn't helpful?

KEVIN: Well, they were bouncing around so much that I had no idea where anybody was in there. It was remarkably convoluted.

MM: Drawing some of these mutants must have been interesting.

KEVIN: Oh, yeah, we designed a new costume for the Toad. We had him wearing it on the cover and never actually introduced it in the series. I have no idea what that's about....

MM: Who put this team together? Was it Fabian's idea to put these particular guys, Mystique and—

KEVIN: Yeah, it was all his idea. Like I said, he was writing *X-Men* for so many years that he was familiar with the whole history of the franchise. This is all things that he wanted to do. I knew nothing. I was a complete novice going in there. I didn't know much about the history.

Below: *X-Men Forever* may not have had a typical cast of characters, but there were two of the original team members involved. Inks by Andrew Pepoy.
Next Page: Batman and Martian Manhunter contemplate on their former teammates. *Formerly Known as the Justice League* #5, page 22. Inks by Joe Rubinstein.

MM: Were you happy with this one?

KEVIN: I was happy that it was wrapped up. I wouldn't point to it as something that I was thrilled with. It had its moments, but it's not quite what I was hoping for it to be.

MM: Do any of these projects ever give you an epiphany about how to avoid—like, "Maybe I won't get myself into something like that next time"?

KEVIN: No, I learned nothing. I just make the same mistakes over and over.

MM: That's rough. At least it was work.

KEVIN: Yeah, it was work, and I got a chance to work on the X-Men, which I was happy for. You've got to do *X-Men* at least once in your life.

MM: Were you looking for a regular series throughout that time?

KEVIN: No, my days of monthly books are probably in the past. Although, we'll see with my next thing.

MM: You were never concerned about going from one-shot to one-shot—"This is going to dry up sooner or later"?

KEVIN: No, I was never concerned, but there were always those rumbling concerns, because you kept hearing the death knell of the comics industry from people about how sales are so low and blah, blah, blah. It's like, "Is there even going to be an industry in a year or two? Will I get a gig?" Hasn't happened yet.

MM: But they always keep you busy. You'll always be in demand, I'm pretty sure of that.

KEVIN: Let's hope so.

Part 5: Return of the League

MM: How did you guys together again for the newer *Justice League* books? Were you hoping you guys would get back together, or was it the last thing on your mind at that time?

KEVIN: Actually, at that particular time I was lined up to do a four-issue series with Marvel which was essentially *Sex in the City* with four Marvel super-heroines. The guy who was writing it had an agent who was negotiating with Marvel to get a better page rate, so while the negotiations were going on, he wasn't turning in any work because his agent was telling him not to hand in any work. So I was sitting there waiting for something to pencil, and at that point [DC editor Dan] Raspler called up and said, "Well, I was talking to Keith, and it seems like he'd be up for it, and DeMatteis is up for it. Would you be up for it?" I said, "You know what? If you can get a script to me in the next couple of weeks, I'll do it now. I've waited so long for this guy to write this other script, I've got nothing to work on other than pinups and covers and other little things. If you can toss something together fairly quickly, count me in." And Keith being the machine that he is had no problem with that.

MM: Was it just like old times again right away?

KEVIN: No, it was actually fairly different. It was kind of, not awkward, but it was different. It was a different situation because back when I was originally doing it, Andy Helfer, who was the editor, had a very strong hand in it, and he was a large part of the driving force behind it. And back then the reason DeMatteis was doing the dialogue was Keith wasn't comfortable with his own dialoguing. You know, he had plot ideas, but he wasn't confident enough in his dialoguing, so DeMatteis came in to write the dialogue. But in the years that passed, Keith became

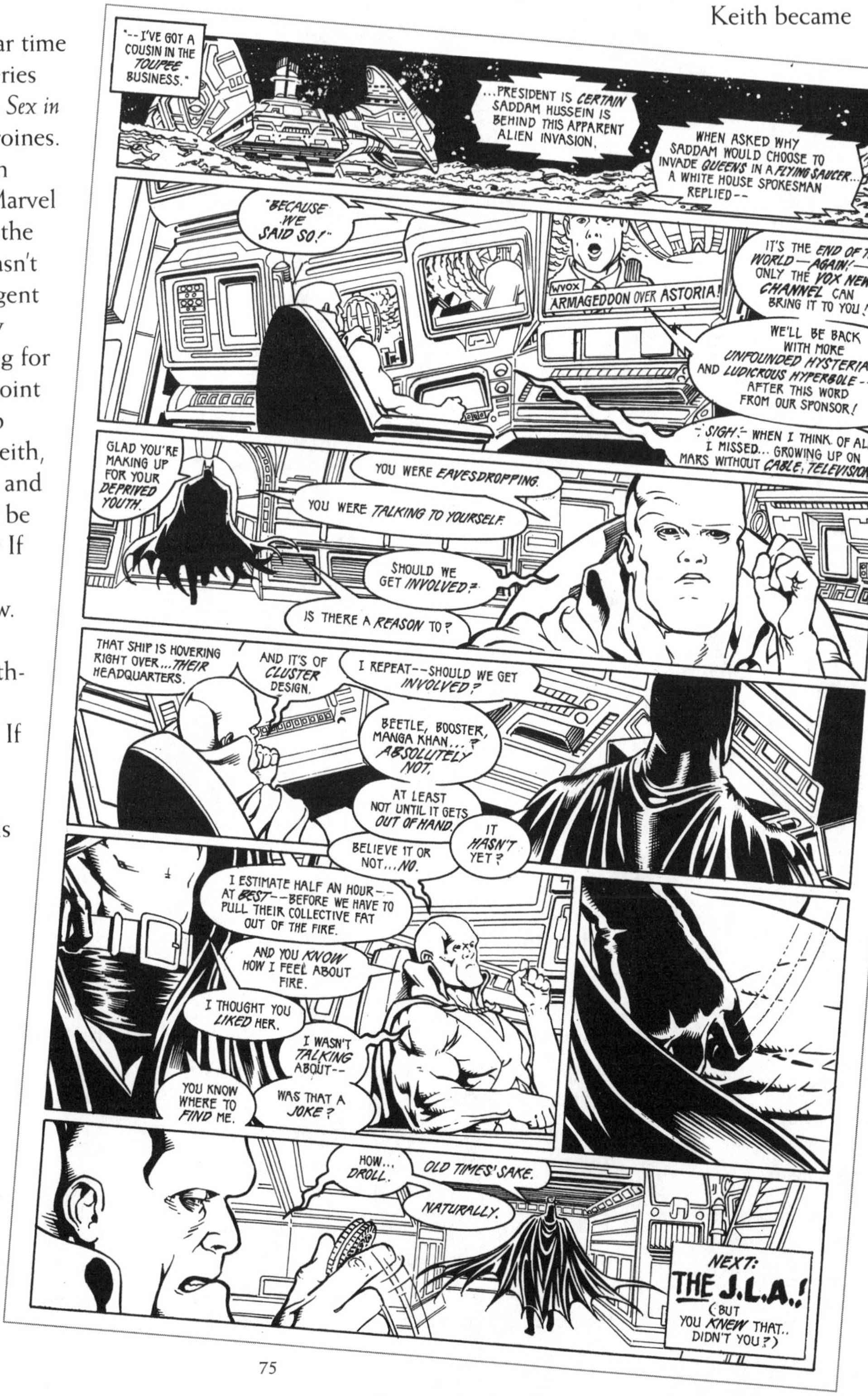

"--I'VE GOT A COUSIN IN THE TOUPEE BUSINESS."
...PRESIDENT IS CERTAIN SADDAM HUSSEIN IS BEHIND THIS APPARENT ALIEN INVASION.
WHEN ASKED WHY SADDAM WOULD CHOOSE TO INVADE QUEENS IN A FLYING SAUCER... A WHITE HOUSE SPOKESMAN REPLIED--
"BECAUSE WE SAID SO!"
WVOX
ARMAGEDDON OVER ASTORIA!
IT'S THE END OF THE WORLD—AGAIN!—AS ONLY THE VOX NEWS CHANNEL CAN BRING IT TO YOU!
WE'LL BE BACK WITH MORE UNFOUNDED HYSTERIA AND LUDICROUS HYPERBOLE--AFTER THIS WORD FROM OUR SPONSOR!
:SIGH:- WHEN I THINK OF ALL I MISSED... GROWING UP ON MARS WITHOUT CABLE, TELEVISION.
GLAD YOU'RE MAKING UP FOR YOUR DEPRIVED YOUTH.
YOU WERE EAVESDROPPING.
YOU WERE TALKING TO YOURSELF.
SHOULD WE GET INVOLVED?
IS THERE A REASON TO?
THAT SHIP IS HOVERING RIGHT OVER... THEIR HEADQUARTERS.
AND IT'S OF CLUSTER DESIGN.
I REPEAT--SHOULD WE GET INVOLVED?
BEETLE, BOOSTER, MANGA KHAN...? ABSOLUTELY NOT.
AT LEAST NOT UNTIL IT GETS OUT OF HAND.
IT HASN'T YET?
BELIEVE IT OR NOT... NO.
I ESTIMATE HALF AN HOUR--AT BEST--BEFORE WE HAVE TO PULL THEIR COLLECTIVE FAT OUT OF THE FIRE.
AND YOU KNOW HOW I FEEL ABOUT FIRE.
I THOUGHT YOU LIKED HER.
I WASN'T TALKING ABOUT--
YOU KNOW WHERE TO FIND ME.
WAS THAT A JOKE?
HOW... DROLL.
OLD TIMES' SAKE.
NATURALLY.
NEXT: THE J.L.A.! (BUT YOU KNEW THAT.. DIDN'T YOU?)

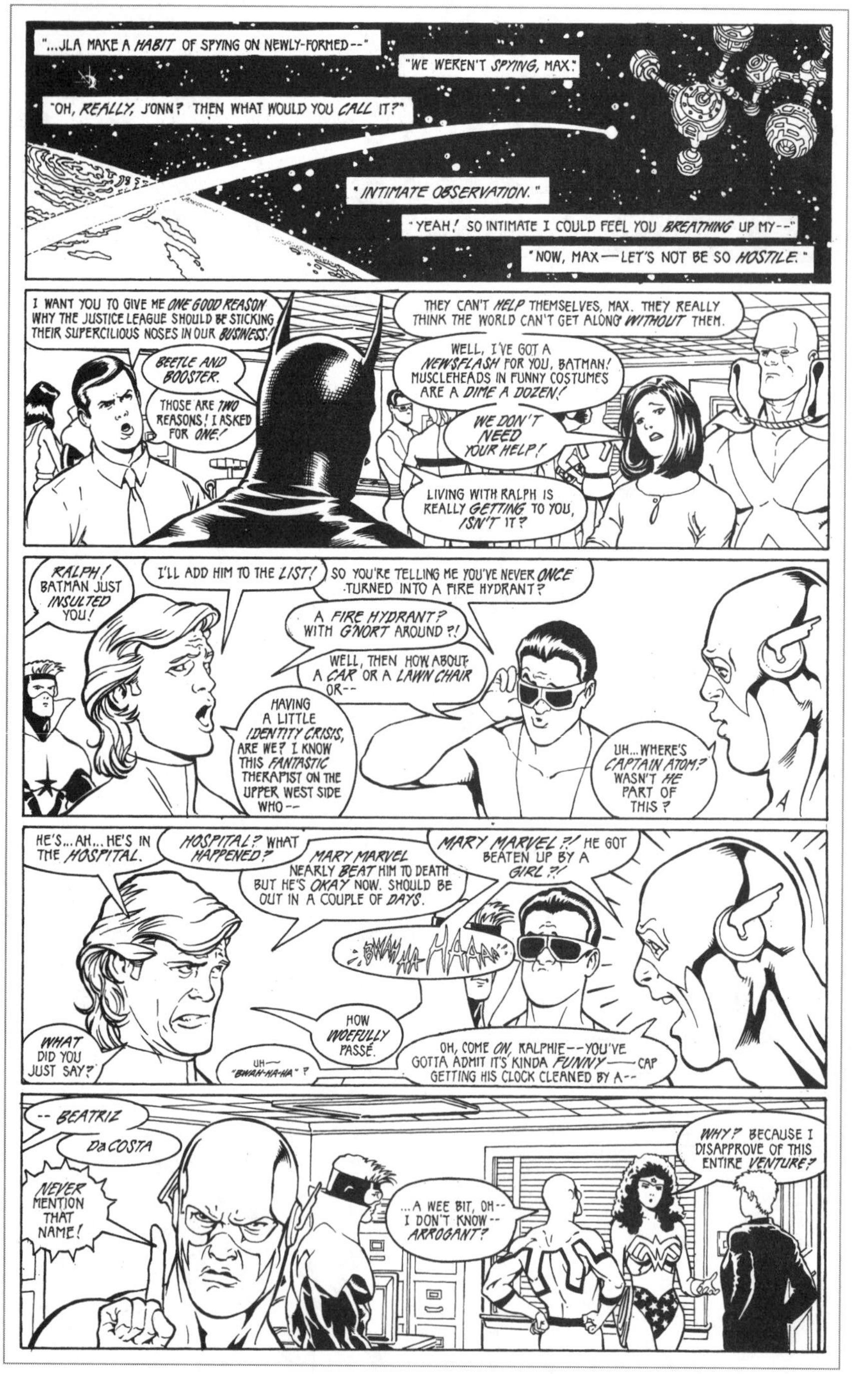
"...JLA MAKE A HABIT OF SPYING ON NEWLY-FORMED--"
"WE WEREN'T SPYING, MAX."
"OH, REALLY, J'ONN? THEN WHAT WOULD YOU CALL IT?"
"INTIMATE OBSERVATION."
"YEAH! SO INTIMATE I COULD FEEL YOU BREATHING UP MY--"
"NOW, MAX—LET'S NOT BE SO HOSTILE."
I WANT YOU TO GIVE ME ONE GOOD REASON WHY THE JUSTICE LEAGUE SHOULD BE STICKING THEIR SUPERCILIOUS NOSES IN OUR BUSINESS!
BEETLE AND BOOSTER.
THOSE ARE TWO REASONS! I ASKED FOR ONE!
THEY CAN'T HELP THEMSELVES, MAX. THEY REALLY THINK THE WORLD CAN'T GET ALONG WITHOUT THEM.
WELL, I'VE GOT A NEWSFLASH FOR YOU, BATMAN! MUSCLEHEADS IN FUNNY COSTUMES ARE A DIME A DOZEN!
WE DON'T NEED YOUR HELP!
LIVING WITH RALPH IS REALLY GETTING TO YOU, ISN'T IT?
RALPH! BATMAN JUST INSULTED YOU!
I'LL ADD HIM TO THE LIST!
SO YOU'RE TELLING ME YOU'VE NEVER ONCE TURNED INTO A FIRE HYDRANT?
A FIRE HYDRANT?! WITH G'NORT AROUND?!
WELL, THEN HOW ABOUT A CAR OR A LAWN CHAIR OR--
HAVING A LITTLE IDENTITY CRISIS, ARE WE? I KNOW THIS FANTASTIC THERAPIST ON THE UPPER WEST SIDE WHO--
UH...WHERE'S CAPTAIN ATOM? WASN'T HE PART OF THIS?
HE'S...AH...HE'S IN THE HOSPITAL.
HOSPITAL? WHAT HAPPENED?
MARY MARVEL NEARLY BEAT HIM TO DEATH BUT HE'S OKAY NOW. SHOULD BE OUT IN A COUPLE OF DAYS.
MARY MARVEL?! HE GOT BEATEN UP BY A GIRL?!
BWAH-HA-HAAA
WHAT DID YOU JUST SAY?
UH— "BWAH-HA-HA"?
HOW WOEFULLY PASSÉ.
OH, COME ON, RALPHIE--YOU'VE GOTTA ADMIT IT'S KINDA FUNNY—CAP GETTING HIS CLOCK CLEANED BY A--
-- BEATRIZ
Da COSTA
NEVER MENTION THAT NAME!
...A WEE BIT, OH-- I DON'T KNOW-- ARROGANT?
WHY? BECAUSE I DISAPPROVE OF THIS ENTIRE VENTURE?

Above: A bit of a class reunion in *Formerly Known as the Justice League* #6. Inks by Joe Rubinstein.
Next Page: Mary Marvel doing her best to fit in with the team. Inks by Joe Rubinstein.

more confident with his dialoguing, so Keith would hand me full scripts, complete full scripts, like a screenplay. I'd get those and I'm like, "What's DeMatteis going to do here? I mean, is he just going to add lines? How is this going to work?" So essentially I penciled it based on Keith's script and DeMatteis would just rewrite the dialogue, and that just really pissed me off. Because I would match the performance of the character to what they say, so I was drawing for different dialogue than what ended up on the page. If I know that this is the dialogue that's going to end up on the page, I'm going to draw things differently. A lot of people just wouldn't ever get it, they wouldn't even see it, but I knew this was very different than what it was supposed to be. And that was frustrating.

MM: You can do conference calls and that sort of thing now.

KEVIN: We ended up working it out. Close to the end of the first mini-series, DeMatteis would send a DeMatteis/Giffen script. I mean, he would rewrite Giffen's script and then give me the finished script. DeMatteis writes dialogue based on the art, but for me it's like telling an actor, "Go up there and do a performance, and we'll put in your words afterwards." It doesn't make sense. I was just so annoyed.

I forget which page it was. It was the first issue of *Formerly Known as the Justice League*, where Max is talking to Fire. Keith's script had Max saying, "You weren't doing..." suggesting she was doing porn. And, she goes, "No, no, no way." So the panel I drew of Max, when he says, "You were doing it, you know," I had him putting the cigar into his mouth kind of orally—and, in fact, they put that image on the back cover of the trade paperback. The first time that I saw it dialogued, with DeMatteis' dialogue, was when I got the actual book, and there was nothing referencing that at all, so the visual gag was just completely gone. I mean, he was still putting the cigar in his mouth, but there was no dialogue about doing porn, so that visual reference was just gone. That drove me nuts.

MM: Were there any other instances?

KEVIN: Yeah, the thing where Max and Beetle are sitting there talking in their offices—there was a page with a lot of close-ups, because I would get Keith's script and I like to break up the panels by emotional beats. I can't stand it when you have it where a character is yelling and the next minute he's saying, "Aw, gee, I'm really sorry," and having both of those lines in the same panel, because that's two different emotions.

MM: You want to show the transition.

KEVIN: Yeah, like, you have one panel where they're angry and the next panel it's a sad face. So I would break up a page based on the emotional beats. I was laying out that page based on what Keith was writing, and it was never exactly the same. Like I said, if I had had DeMatteis' dialogue, I would have paced it differently.

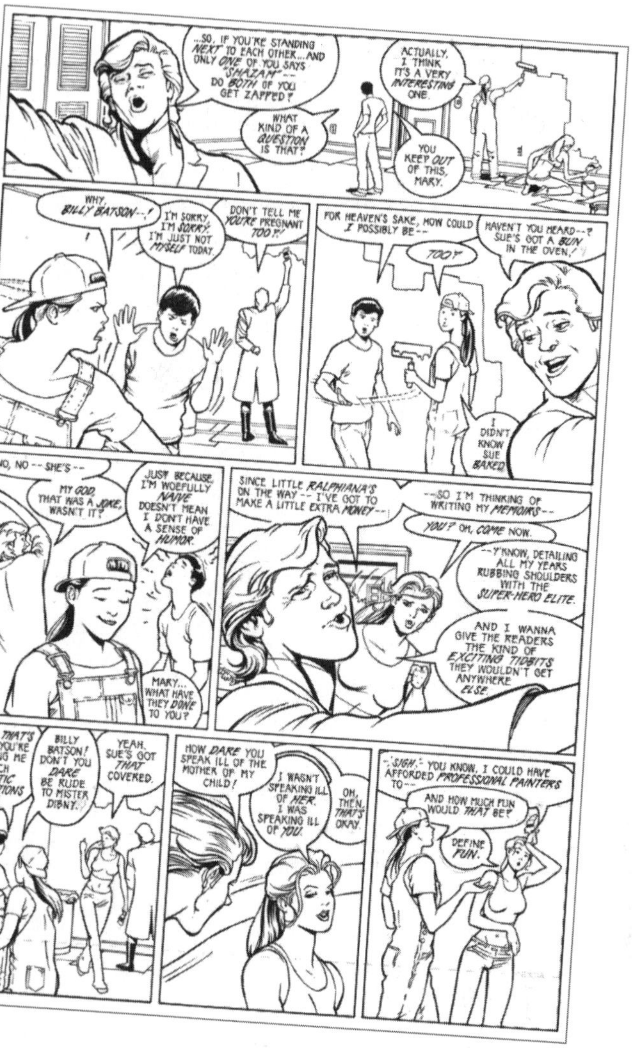

...SO, IF YOU'RE STANDING NEXT TO EACH OTHER...AND ONLY ONE OF YOU SAYS "SHAZAM"-- DO BOTH OF YOU GET ZAPPED?
WHAT KIND OF A QUESTION IS THAT?
ACTUALLY, I THINK IT'S A VERY INTERESTING ONE.
YOU KEEP OUT OF THIS, MARY.
WHY, BILLY BATSON--!
I'M SORRY, I'M SORRY. I'M JUST NOT MYSELF TODAY.
DON'T TELL ME YOU'RE PREGNANT TOO?!
FOR HEAVEN'S SAKE, HOW COULD I POSSIBLY BE--
TOO?
HAVEN'T YOU HEARD--? SUE'S GOT A BUN IN THE OVEN.
I DIDN'T KNOW SUE BAKED.
NO, NO -- SHE'S --
MY GOD, THAT WAS A JOKE, WASN'T IT?
JUST BECAUSE I'M WOEFULLY NAIVE DOESN'T MEAN I DON'T HAVE A SENSE OF HUMOR.
MARY... WHAT HAVE THEY DONE TO YOU?
SINCE LITTLE RALPHIANA'S ON THE WAY -- I'VE GOT TO MAKE A LITTLE EXTRA MONEY--
--SO I'M THINKING OF WRITING MY MEMOIRS--
YOU? OH, COME NOW.
--Y'KNOW, DETAILING ALL MY YEARS RUBBING SHOULDERS WITH THE SUPER-HERO ELITE.
AND I WANNA GIVE THE READERS THE KIND OF EXCITING TIDBITS THEY WOULDN'T GET ANYWHERE ELSE.
AND THAT'S WHY YOU'RE ASKING ME SUCH IDIOTIC QUESTIONS?
BILLY BATSON! DON'T YOU DARE BE RUDE TO MISTER DIBNY.
YEAH, SUE'S GOT THAT COVERED.
HOW DARE YOU SPEAK ILL OF THE MOTHER OF MY CHILD!
I WASN'T SPEAKING ILL OF HER. I WAS SPEAKING ILL OF YOU.
OH, THEN, THAT'S OKAY.
SIGH. YOU KNOW, I COULD HAVE AFFORDED PROFESSIONAL PAINTERS TO--
AND HOW MUCH FUN WOULD THAT BE?
DEFINE FUN.

MM: By the time you caught onto this thing, it was already towards the end of the series.

KEVIN: Yeah, it was about the fourth issue that, "We've got to change this. I've got to know what's being said."

MM: There wasn't any power struggle between DeMatteis and Giffen?

KEVIN: No, no, there never was.

MM: I'm surprised they don't talk about what they're going to write about together.

KEVIN: Well, that's the way it works. As far as I know, they talk to each other, but I don't think they sit there and, "We'll do this, we'll do this, we'll do this." I mean, they might do that with the *Heroes Squared* stuff or some of the other projects they have lined up. With *Justice League*, Keith just comes up with the ideas, and DeMatteis writes the dialogue, and then I draw it.

MM: So you have no say in, like, who's going to be on the team or anything like that?

KEVIN: Ummm... no.

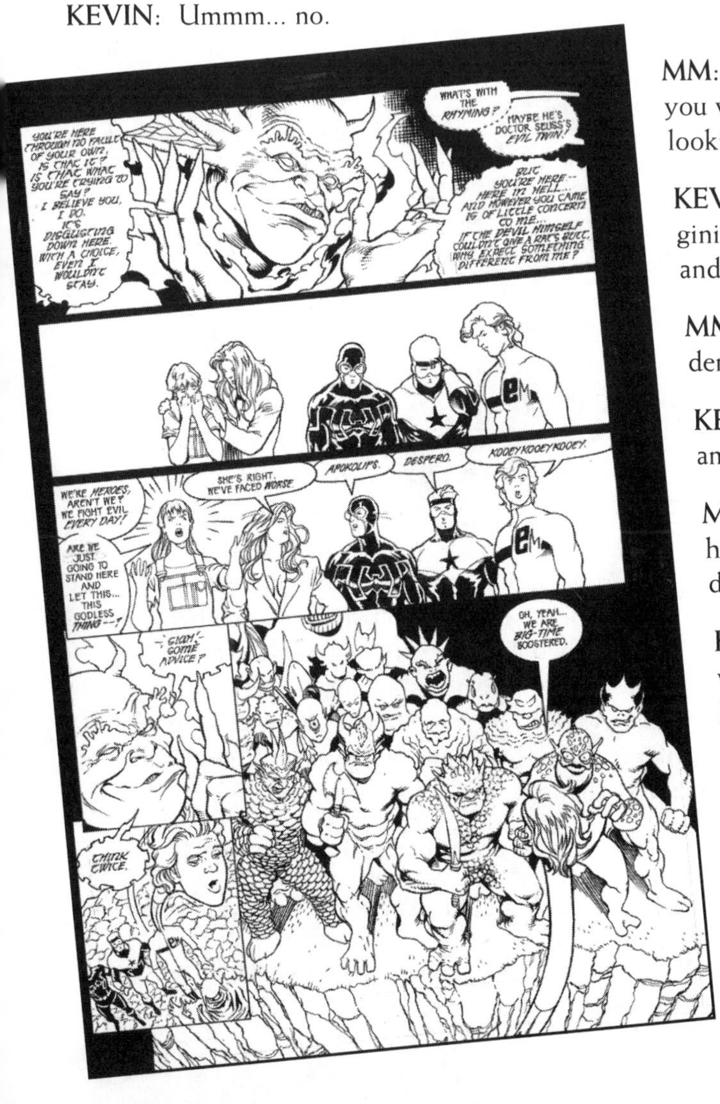

YOU'RE HERE THROUGH NO FAULT OF YOUR OWN; IS THAT IT? IS THAT WHAT YOU'RE TRYING TO SAY? I BELIEVE YOU, I DO. IT'S DISGUSTING DOWN HERE. WITH A CHOICE, EVEN I WOULDN'T STAY.
WHAT'S WITH THE RHYMING?
MAYBE HE'S DOCTOR SEUSS'S EVIL TWIN!
BUT YOU'RE HERE-- HERE IN HELL... AND HOWEVER YOU CAME IS OF LITTLE CONCERN TO ME... IF THE DEVIL HIMSELF COULDN'T GIVE A RAT'S BUTT, WHY EXPECT SOMETHING DIFFERENT FROM ME?
WE'RE HEROES, AREN'T WE? WE FIGHT EVIL EVERY DAY!
SHE'S RIGHT. WE'VE FACED WORSE.
APOKOLIPS.
DESPERO.
KOOEY KOOEY KOOEY.
ARE WE JUST GOING TO STAND HERE AND LET THIS... THIS GODLESS THING--?
SIGH. SOME ADVICE?
OH, YEAH... WE ARE BIG-TIME BOOSTERED.
THINK TWICE.

MM: But you were looking forward to drawing Mary Marvel?

KEVIN: Like I said earlier, Keith wanted to have her lose her virginity in that story. He wanted her to start out in the white outfit, and then she wears the red outfit after she loses her virginity.

MM: There was a lot of that stuff in the sequel, too, with demons hitting on her all the time, even a little bondage.

KEVIN: Yeah. She's the kind of Pollyanna-ish character amongst these lunatics.

MM: Were you surprised when you were drawing this book how much you had grown as an artist, comparing to what you did 13 years earlier?

KEVIN: Yeah. We were talking to some people and they would say, "Wow, it's like going back in time. It's like you guys have never stopped." And I'd like to think we got better!

MM: I think your art really delivered on that first series. It was very good throughout.

KEVIN: I was fairly happy with it, I think.

MM: Did you make any art corrections or anything because of those dialogue changes?

KEVIN: No, because I didn't know about it until, I think it was the fifth or sixth issue. I don't remember where it was.... It got to the point where I would lay it out on the board and then I would have it lettered, because I personally find it extremely annoying when you bust your ass working on something in the background just to have it covered up by word balloons. It's just a monumental waste of time. And especially with these books, where there were so, so, so many word balloons on these things. So many square inches got covered up. It just seemed kind of redundant to be spending the time to be drawing every brick on a building, and then it's just gone and no one sees it. So there was a point, I would do layouts, I would get the lettered board back, and then I might make some changes because the dialogue was slightly different. But by the time we got to the second mini-series we had all that stuff ironed out.

MM: Did you have a lot of anticipation for the series when it came out?

KEVIN: Not really, no.

MM: So you were surprised that it got a nice reception?

KEVIN: Umm... somewhat. I understood the nostalgia factor, so it really was just a matter of will we do a good job with it. I thought we did okay.

MM: Were you kind of hoping this was going to be a one-time reunion and that's it?

KEVIN: I really wasn't thinking about it as far as, "This is it and it'll never happen again." Although, I think now it'll never happen again. [*laughter*] With the death of Blue Beetle and Max, it was like, "That's it. The door's closed on that."

MM: Were you surprised about that, when they killed them off?

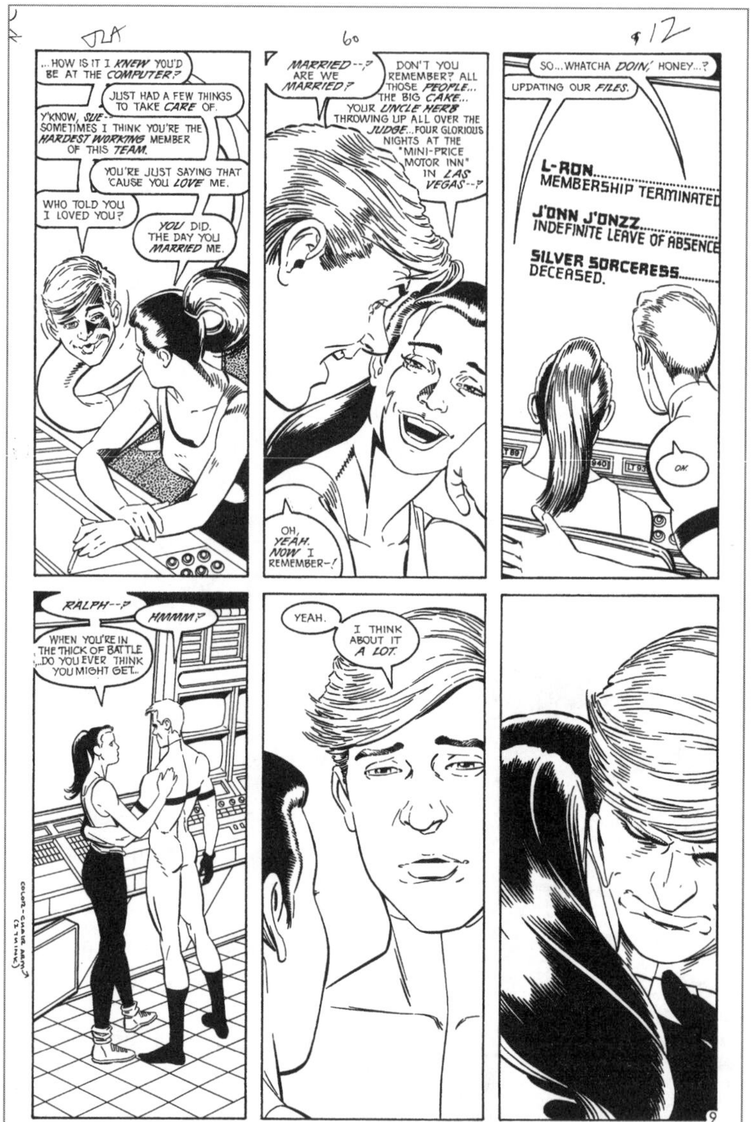

JLA
60
#12
...HOW IS IT I KNEW YOU'D BE AT THE COMPUTER?
JUST HAD A FEW THINGS TO TAKE CARE OF.
Y'KNOW, SUE-- SOMETIMES I THINK YOU'RE THE HARDEST WORKING MEMBER OF THIS TEAM.
YOU'RE JUST SAYING THAT 'CAUSE YOU LOVE ME.
WHO TOLD YOU I LOVED YOU?
YOU DID. THE DAY YOU MARRIED ME.
MARRIED--? ARE WE MARRIED?
DON'T YOU REMEMBER? ALL THOSE PEOPLE... THE BIG CAKE... YOUR UNCLE HERB THROWING UP ALL OVER THE JUDGE...FOUR GLORIOUS NIGHTS AT THE "MINI-PRICE MOTOR INN" IN LAS VEGAS--?
OH, YEAH. NOW I REMEMBER--!
SO...WHATCHA DOIN,' HONEY...?
UPDATING OUR FILES.
L-RON.......... MEMBERSHIP TERMINATED
J'ONN J'ONZZ.......... INDEFINITE LEAVE OF ABSENCE
SILVER SORCERESS.......... DECEASED.
RALPH--?
HMMM?
WHEN YOU'RE IN THE THICK OF BATTLE ...DO YOU EVER THINK YOU MIGHT GET...
YEAH.
I THINK ABOUT IT A LOT.
9

KEVIN: Yeah, yeah, because first off, killing off Sue. Sue died, what, before the second mini-series came out?

MM: Yes.

KEVIN: Right. So....

MM: You guys had agreed to do a second mini-series and they did this, right?

KEVIN: Yeah, they greenlit the second mini-series while we were on, like, the fourth issue of the first one. I don't even know if the first issue had come out yet, but they were like, "Yeah, you can do another six." DiDio came up to me and said, "All right, this is what we're thinking of doing. We're going to have the second mini-series come out immediately after the first one. It'll be three double-sized issues, because we want to have the last issue out before *Identity Crisis* comes up, because, obviously, we can't have Sue prancing around in this story if she's actually dead." So I was like, "Oh, okay. Who are you going to get to pencil it? There's no way I'm getting that volume of work done in the amount of time we're talking about." And I was very happy with the art for the second mini-series. I was very happy with the idea of "I'll do the first double-sized thing and you can get other artists to do the other two. I'm fine with that; I've got no problem with that." They were like, "No, no, no. It's got to be the team. Got to be the team." So when it materialized that it was never going to be done before *Identity Crisis*, at that time it was lumped into the *JLA: Classified* thing.

MM: Was it a let-down having it be part of *Classified*?

KEVIN: Yeah. You don't want your first issue to be #4.

MM: It's almost like being in *Marvel Comics Presents* or something.

KEVIN: Yeah. I understood why; I understood the necessity of it, but....

MM: But it still could have been its own series. That's what I don't understand, because your first series did very well by itself. It didn't need to be lumped in there with miscellaneous stories.

KEVIN: Their decisions are made above my pay rate.

MM: I'm thinking *Identity Crisis* is not your favorite series?

KEVIN: Nah, it was a fine series.

MM: I thought it was kind of strange seeing the characters you guys played with, seeing them in these serious kinds of situation.

KEVIN: I had no problem with that. I think that's fine. I mean, I was for us doing more dramatic moments in our book. I was never a big fan of the constant, non-stop comedy. I like a lot of humor. I mean, anything I do is going to have humor in it—that's just how I am. I like a lot of humor. But, I like it balanced with gravitas. It's kind of like—to use James Bond as a reference—Connery had a lot of funny lines, but he also had the gravitas to go with it, whereas Roger Moore was just spouting off funny lines but didn't have that gravitas.

MM: Well I think that's one of the things you guys did right.

KEVIN: Yeah!

MM: *Identity Crisis* had some of that stuff, and I read the first and was, like, "Wow! This is *too* serious."

KEVIN: Well, I don't mind it, because these guys are dealing with life and death stuff every day, so they should be serious. I was never a big fan of the [Justice League] villains being funny. Almost like the Joker or someone like that. Blue Beetle and Booster Gold and Fire and

those guys can be funny as hell, but I would have preferred there to have been menace to the villains. I mean, you want to have some sort of reality connection. When people are making quips during what are supposed to be tense situations, it's suddenly not as tense anymore.

MM: You guys had some of that stuff in the second series, though. Like when Guy finds Ice and he starts crying and getting all emotional.

Previous Page: Sue and Ralph long before *Identity Crisis*. Page 9 of *Justice League America #60*. Inks by Terry Austin.
Below: Guy has his moments, but for the most part he's just a jerk. Inks by Joe Rubinstein.

Justice League and all related characters ™ and ©2007 DC Comics.

JLA
60 MAR
16 21
CATHERINE!!!
YOU KNOW I'M GONNA FIND YOU, WOMAN-- AND WHEN I DO--!
THERE AIN'T NO USE IN HIDIN' FROM ME! YOU KNOW AND I KNOW THAT THERE JUST AIN'T NO WAY YOU'RE NOT MAKIN' ME TEAM LEADER!!
CATHERINE, DAMMIT-- WHERE THE HELL ARE YOU?!
YOU'RE GETTIN' ME MAD NOW! AND I JUST MIGHT--
SOB
WHIMPER
...MIGHT...?
HEY-- I'D KNOW THOSE SNIFFLES ANYWHERE!
AW, JEEZ-- IT'S MY HONEY!
SHE'S REALLY TAKIN' THIS SILVER SORCERESS THING HARD.
I OUGHTA TAKE THE POOR KID IN MY ARMS...GIVE 'ER A LITTLE LOVE AN' COMFORT. AN' I WILL, TOO--
--RIGHT AFTER I'M DONE STRAIGHTENIN' OUT THAT FRENCH FLOOZIE!!
CATHERINE!! CATHERINE, DAMMIT, IF YA DON'T SHOW YER FACE, I'M GONNA HAVE T' USE MY RING T' FIND YA!
CATHERINE!!!
16
COLOR-GREEN LIGHT FROM RING

Above: Guy goes from one extreme to another in this flashback to *Justice League America* #60. Inks by Terry Austin.
Next Page: Beetle and the gang return from Hell, but can't escape *Infinite Crisis*. Inks by Joe Rubinstein.

Justice League and all related characters ™ and ©2007 DC Comics.

KEVIN: Yeah, that last page.

MM: That came out of nowhere, but it was kind of sweet.

KEVIN: Oh, I liked that. I was very happy with that. The original description had the two of them in the foreground and the other characters in the background looking somber or something. No, no, no. I wanted to get right in there. I wanted it to be completely about what these two were going through.

MM: That was a really sweet moment, and the way you built it up I thought was really nice, too. And for one issue Guy's not a total jerk.

KEVIN: Yeah, you had sympathy for him. He can still be a jerk, but, there's another side to him that creates a little empathy.

MM: She was the love of his life.

KEVIN: Yeah, I liked that. It was actually my idea to send them to Hell. When we were talking about a second mini-series, I said, "Let's call it *The Justice League Goes to Hell.*" Because I didn't want to draw buildings. [*laughter*] I just wanted to draw easy backgrounds. "Let's send them to Hell. Have them fighting monsters and demons in caves." And then, of course, Giffen has them working at Burger King and I had to draw buildings anyway. [*laughter*]

MM: Were you happy with the way the series was treated? Was it sitting around for a long time?

KEVIN: No, no. Well, the first few issues were sitting a long time before we finished the last batch, but nah.

MM: It's not likely that you guys are going to come back to DC to do anything anytime soon.

KEVIN: Well, I have no animosity toward DC.

MM: But you don't have "your" characters any more. Could you see yourself—

KEVIN: I don't think we'll be doing those characters. You asked me earlier about how I feel about Blue Beetle being killed. There was all this Internet buzz about, "I think they're killing Blue Beetle." They never told me. I had no idea. So I was up in the office one day and I'm asking them—this was the day that the make-readies came out for *Infinite Crisis*, the one where Beetle gets shot—and Dan DiDio puts his arm around me and walks me over to his office and gives me a copy. He was, like, "Yeah, Blue Beetle gets killed, but that's not the worst part." "It's worse than that?" He shows me Max Lord shooting Beetle in the head. "Oh, f*ck." That ticked me off. That really ticked me off, because saying Maxwell Lord was some evil guy who was scheming us all along completely negated every creative decision we made about Max while doing the mini-series. When I was drawing him, he was a cross between Donald Trump and Bill Murray. He was not evil. The guy I was drawing was not an evil guy. So now this thing comes out and it says, "Everything you guys did with that ain't true."

MM: A complete 180 degrees on your characters.

KEVIN: Yes, exactly. That really ticked me off. But, I don't own the character, so there was nothing I could do about it. I know that DC wasn't that thrilled about it either, in terms of the fact that we had the second mini-series coming out while that book was out showing Max differently. I'm sure they would have liked to have had that consistency all through it.

MM: Why Blue Beetle? There are so many other characters in the DC Universe. I guess Meltzer really liked your characters?

KEVIN: Or he didn't. When I found out about Max killing Beetle, I wasn't done with the second mini-series, and I intentionally changed the last panel of the mini-series. Originally it was a shot of Fire and Mary Marvel flying away from the strip mall, but I decided, no. I made it as a shot of Max and Beetle standing side by side, laughing. Because those were our characters. Not the evil guy shooting people in the head.

MM: Well, Max always had those kinds of undertones. Didn't he have that in the beginning? You guys presented a mysterious background for him.

KEVIN: Yeah, originally he was going to be more of a menace, but then over time he just became, like I said, the Bill Murray/Donald Trump character—the huckster, the con man.

MM: And he made a great team with L-Ron.

KEVIN: Yeah. I always pictured the voice of Crow [*from* Mystery Science Theater 3000]. I have a picture of one of those robots in reverse as L-Ron.

MM: What about the darker Blue Beetle costume. Did you have to design that or was it given to you?

KEVIN: Yeah, that was mine. I wanted to change his costume in the first mini-series, because, specifically, Keith told me that Blue Beetle in this one was going to be more mature, he wasn't going to be as silly. I thought, "Well, if he isn't going to be that silly, then he probably shouldn't be wearing such a silly costume." At least something a little more mature. So, for me, it was a compromise. It's the exact same costume except the blues are black and the blacks are blues. It's just an inversing of the color scheme, which in the end just turned out to be a pain in the ass to draw. And in the end not really such a great idea, but I wanted it to reflect more of a grown-up approach for him. Honestly, I would have loved something more along the lines of what they did with the new Blue Beetle. I thought he should have some kind of body armor. Beetles have body armor, exoskeletons. And also Blue Beetle is a high-tech guy, he's an inventor. He's not a fighter on Batman's level, so he really should have had some sort of body armor-type costume.

MM: That's true.

KEVIN: I'd like to make another little point, another trivia thing. I was really toying around with the idea—I didn't do it—but when I found out that Max had killed Blue Beetle and I had to finish the second mini-series, what I was going to do was, the team's been in another dimension and then they come back to their dimension. What I was planning on doing was, when Blue Beetle comes back to their dimension, he's wearing the bright blue costume rather than the black costume, so people might think, "Oh, it's the Blue Beetle from a different dimension that got shot! It wasn't the actual one!" [*laughs*] I didn't do that.

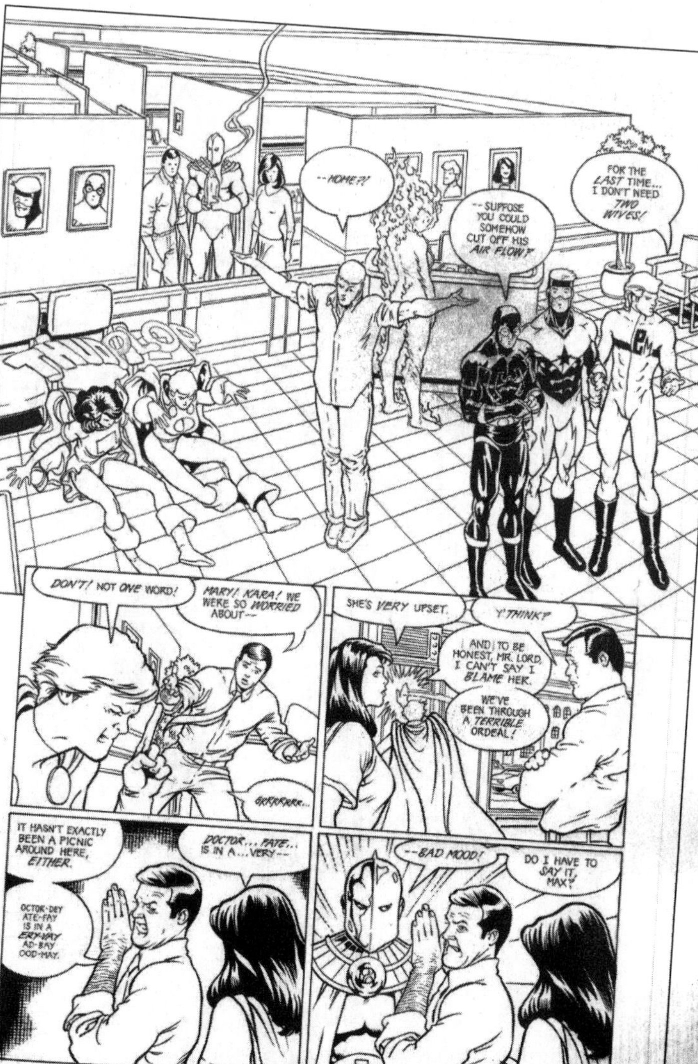
--HOME?!
--SUPPOSE YOU COULD SOMEHOW CUT OFF HIS AIR FLOW?
FOR THE LAST TIME... I DON'T NEED TWO WIVES!
DON'T! NOT ONE WORD!
MARY! KARA! WE WERE SO WORRIED ABOUT--
GRRRRRR...
SHE'S VERY UPSET.
Y'THINK?
AND TO BE HONEST, MR. LORD, I CAN'T SAY I BLAME HER.
WE'VE BEEN THROUGH A TERRIBLE ORDEAL!
IT HASN'T EXACTLY BEEN A PICNIC AROUND HERE, EITHER.
DOCTOR... FATE... IS IN A... VERY--
OCTOR-DEY ATE-FAY IS IN A ERY-VAY AD-BAY OOD-MAY.
--BAD MOOD!
DO I HAVE TO SAY IT, MAX?

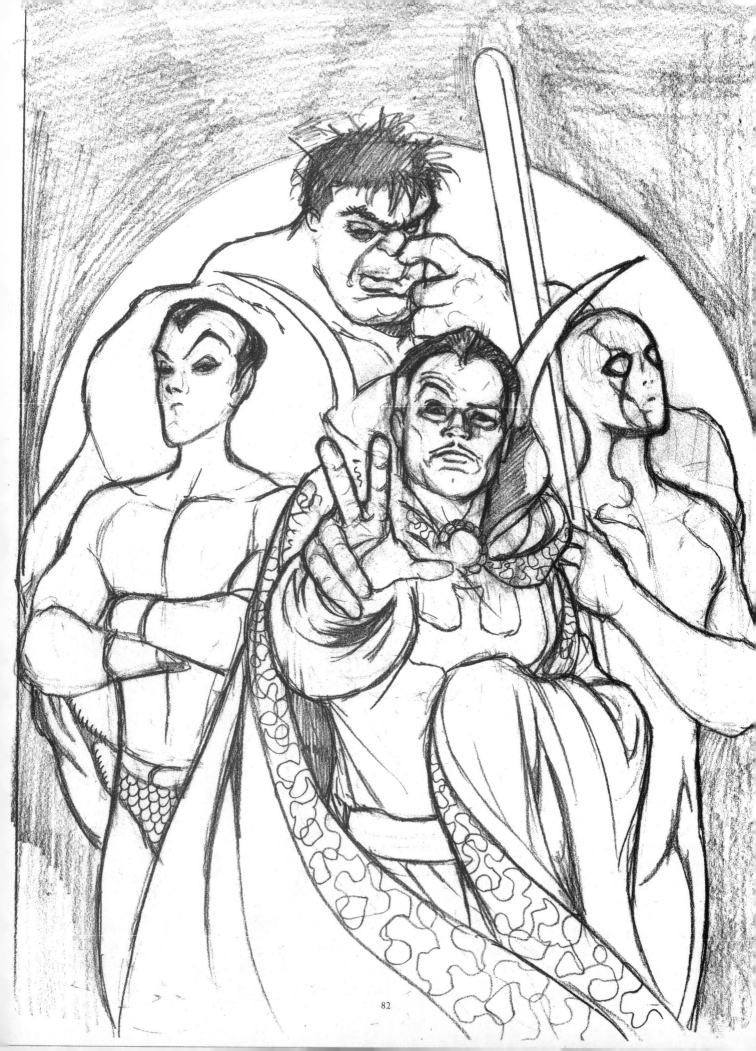

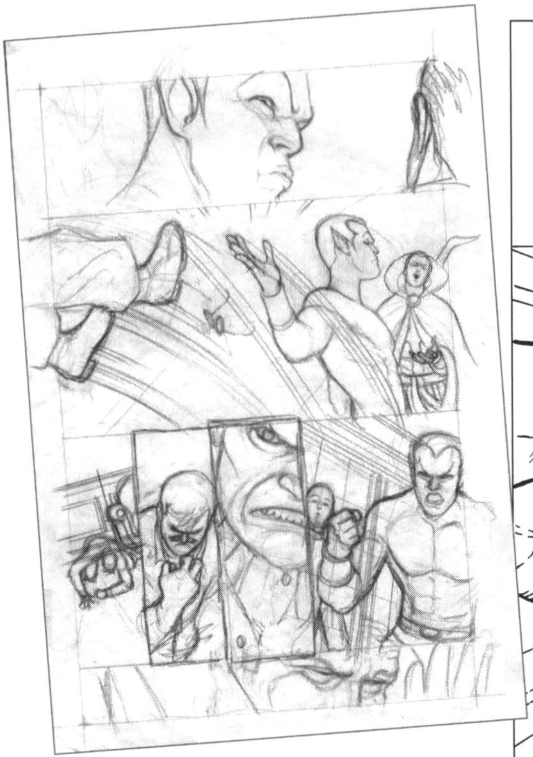

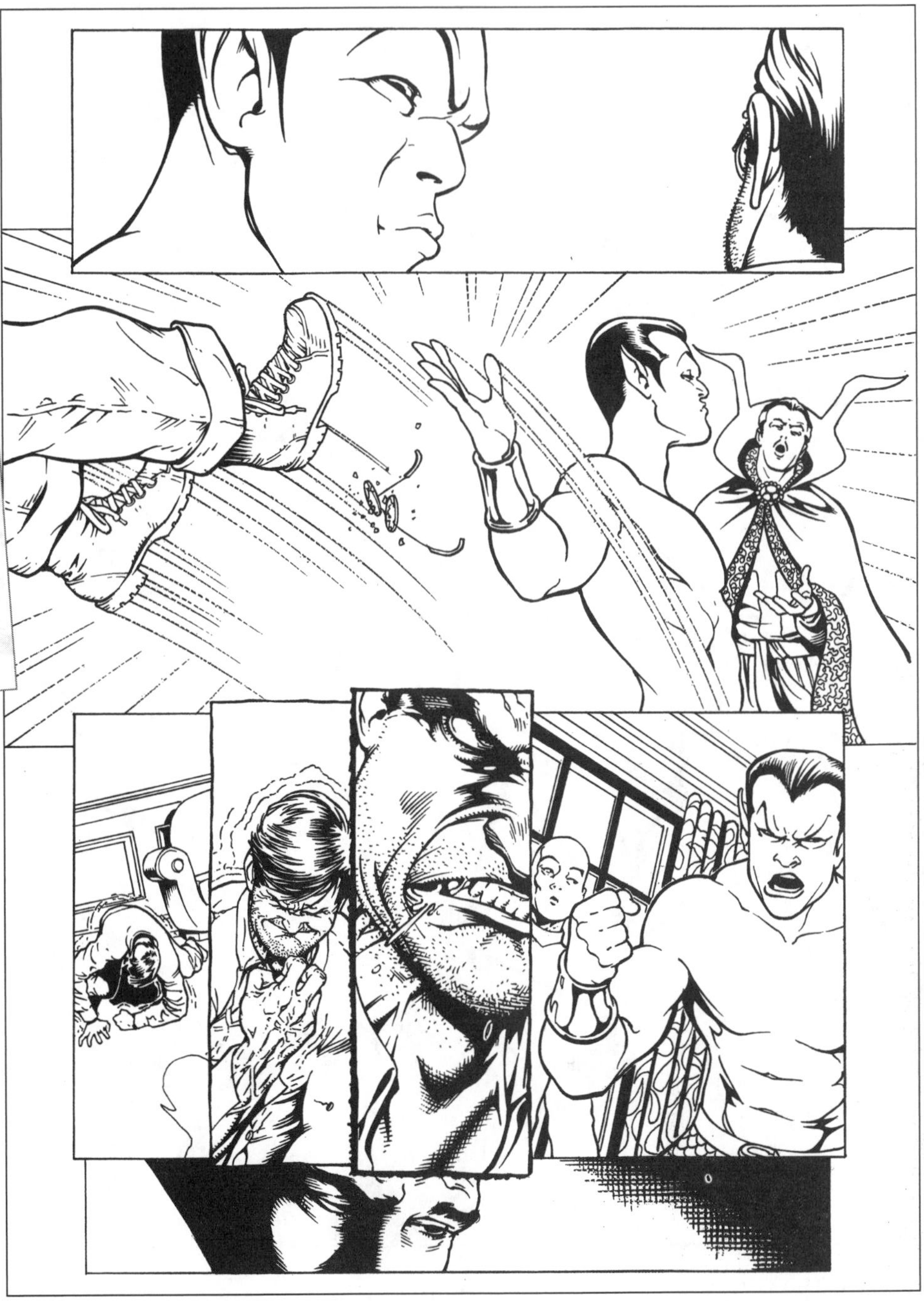

MM: How did *The Defenders* comic get started?

KEVIN: Well, we were still working on the second mini-series, when Giffen started talking to Marvel about doing things over there, and after that, it went back and forth. At first they offered us *Great Lakes Avengers*, and I was like, "I don't want to do every D-list super-hero team out there." Then they offered *Guardians of the Galaxy*, and I thought, "Oh, that might be cool." They showed me some of the characters. "That might be a fun thing to do." I think Keith asked me what would be the one thing I'd love to do, and looking at *Defenders*, those were my favorite books. "That would be something I'd love to do." And then we ended up getting it.

MM: Did you right away have in mind what you wanted to do with each character, what look you were going to give them?

KEVIN: Well, sort of, I guess. There was a lot of flak online about how I drew Sub-Mariner. I was really an idiot. Maybe I just didn't look that closely at it afterwards, but I was basing it on what I remembered Bill Everett's Sub-Mariner was, which was a slightly bigger head and a leaner body. I just pictured him with a swimmer's body. I don't think he has to be a big, massive, muscular kind of guy. He's a fish man, and I just wanted—if I could have given him webbed hands, I would have given him webbed hands.

MM: Well, he was the most exciting character that you illustrated, I think. I liked the way he looked. I liked it so much I thought you should do a series.

KEVIN: Well, yeah, he is fun to "animate." I always pictured Yul Brynner from *The King and I*. That sort of proud, strutting kind of guy.

MM: The series really focused on three of the four original Defenders.

Previous Page: Kevin's layout for *Defenders* #1. **Above:** Layouts and finished inks for page 18 of *Defenders* #1. The "inks" were created in Photoshop off of Kevin's pencils.

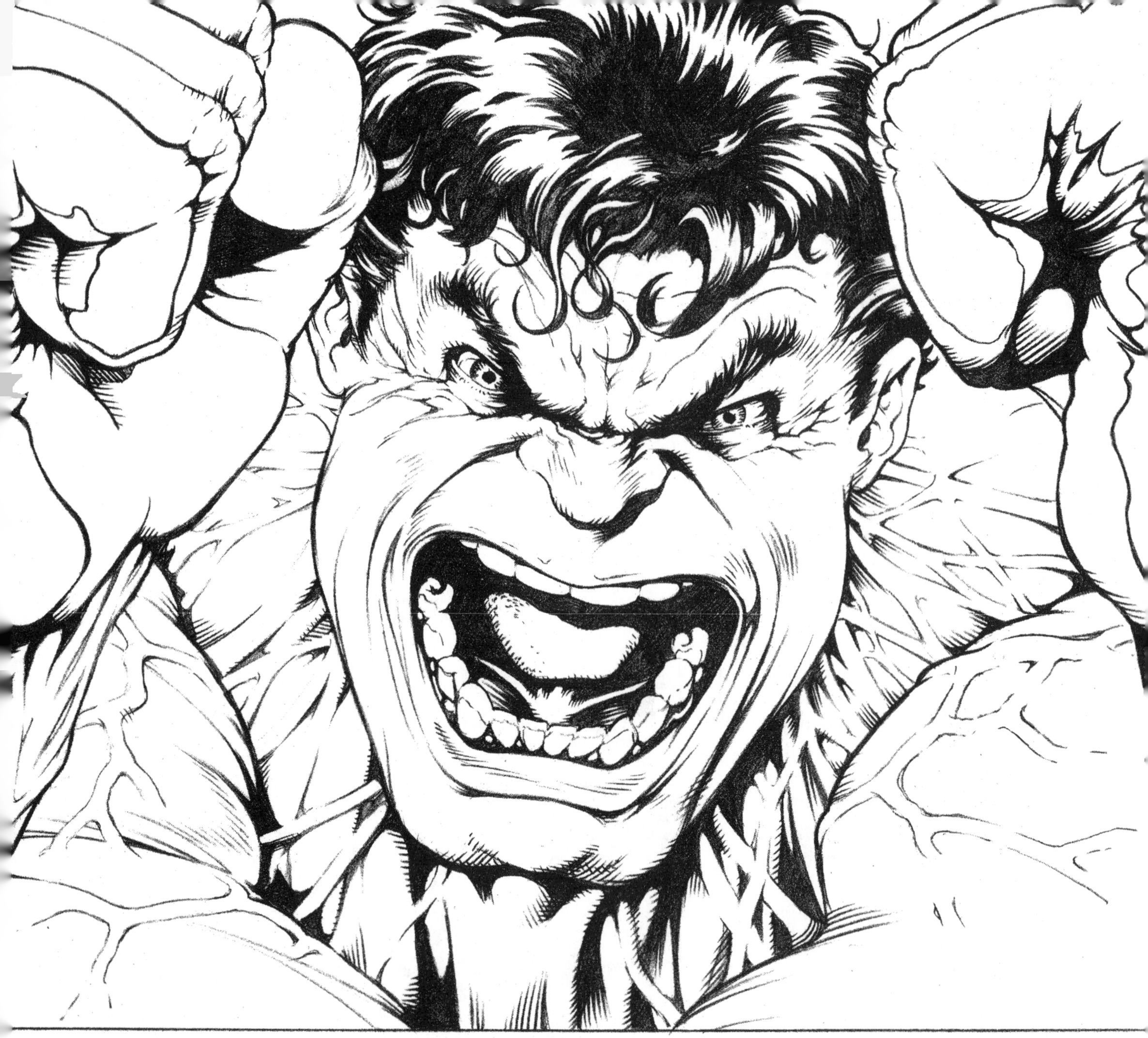

KEVIN: Yeah, Silver Surfer had nothing to worry about.

MM: But there were a lot of comments about the way you drew the Silver Surfer.

KEVIN: Yeah, yeah, but he's an alien.

MM: He was really spaced out.

KEVIN: I didn't really get to do him doing anything except, like, reacting to surfers. I didn't get a chance to draw him blasting things or being angry or anything. It was just sort of like he was a Zen Alien. As much of a fan of John Buscema as I was, all of his characters have pretty much the same body shape, and I'm not a fan of that. I think that the characters should be different. Obviously Spider-Man is built differently from Captain America. I didn't see any need for the Silver Surfer to be a big, muscular kind of guy. There was no real need for it. Like I said, he's an alien. He's trying to understand Earth.

MM: Did Marvel have any problems with the way he looked?

KEVIN: No.

MM: He finally looks like an alien, not some guy in a Speedo.

KEVIN: Oh, yeah. I mean, I think I've drawn him like I last drew him, but, like I said, he's an alien, who is probably a little more like this. Probably a smaller nose, probably not a lot of features on his face, just very smooth.

MM: Who made the decision that you would ink yourself on the series?

KEVIN: Umm, the editor. I handed in the first cover and he was like, "Wow, I had no idea your work was so clean. Have you ever thought of having it scanned in and being brought off the pencils?" I was like, "I can do that? Then, yeah, let's do that."

MM: You learned how to do that with this series, *The Defenders*?

KEVIN: I wasn't really changing all that much, because I've always penciled very tightly, so there really wasn't that much of a change for me on this. And, a lot of what I imagine the work that had to be done was done at Marvel, because for the first few issues I just handed it in because my scanner wasn't working. I had to get a new scanner, so I just handed in the pencils, and then they would come out looking inked. But, yeah, the first time getting my feet wet in that environment was with *The Defenders*.

MM: Were you very proud of how the art looked when you saw it in production?

KEVIN: Yeah, I was amazed that it looked like it was inked. I'm like, "Wow! Look at that! It looks inked!"

MM: And from now on will it be that way?

KEVIN: Yeah! I mean, why not?

MM: Was this *Defenders* series a bigger success than the two *Justice League* mini-series?

KEVIN: Nah. I think it was fun when we did it, but in the long run I don't think it turned out to be that big a deal. I don't think we translated as well over to Marvel working with those characters. But I knew there would be people, purists, who feel you can't make fun of these guys, and you can't be funny with these characters. But it's just a five-issues series, it's just one version of *Defenders*, someone else will coming along and do another version of *Defenders*, so it's not like this is the way it'll be from now on. I look at it as the *Star Trek IV* of *Defenders*. A little like that, a little more light-hearted series.

MM: Three of the four characters didn't even have their own series. I don't know why people were complaining, because you guys brought some excitement to those characters that they hadn't had in a while.

KEVIN: I was reading a lot of the Internet stuff, and some of the people on the Internet just get really pissy about that. I was reading stuff online in some of the chat rooms, on the message boards, I'm like, "Wow! There are some pissed off people out here." But, everyone—especially with these iconic characters—has their own vision of what they should be, and you can't match everyone's vision. Some people liked it, some people didn't. I mean, that's how it works.

Previous Page: Hulk mad! Pencils for the opening page of *Defenders* #2. **Below:** Page 2 of *Defenders* #2.

Defenders ™ and ©2007 Marvel Characters, Inc.

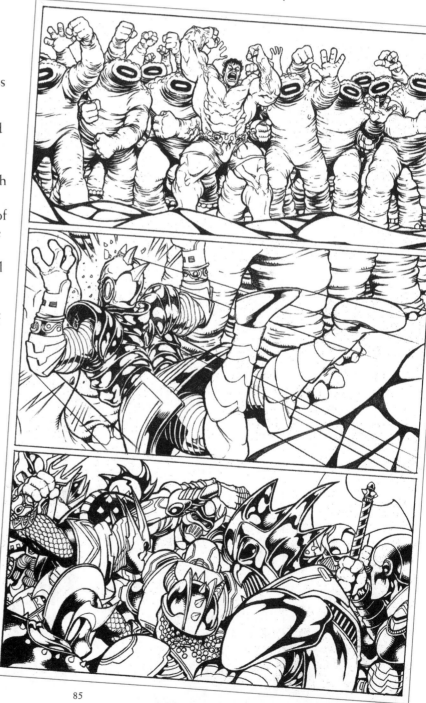

MM: What were some of the best things about working on *The Defenders*, that you enjoyed drawing?

KEVIN: Well, I enjoyed drawing Umar. I wasn't too thrilled about them putting a bikini on her while she's bathing.

MM: Did you draw her nude?

KEVIN: Yeah, I mean, she's *bathing*, she's nude. Y'know, as I am when I bathe. I don't wear a bathing suit. I drew her nude. I didn't show anything. I mean, I know the ground rules: you don't show the erogenous zones.

MM: They still art-corrected it?

KEVIN: Yeah!

MM: Did they go through you or did they just do it?

KEVIN: No, no, they did it. The editor was very embarrassed by it.

MM: They had Storm doing that kind of stuff for years.

KEVIN: Yeah. He was very embarrassed. He was like, "I'm really sorry they did this. I don't know why, but that's what they said." I was like, "Okay, whatever." You can show Wolverine gutting people, but heaven forbid we should see the side of a breast. I found it a little odd.

MM: What are you working on now?

KEVIN: I'm doing a fill-in issue of *Superman/Batman*, it's a fun little story. I was actually working on something else before I started the *Superman/Batman* thing, but the project was unscheduled, so

Above: Kevin's layouts for page 5 of *Defenders* #2, showing a bathing—not swimming—Umar.
Right: Solomon Grundy hate Super... Power... whoever you are! From *Superman/Batman* #27—a fun identity swap story.

Umar ™ and ©2007 Marvel Characters, Inc.
Huntress, Power Girl, Solomon Grundy ™ and ©2007 DC Comics.

the editor was like, "Sure, sure, that's fine to do it." And especially since it's a project for DC. The project is a three-issue story. I'm not going to do a monthly series. I'm not there yet. Six-issue arcs are good for me for now.

MM: But you also want to do more writing, as well?

KEVIN: Yeah, yeah.

MM: Do you see yourself doing more creator-owned or creator-driven projects? Something written by you and drawn by you?

KEVIN: Obviously not exclusively from now on, but yeah. Those are the projects that I enjoy doing the most. Not because I'm the greatest writer, but because it's more personal, it's more from my own imagination. That's much more satisfying than illustrating somebody else's idea.

Part 7: Storytelling and the Creative Process

MM: Who influenced you? Which guys really sparked your imagination when you were growing up?

KEVIN: Well, I remember Neal Adams. I specifically remember, I think it was *Conan* #37. But I was reading *Conan* religiously back then, so I was used to seeing John Buscema when that issue came out. "Wow! Look at this!"

MM: Yeah, there was a little Frazetta in there.

KEVIN: Yeah! I was like, "Wow, look at this! It's so cool!" I just remember being blown away by that. I remember an *Avengers Annual* that Michael Golden did.

MM: Oh, *Avengers Annual* #10, the one with Rogue.

KEVIN: Yeah, I remember really being blown away by that.

MM: What was the attraction, though?

KEVIN: I don't know. It was just the amount of detail, and that really impressed me.

MM: Very story-heavy story without many splash pages. There aren't a lot of stock pages in there.

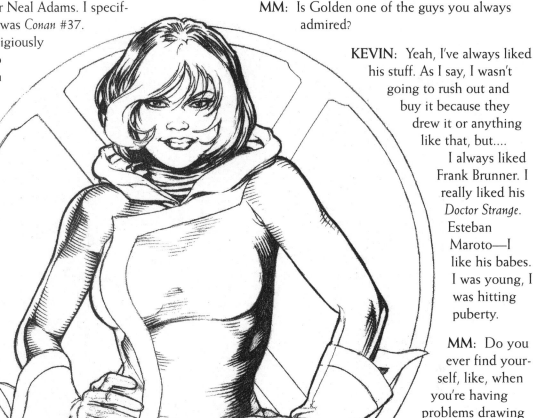

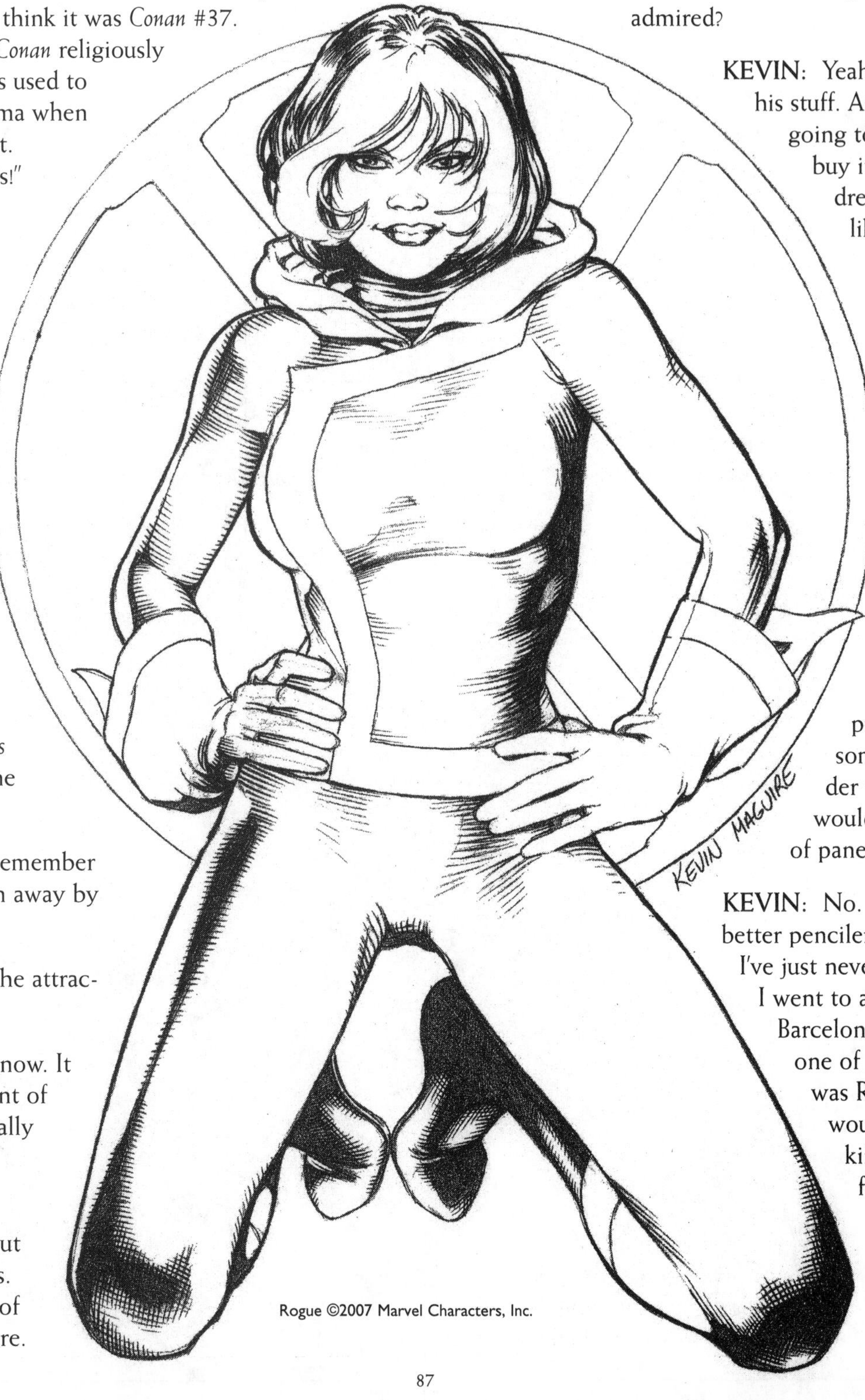
KEVIN MAGUIRE

KEVIN: Yeah, yeah. I just remember the amount of detail and.... it was really impressive.

MM: Is Golden one of the guys you always admired?

KEVIN: Yeah, I've always liked his stuff. As I say, I wasn't going to rush out and buy it because they drew it or anything like that, but.... I always liked Frank Brunner. I really liked his *Doctor Strange*. Esteban Maroto—I like his babes. I was young, I was hitting puberty.

MM: Do you ever find yourself, like, when you're having problems drawing something, "I wonder what Neal Adams would do in this sort of panel here?"

KEVIN: No. I'd probably be a better penciler if I did, but no. I've just never been that way. I went to a convention in Barcelona back then and one of the people there was Ron Garney. He would pick up all kinds of books by famous illustrators and be looking at those in detail, and he had that curiosity, but I

Book JUSTICE LEAGUE COVER SKETCHES Issue # Story Page # #

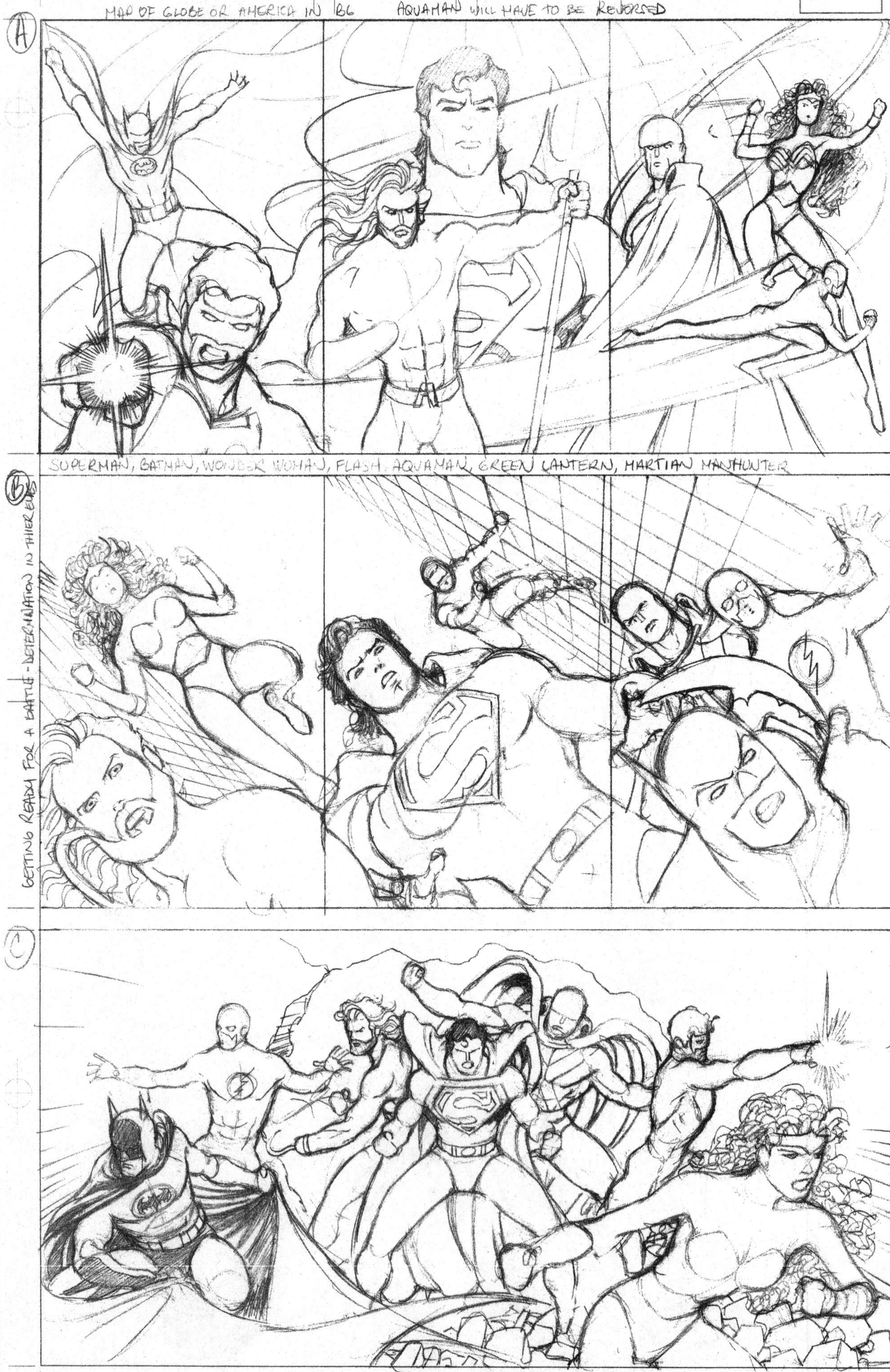
MAP OF GLOBE OR AMERICA IN B6 AQUAMAN WILL HAVE TO BE REVERSED
A
SUPERMAN, BATMAN, WONDER WOMAN, FLASH, AQUAMAN, GREEN LANTERN, MARTIAN MANHUNTER
B
GETTING READY FOR A BATTLE - DETERMINATION IN THIER EYES
C

06/30/95 / PO #41793 #6485 / 6531

Strathmore Stock

Virginia Romita

didn't. Again, probably to my detriment, because there're probably all kinds of things that I could learn from looking at the work of other people, but, I don't know, it just happened.

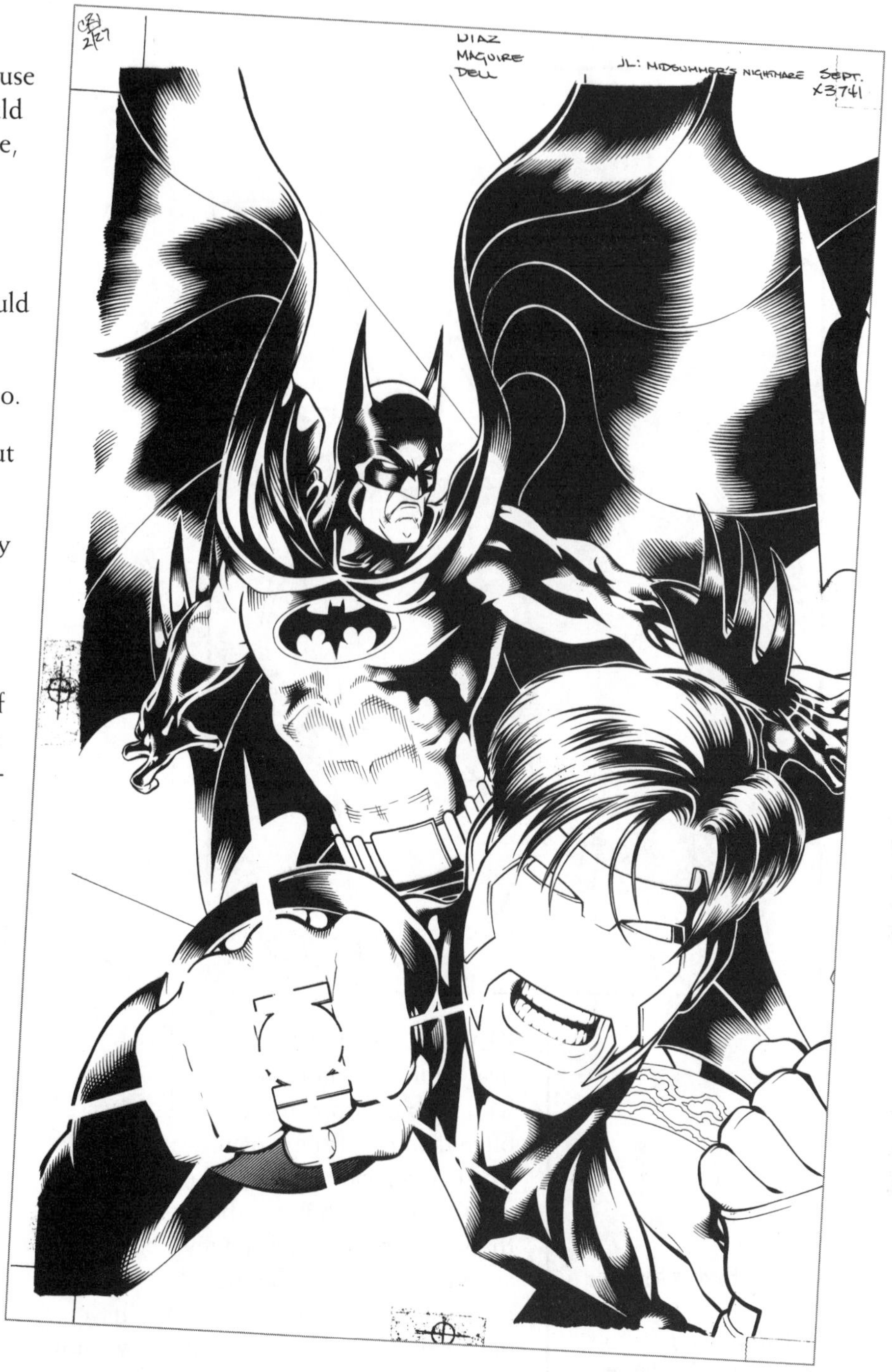
DIAZ
MAGUIRE
DELL
JL: MIDSUMMER'S NIGHTMARE SEPT.
X3741

MM: When you see your art, do you see anybody that looks kind of similar to you? If you were to classify yourself in a certain group, would you be closer to what Michael Golden does?

KEVIN: No, I wouldn't say Michael Golden, no.

MM: I look at your work and I can't figure out who you are.

KEVIN: That's probably because I don't really follow or look at very many people.

MM: Because with Art Adams, you see a little Michael Golden in his stuff, and I guess if you look at John Buscema, you can see a little bit of whoever it was who influenced him. You don't see any real influences in your art. You see a little animation, maybe, and sometimes—

KEVIN: Yeah, like I said, I wasn't really that sort of guy, looking at other people's work and examining it. Everything was kind of instinctive.

MM: Have you learned more from film than comics? When you're doing a comic, do you think more of a shot than a picture?

KEVIN: Yeah, a little. But also I breakdown stories by emotional beats, which is especially difficult with a lot of the *Justice League* stuff, because the emotional beats go back and forth with the characters. They'll be yelling, and then they'll be crying. I mean, there's so much going on that breaking down the panels, I remember going, "Just make lots and lots of panels."

MM: Do you ever sketch on your own? Do you doodle or practice?

KEVIN: No.

MM: When did that start? Once you became a professional, you're too busy to do that?

KEVIN: Yeah. I used to draw for fun and entertainment, and now when I'm done with drawing, a day's work... I just don't feel like drawing stuff for myself.

MM: If you're watching a film and you see a certain expression that John Wayne made or a nice visual shot, you don't want to draw it down or anything?

KEVIN: No, not really.

MM: Your art has progressed since you started. How would you say that's happened then? Are you just keeping at it?

Previous Page: Cover layout options for *JLA: Midsummer's Nightmare* #1-3. Option A was chosen for the triptych. **Above:** Inks for the first cover. Note that for the final drawing Batman was brought more into the forefront and given a more dramatic pose. Inks by John Dell.

Above: Kevin's layout—shown at actual size—and pencils for *JLA: Midsummer's Nightmare* #2. Note that Aquaman has been reversed to put the hook on the proper hand, and Superman has been slightly enlarged.
Right: And the final version. Inks by John Dell.

KEVIN: Yeah, I see too many things I'm not happy with. I'm not happy more often than not. I'm my own worst critic, and I look at a page and I see what's wrong with it, for the most part. So that's probably the reason why I don't draw as much as a lot of other people. I do a lot of erasing, a lot of nit-picking. You have a picture in your mind's eye that you want it to be, and it works sometimes. Sometimes it comes out looking better than I expected it to look, and those are the happy moments.

MM: You're your own person; you don't need to see what Joe Madureira is doing or any of the other artists in the field?

KEVIN: I don't think about my place within the industry as much as I just think about the needs of a specific panel. I make competition with myself, not with any-body else, so I'm not as aware of what other people are doing.

MM: When you're at your drawing table, what sort of material do you keep in your apartment? Do you keep a lot of reference material?

KEVIN: I've got some reference books. Lately I've been finding that the best reference is obviously the Internet and DVDs— just use the freeze frame at certain points.

MM: That helps you with anatomy or posing techniques?

KEVIN: No, it helps me with cars, trucks, buildings, and inanimate objects. The stuff I need to draw.

MM: You like drawing people, you don't like drawing—

KEVIN: I love drawing people, I hate drawing *stuff*.

MM: Like cars and planes....

KEVIN: Cars, vehicles, strip malls, office spaces.

MM: Well, how did you work on your anatomy, then? You just developed over time?

KEVIN: Yeah. Still not perfect, yet.

MM: I think that your figurework is as good as it's ever been.

KEVIN: It's always getting better, but I still don't think it's perfect yet.

MM: Do you have a list of filmmakers that you like? Maybe your five favorite ones.

KEVIN: Five filmmakers?

MM: Yeah, the ones that might have inspired you in terms of storytelling.

KEVIN: Hmm... okay. I like John Lasseter. I don't know how much of an influence the filmmakers are on me, but John Lasseter's a favorite. Have you—?

MM: Yeah, the *Toy Story* person.

KEVIN: Yeah, yeah. I just think as far as storytelling goes, he's just got it down. He's a Spielberg of his generation in terms of just putting together something that's extremely entertaining, but also very smart and that doesn't dumb anything down. I'm really looking forward to *Cars* this weekend. I just remember being in a theater opening night of *Toy Story* 2, and 2/3 of the way through the movie, "What the hell is Woody going to do now? How is he going to solve this problem? Man this guy is a freaking master." Y'know, I'm looking at a bunch of ones and zeroes on the screen and I'm caring about what's happening.

MM: He has a very smooth way of telling a story, too.

KEVIN: Yeah, yeah. And they work very, very hard, and they go over and over and over again. I was reading how, when they decided to make *Cars*, he had his animators get inside NASCAR cars so that they could feel what it's like to be in a car going that fast—that helps translate it on the screen. And it takes that kind of homework and research to create that feeling. For the audience, that just really pays off. So I'm a big fan of his.

Obviously, Steven Spielberg. Even though a lot of his films haven't been blowing me away. I like Robert Rodriguez because I like his work method—being outside the studio system and making the kind of movies he wants to make basically out of his home. They're like big home movies. I like that.

MM: He also likes to work cheap and fast.

KEVIN: And in some cases that's good, in some cases that's not good. Who else?

MM: What about any of the classic guys like John Ford or Howard Hawks? Are you into those guys?

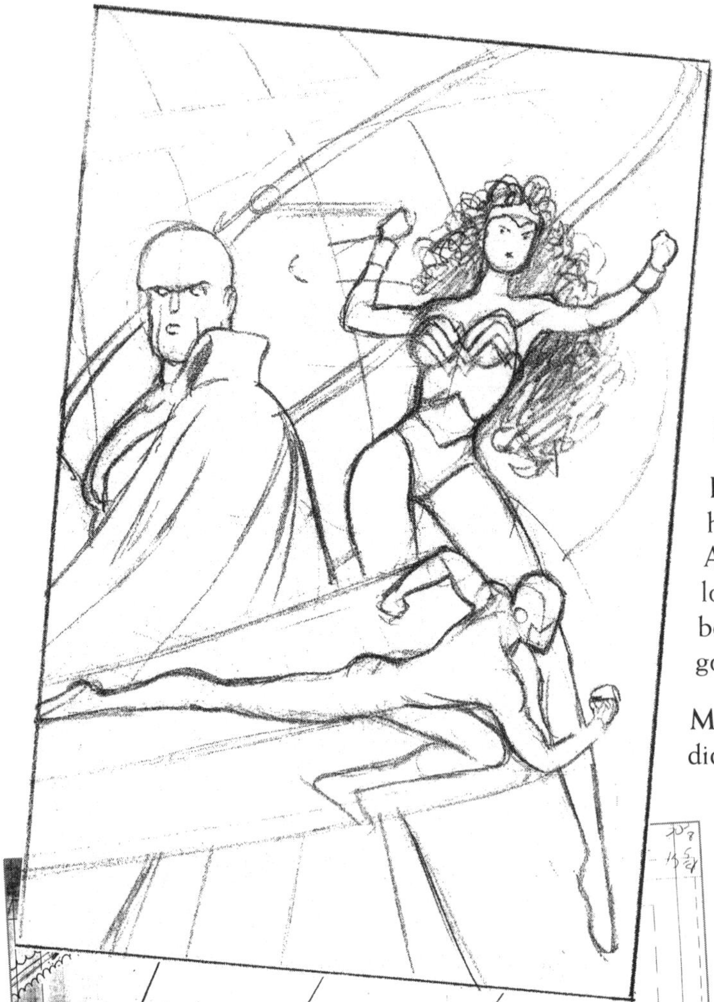

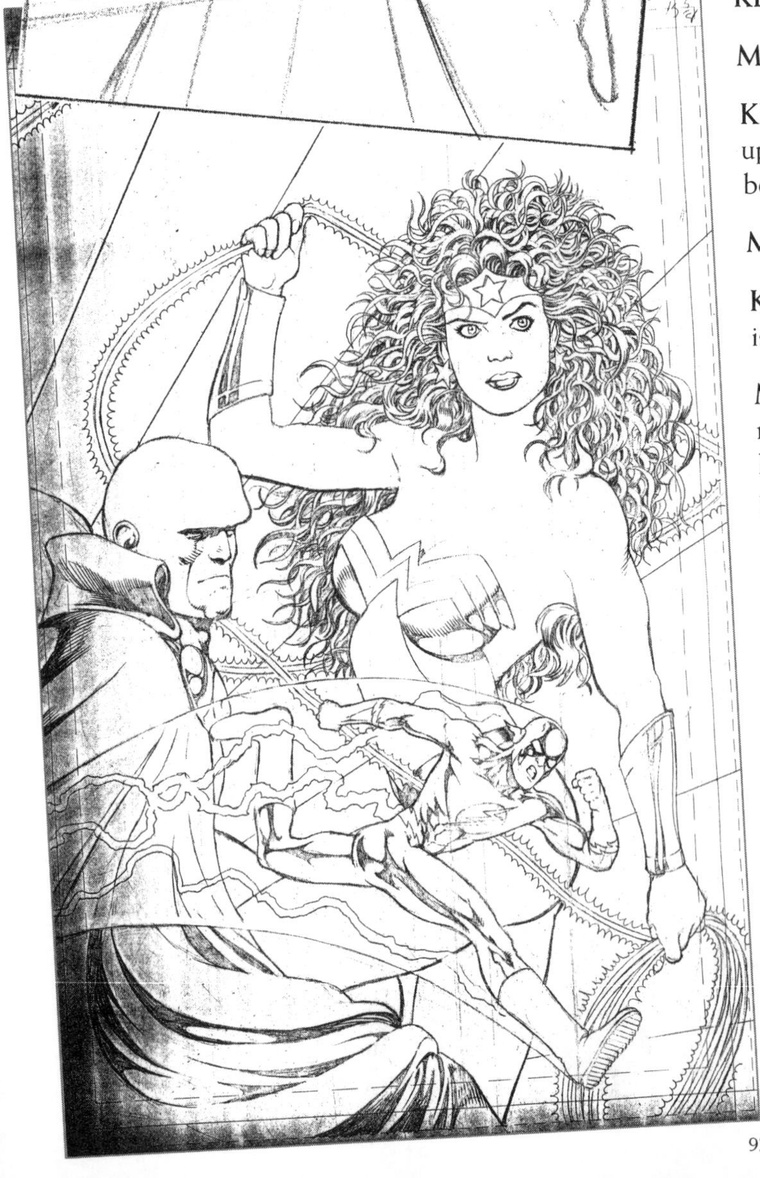

KEVIN: Yeah, but I respond more to the movies themselves rather than the filmmaker. Hitchcock obviously had this imprint style.... Who else? I wasn't expecting this question.

MM: All right, I just wanted to throw you off guard a little bit.

KEVIN: A little bit.

MM: You and Fabian are very different types of people; Fabian's a very conservative-type next to you.

KEVIN: Fabe's got the house, the two kids, the mortgage, he's the soccer coach. He's the productive creating machine. And I absolutely admire him and his ilk for that, but I'm just a lot more.... Again, it goes back to the whole self-esteem thing, because in the back of my mind, it's like it's never going to be good enough, it's never going to be good enough, and....

MM: But there's also a lot of yourself in your art. When you did do a page, that's something I think Fabian wouldn't understand—there's an attachment there, I guess.

KEVIN: Mm-hmm. Yes.

MM: But you can't let go, it's never good enough?

KEVIN: That's part of it. I'm probably not going to end up, at this point in my life, having kids, so this is what I'll be remembered for. Everything that goes out—

MM: These books are your kids.

KEVIN: Yeah. Whereas for Fabe, "This is my job and this is a paycheck." He has that.

MM: I was telling him that there are some people who really believe in doing things for the sake of the art. But he says that it is just a job—that you've got to do what you've got to do to pay the bills.

KEVIN: But he's right, though. And you've also got to remember, he used to be an editor at Marvel and editor-in-chief at Valiant, so he's very well-versed on the other side of that, being in charge of the business and publishing end and making sure that things get out on time. I'm sure that if I spent a few years as an editor somewhere, I'd probably be more like, "It has to be in now!" Y'know? "You're paying for this, it's publishing!"

MM: "Who cares about the story? Hand it in already!"

KEVIN: Yeah, for the most part. A lot of times it's just got to be out; he's right, he did this. And that's why I have a lot of respect for people like McFarlane who, even though he was making millions of dollars, he sat by that drawing board every day and he produced. I'm not a huge fan of his art, but I'm a huge fan of his work ethic. He had a book coming out every month. That's really what it comes down to: the discipline. Rolling up your sleeve, "I'm sitting down now, and I'm going to do this for 'x' amount of hours."

MM: But I don't think that you're the kind of guy who could live with yourself with some other guy inked your work and it was crap.

KEVIN: Yeah.

MM: There are some artists like Art Adams who can't take it when things don't come out like he envisioned it in his head.

KEVIN: Yeah, again, that's the eternal struggle. But it's part art and it's part business. You have to find that balance of good art on a regular basis. I'm still struggling to find that. I would still love to find a way to do a page a day. If I did a page a day, my life would be completely different.

MM: You're more proud of yourself than most guys are.

KEVIN: Not always, not always, no. It's a piece by piece thing. The first two years of *Justice League* I didn't like what I did at all. I liked the first few issues of *Captain America*. But there are conventions when people hand me things to sign and I'm like, "Oh, God, I did this? Oh my God." I just hate that.

MM: In your work schedule, do you set goals for yourself?

KEVIN: Yeah, but I never meet them. It's never worked for me. I don't know why. Obviously, if I could, I'd be far more productive, but it's very tough for me.

MM: What works more, having a deadline looming over your head, perhaps?

KEVIN: That helps. I mean, that's obviously a big motivator. When they are like, "It's coming out next week!" Yeah, that helps. I don't know. I'm curious to see what happens with the project I'm doing after the three-part story I mentioned, because it's something that I'll be writing as well, and that's the stuff I always get into more.

MM: What do you find works for you when you're working? You said you like to

feel comfortable. Do you like to set a mood around the room, or your art table a certain way?

KEVIN: Well, I have a TV on the news station. I'm sort of fond—or at least I used to be—of working late at night. That's when I'm most focused. I'm less distracted very late at night.

MM: Well, do you have the TV on and you just draw and listen, I guess?

KEVIN: Yeah. I should probably just be listening to music. Early on I listened to talk radio.

MM: Are there ever those projects you're working on where you can't stop?

Previous Page: Layout and pencils for the third issue of *JLA: Midsummer's Nightmare*. In the layout there is no dominant figure, but Kevin focuses on Wonder Woman in the pencil stage. With Wonder Woman facing to the left now, Martian Manhunter is redrawn to face the right, and Flash is pushed down a bit. **Below:** Normal guy vs. super-guy—a lesson in comic book anatomy.

Justice League ™ and ©2007 DC Comics.

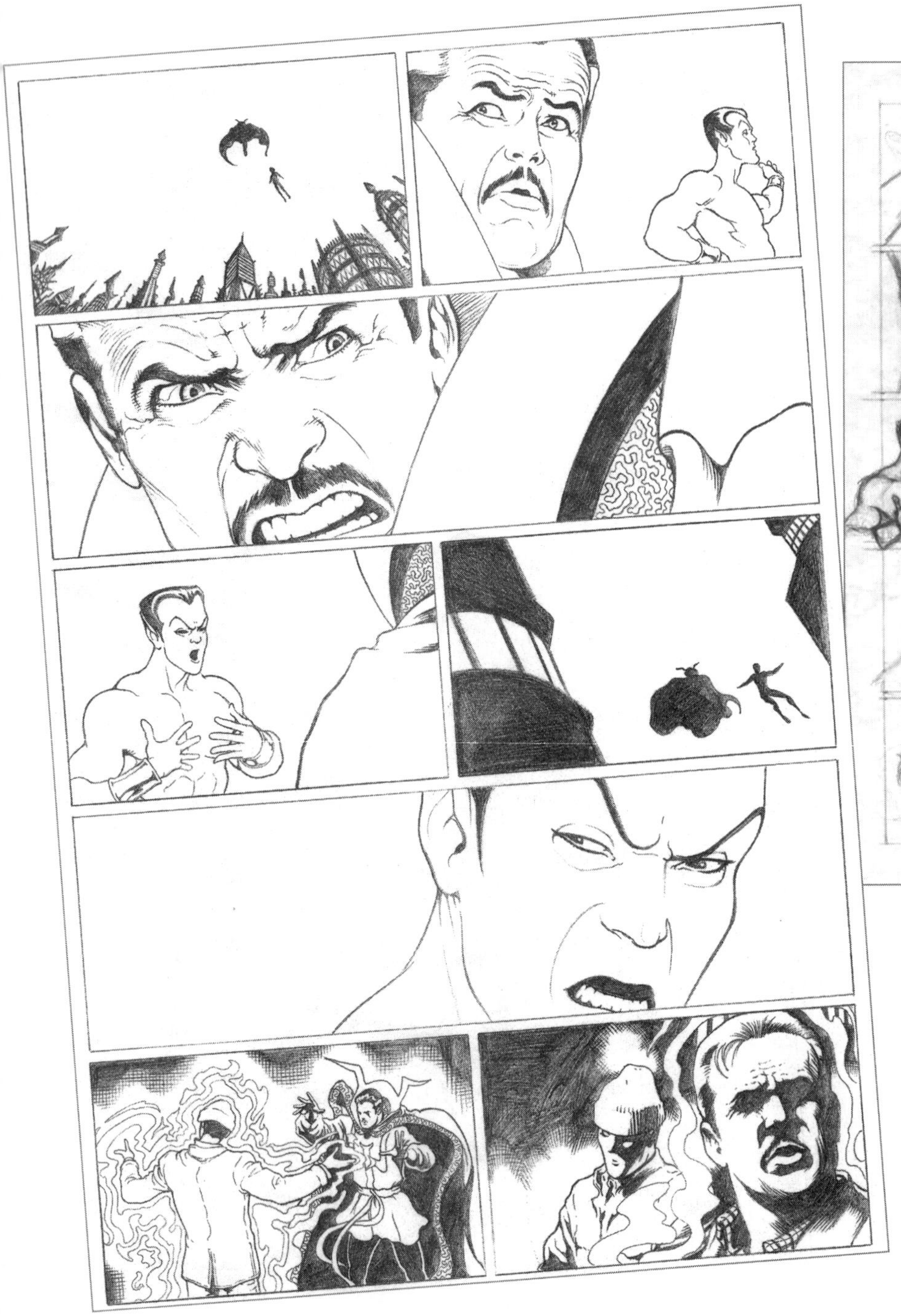

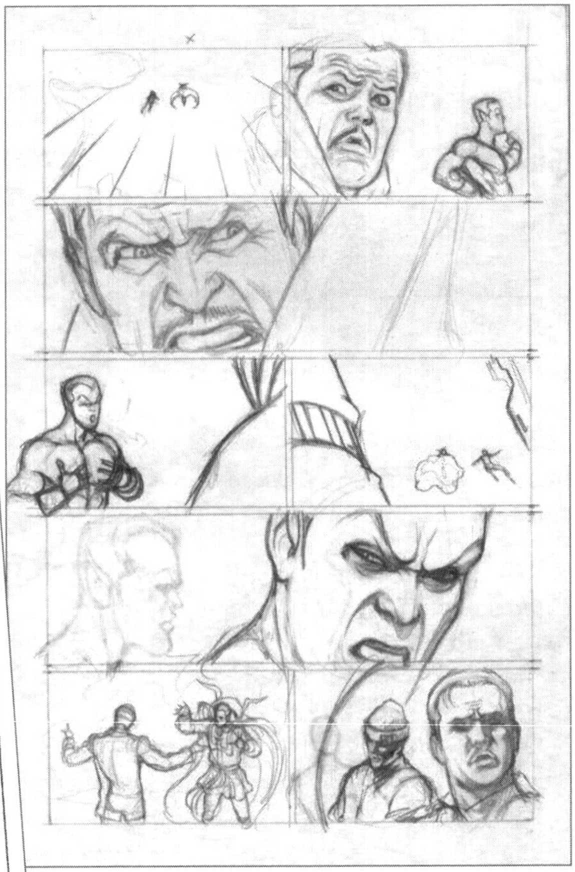

Above: Layouts and pencils for *Defenders* #3, page 20. Notice that Namor was repositioned in panel 5 during the layout stage.
Next Page: Page 12 of *Defenders* #4 opens with a dramatic shot from the villains' POV.

KEVIN: Umm... no. Isn't that sad. [*laughter*] I really wish I did. I really do.

MM: Do you break down a story before you start working on it?

KEVIN: My system changes on every book.

MM: Preliminaries?

KEVIN: Not really, no.

MM: For *The Defenders* I think I saw some sketches.

KEVIN: Sketches?

MM: Your art dealer had some preliminaries and things like that.

KEVIN: Only layouts.

MM: Layouts for pages, yeah.

KEVIN: Yeah, sometimes I would lay it out on a separate sheet of paper and then lightbox it onto the board.

MM: But that's not usually what you do?

KEVIN: It's a 50/50.

MM: But usually you just go straight to the board?

KEVIN: Fifty percent of the time.

MM: Okay. What brand of pencil do you use?

KEVIN: Lately I've been using a mechanical pencil, because I'm scanning the pages into the computer and everything, so it has to be a clean, sharp line, as opposed to a fuzzy line. Then I just have to go in there and clean it up microscopically in the computer. Or it's just a #2.

MM: What kind of software are you using on the computer?

KEVIN: Photoshop.

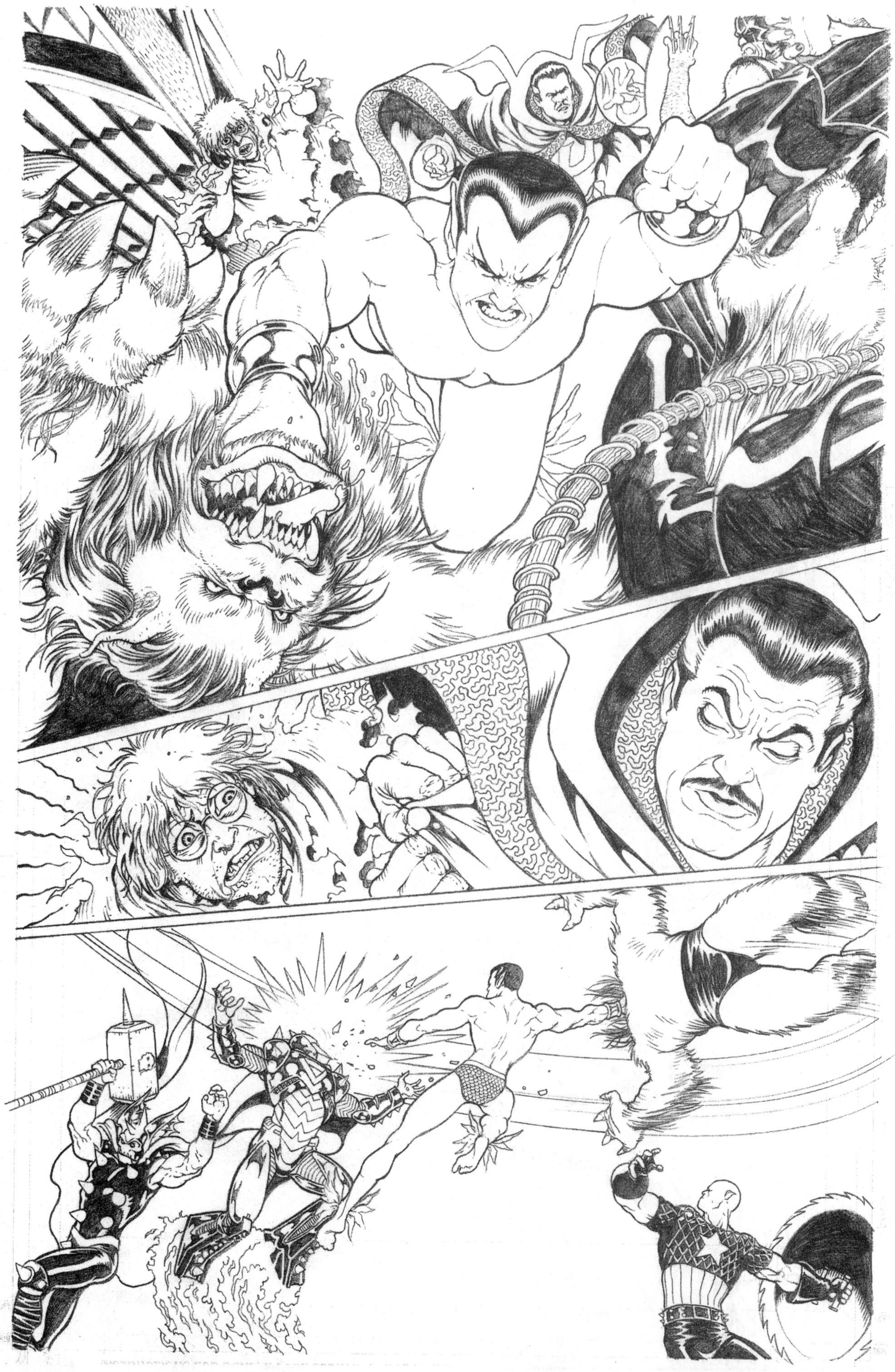

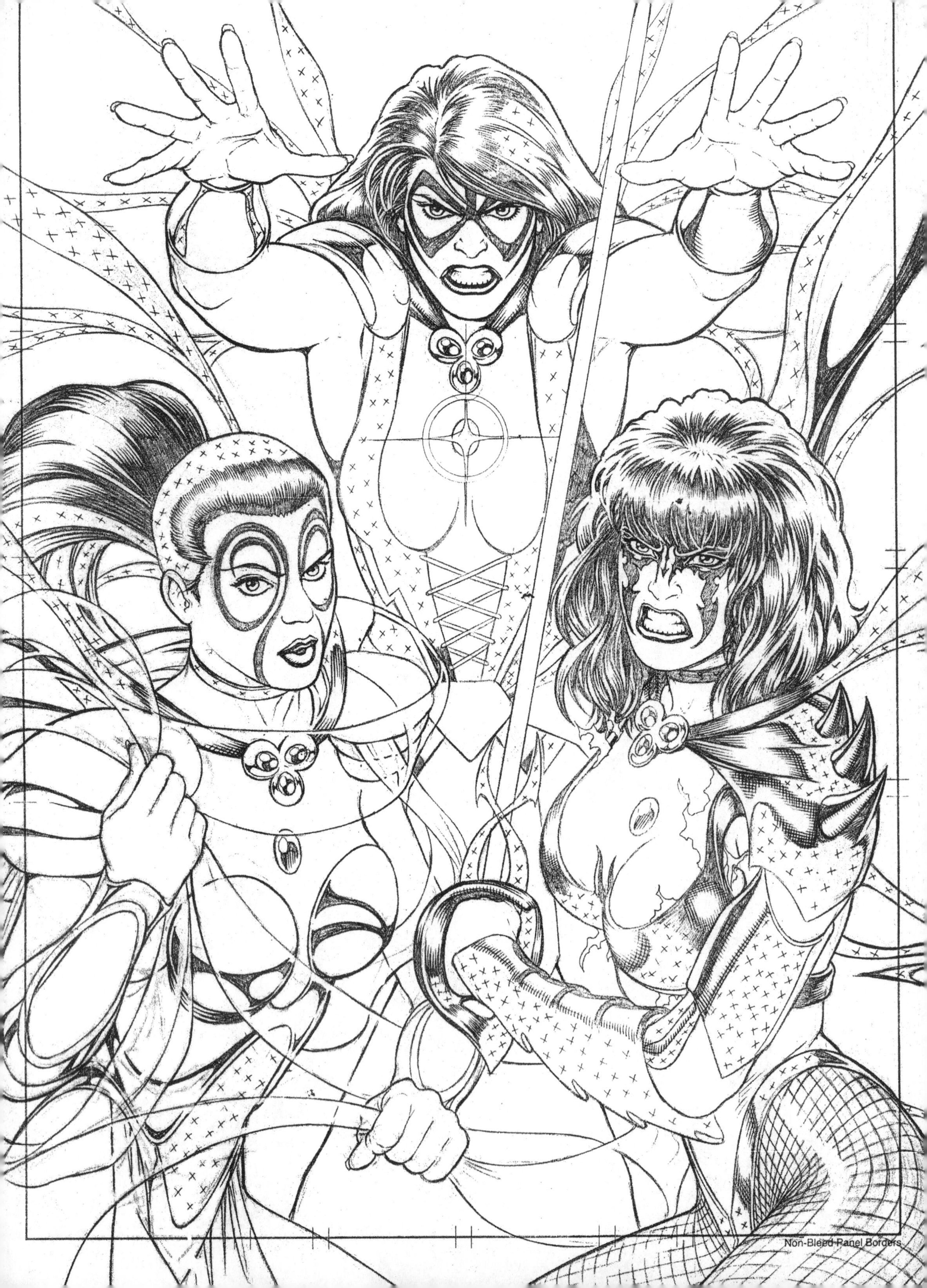
Non-Bleed Panel Borders

MM: Are you going to try to draw with a Wacom tablet?

KEVIN: I know Brian Bolland does it that way, but no.

MM: Have you experimented with that?

KEVIN: The most experimental I get with it is just doing corrections on the computer. Like, if I scan in a line and the line breaks up, then I finish it on the computer.

MM: What do you feel about it? Do you get the kind of line that you're looking for when you do those corrections?

KEVIN: No, it's just with things like a panel border—if the line was too faded when I scanned it in, then that line's broken up and I'll just go in with the mouse and fill in the line. But I haven't been doing any actual drawing in the computer.

MM: You don't think that's going to happen anytime soon?

MM: No, not really. Plus, I like having original pages, y'know? If you do it with the computer, that's it.

MM: You lose that income.

KEVIN: There's no original art.

MM: And when you've got the actual drawing in your hand, it feels like you've done something, doesn't it?

KEVIN: Yeah.

MM: You talked about this a little in the beginning—when were you diagnosed with ADD?

KEVIN: It was back in the '90s.

MM: Were you depressed at the time, or did you have to go to a doctor?

KEVIN: I just started hearing about it and reading about it, and just, "Y'know, that sounds like me. The habits that someone like that has, that's exactly like me."

MM: Was there anything you can do, though, to focus?

KEVIN: Nothing, really. I've been trying everything from therapy, to subliminal hypnosis, to different kinds of medications and all that. There really isn't anything that's allowed me to—I describe it as "getting into

Previous Page and Below: Kevin's pencils and inks for the cover of *Trinity Angels #1*.
Left: Kevin himself.

Trinity Angels ™ and ©2007 respective owner.

the zone," where you're just there, and you're focused on the work, and you sit there drawing and you look up and it's been, like, three hours. I never have that.

MM: Are there ever times that drawing is enjoyable for you? I mean, it's something, you're good at it.

KEVIN: The enjoyable part comes when you look at something when it's done and you think that it looks better than you expected. I forgot who said it, but someone said, "I hate writing, but I love having written." And that kind of sums it up.

MM: Does it give you a sense of pride to see the page done—?

KEVIN: Yeah, yeah. I mean, you say, "Yeah, I did that," and that's satisfying. But the whole process of doing it, to me it's just mind-numbingly tedious.

MM: Is a lot of it just trying to figure out what you're going to do on the page? Do you think a lot before you actually start?

KEVIN: Well, I read the script and just do it as I feel, as it comes to me. There are some times where I will go ahead and lay out little thumbnails for what I want it to be, and then when I start drawing I have different ideas and I do something different. But, no, there's not a great deal of pre-planning.

MM: Do you have any regrets about being a comic book artist?

KEVIN: Oh, no. No, no, no. There's a creative satisfaction to it that you don't get being, like, an accountant or pizza maker or whatever. You have people who admire what you do, and that's very satisfying. It's nice to know you've had some kind of ripple effect. As tiny as it may be, it's nice to feel that someone's responded to what you've done. But I haven't been able to divorce myself from it.

Below: Layout for *Superman/Batman* #27, page 4.

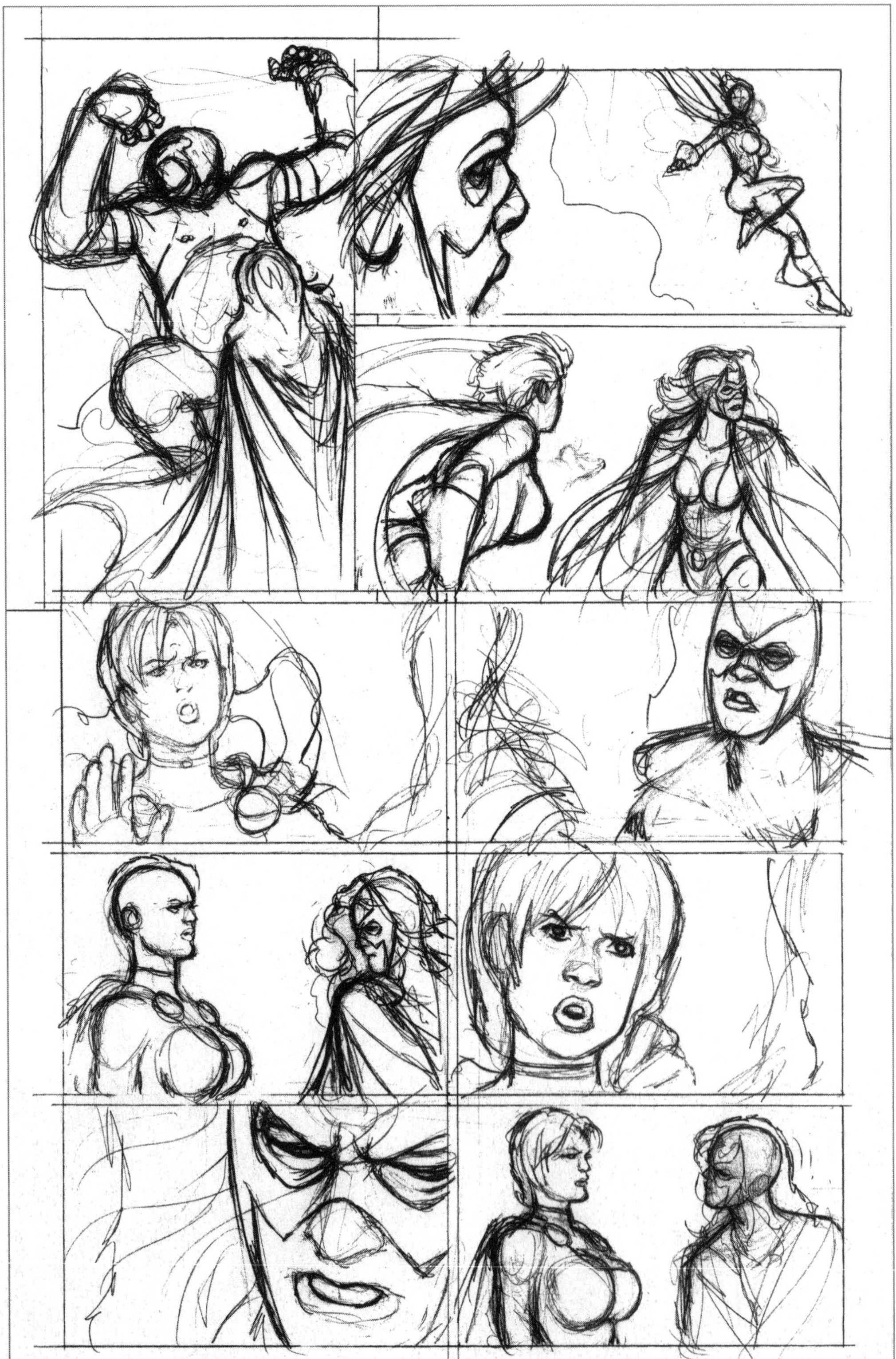

Kevin Maguire

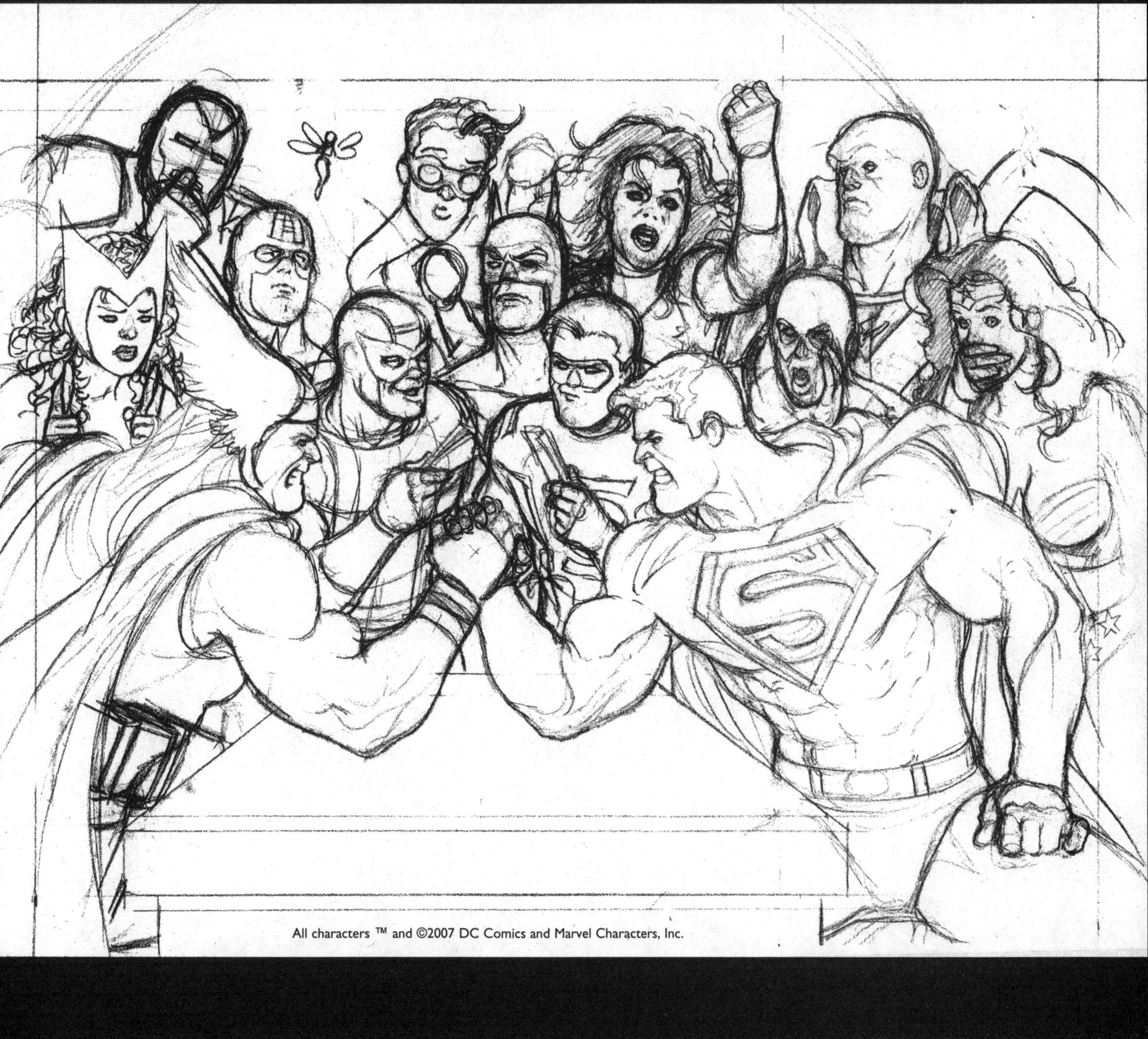

All characters ™ and ©2007 DC Comics and Marvel Characters, Inc.

Art Gallery

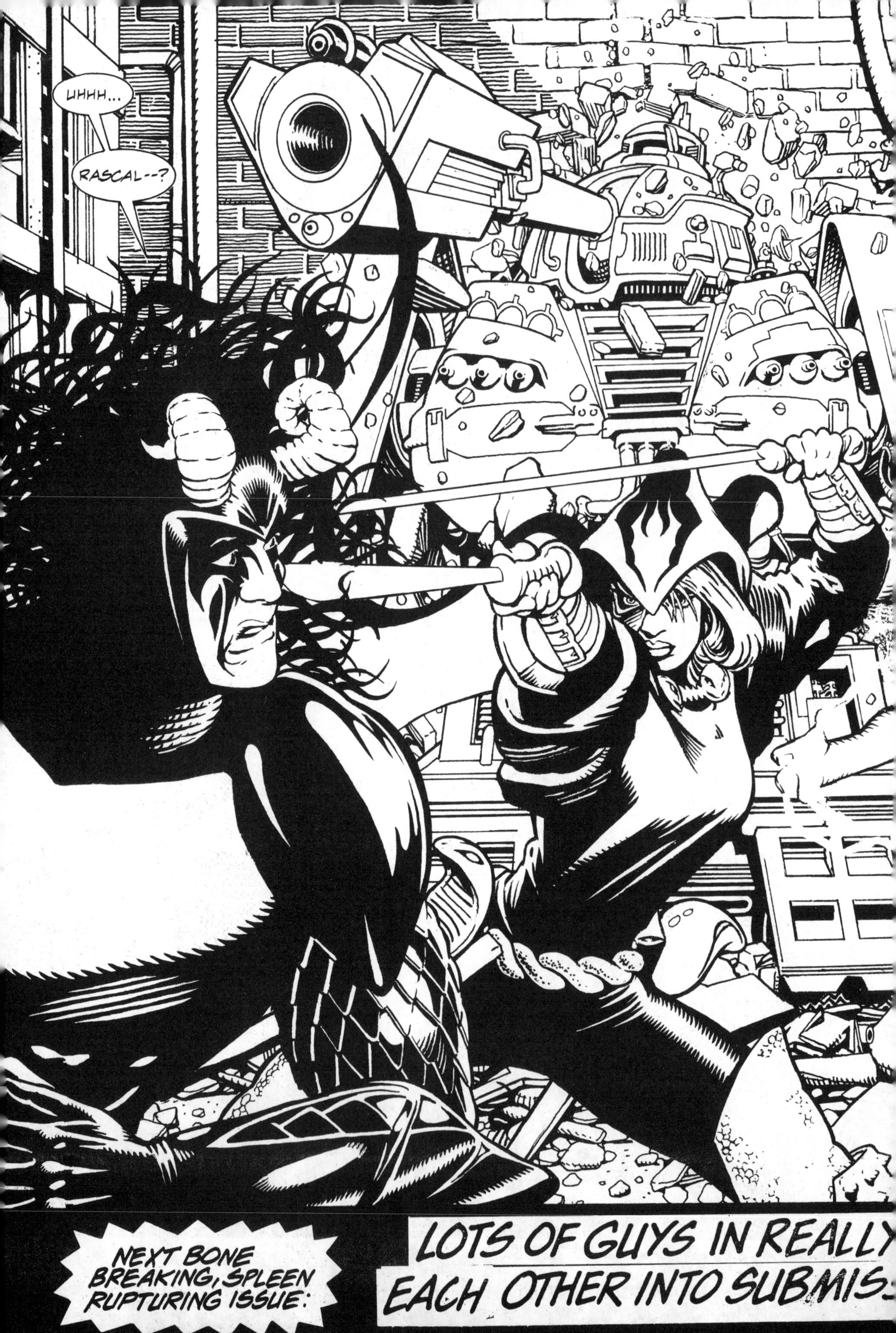
UHHH...
RASCAL--?
NEXT BONE BREAKING, SPLEEN RUPTURING ISSUE:
LOTS OF GUYS IN REALLY
EACH OTHER INTO SUBMIS

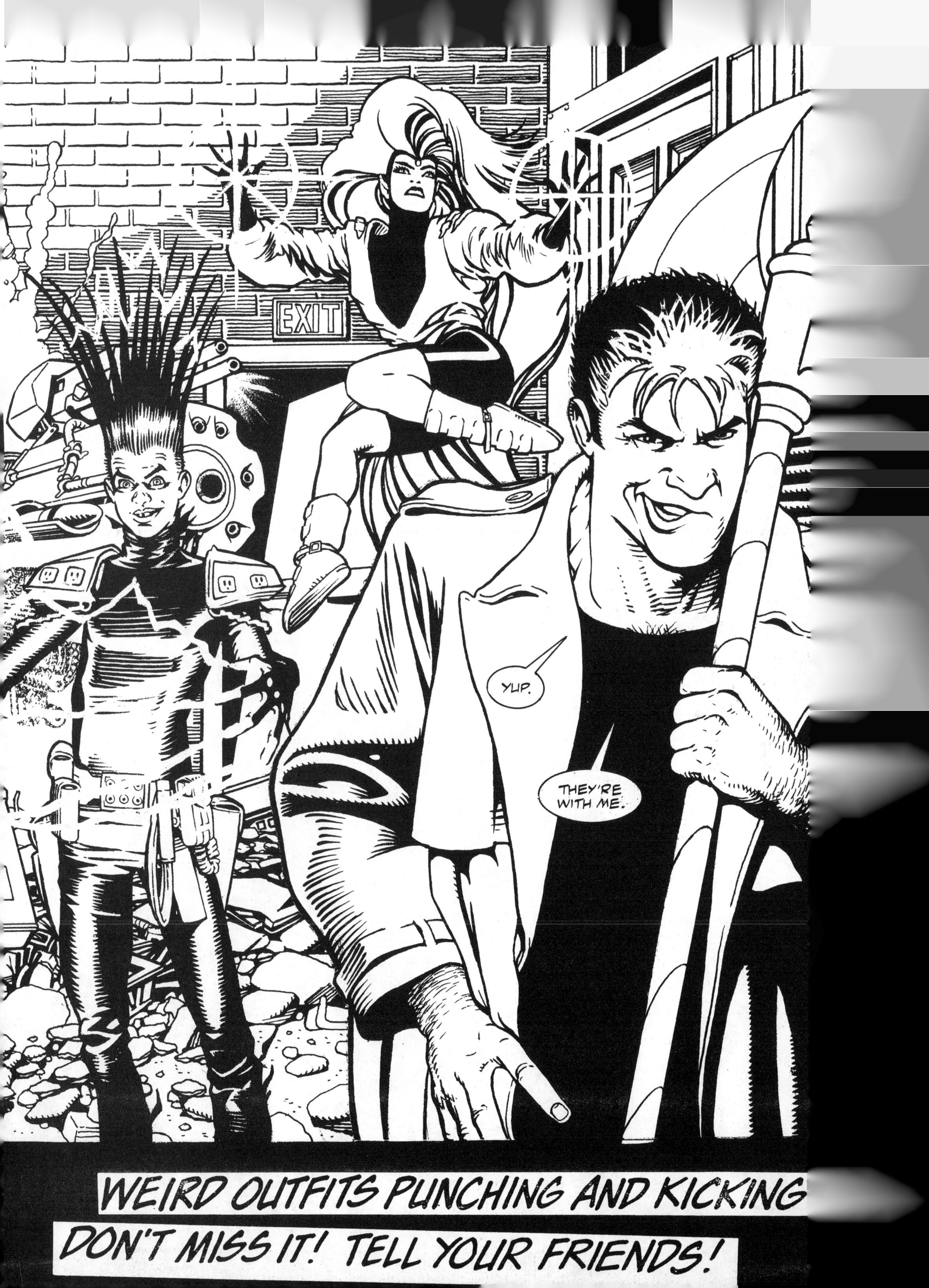
YUP.
THEY'RE WITH ME.
WEIRD OUTFITS PUNCHING AND KICKING
DON'T MISS IT! TELL YOUR FRIENDS!

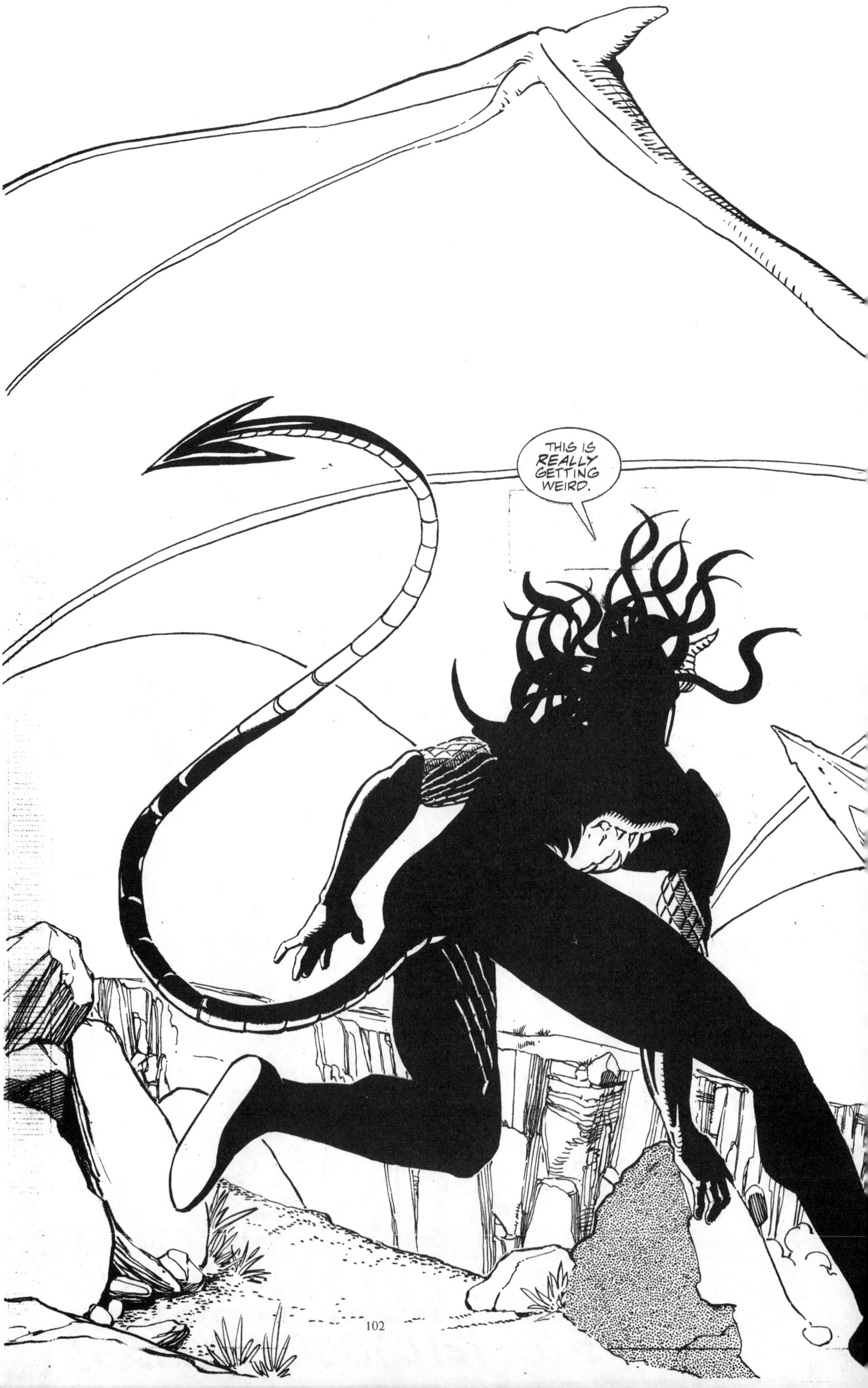
THIS IS REALLY GETTING WEIRD.

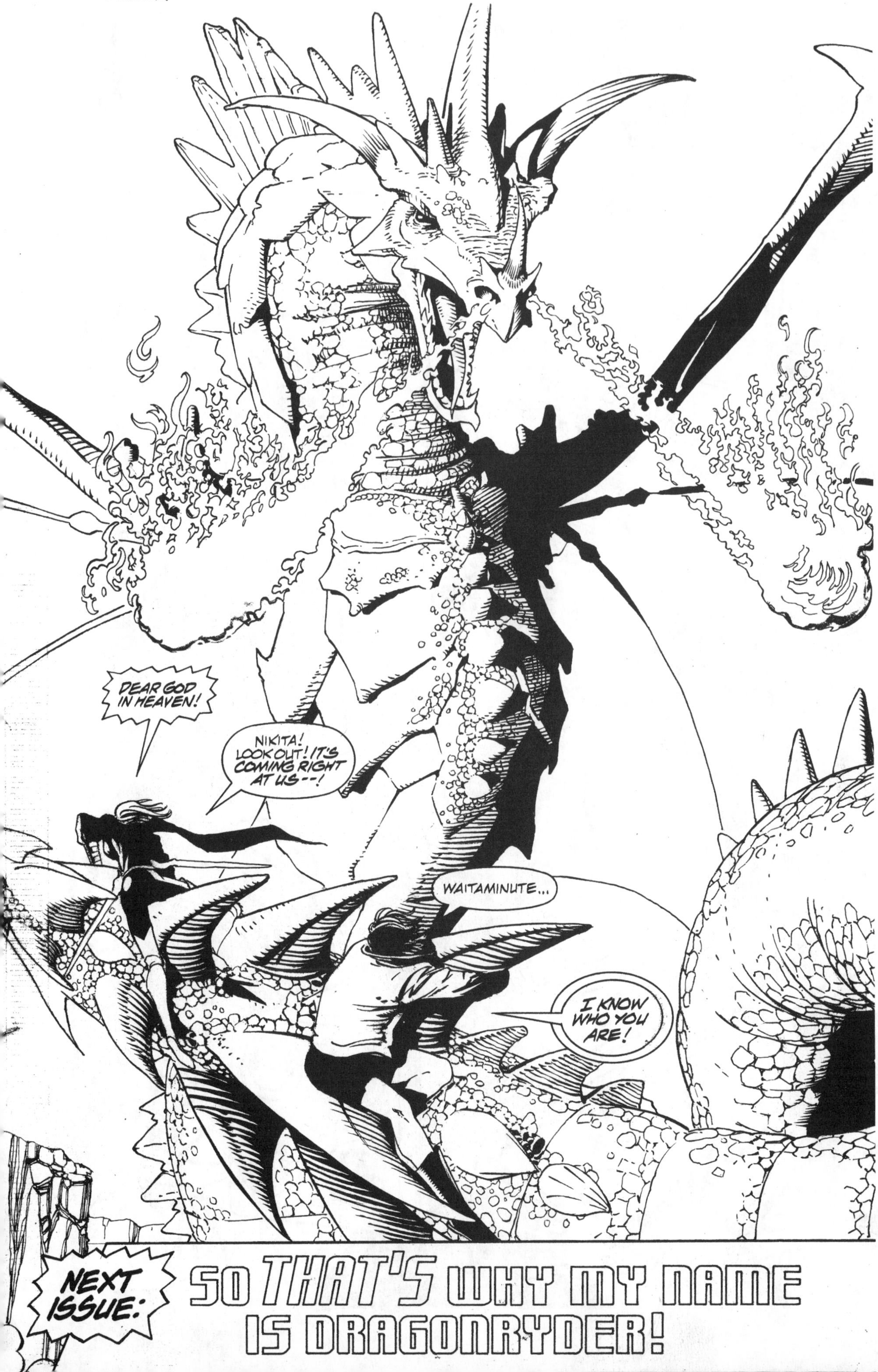
DEAR GOD IN HEAVEN!
NIKITA! LOOK OUT! IT'S COMING RIGHT AT US--!
WAITAMINUTE...
I KNOW WHO YOU ARE!
NEXT ISSUE:
SO THAT'S WHY MY NAME IS DRAGONRYDER!

STRIKEBACK 1 2 4 COVER

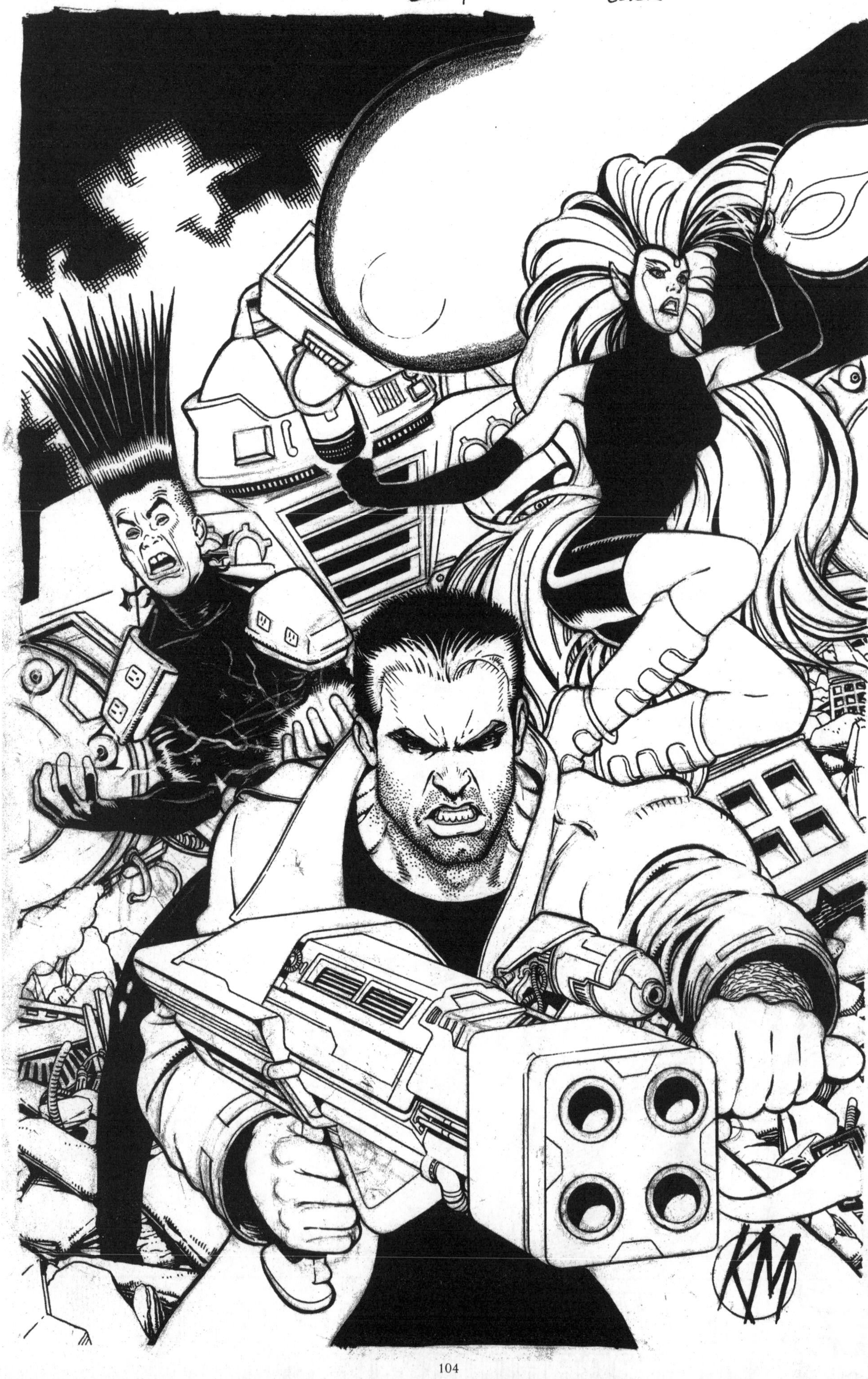

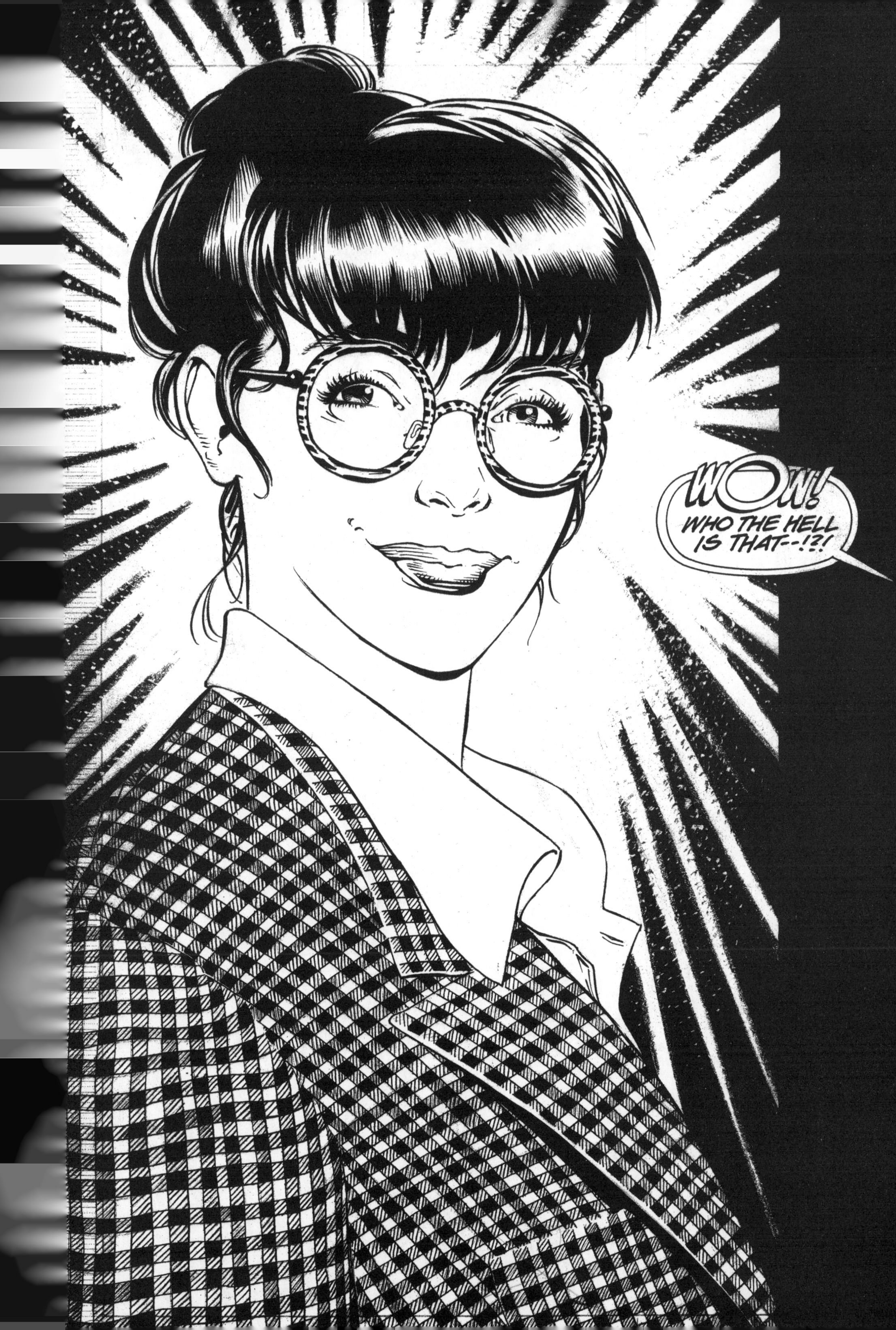
WOW! WHO THE HELL IS THAT--!?!

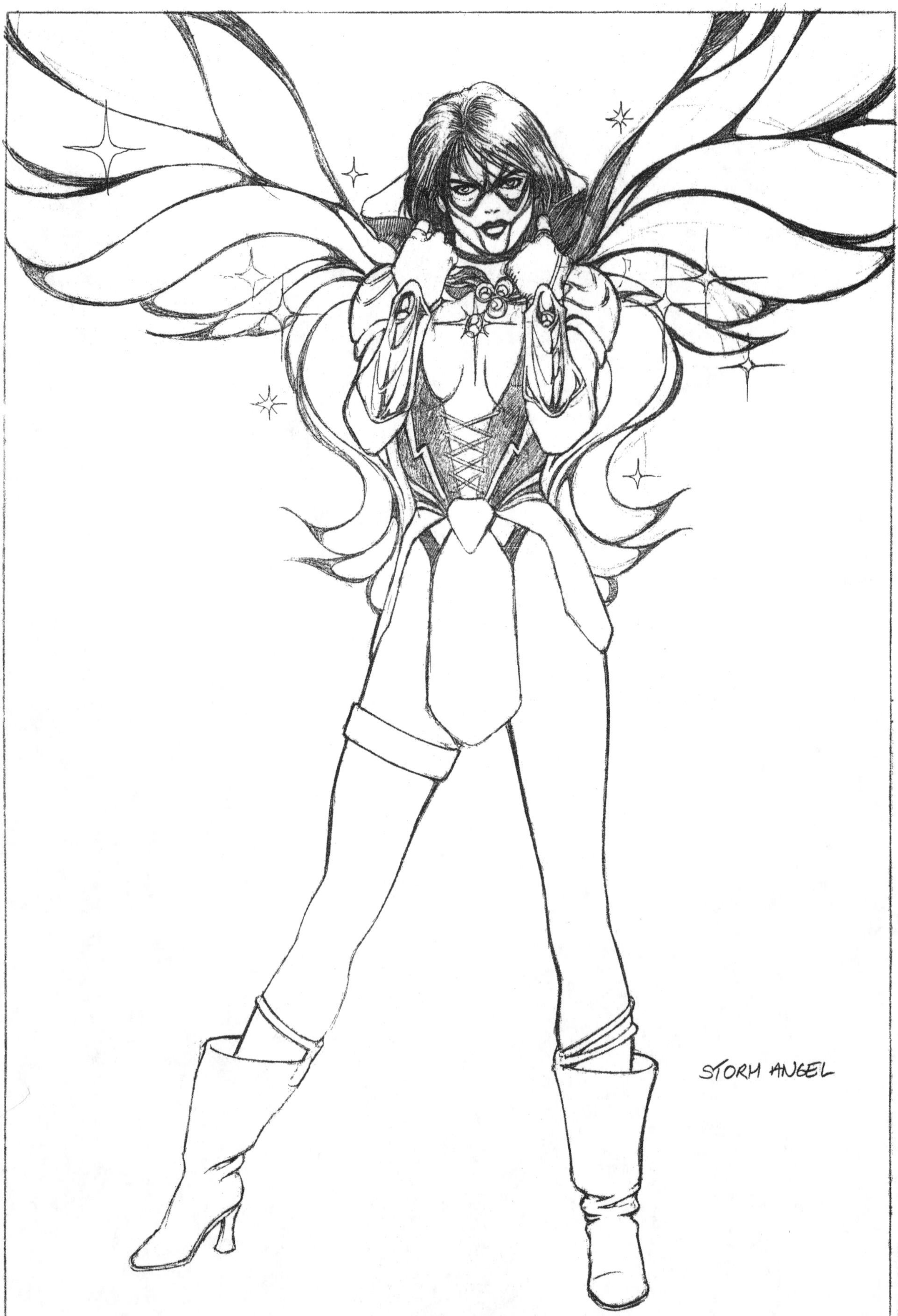
STORM ANGEL

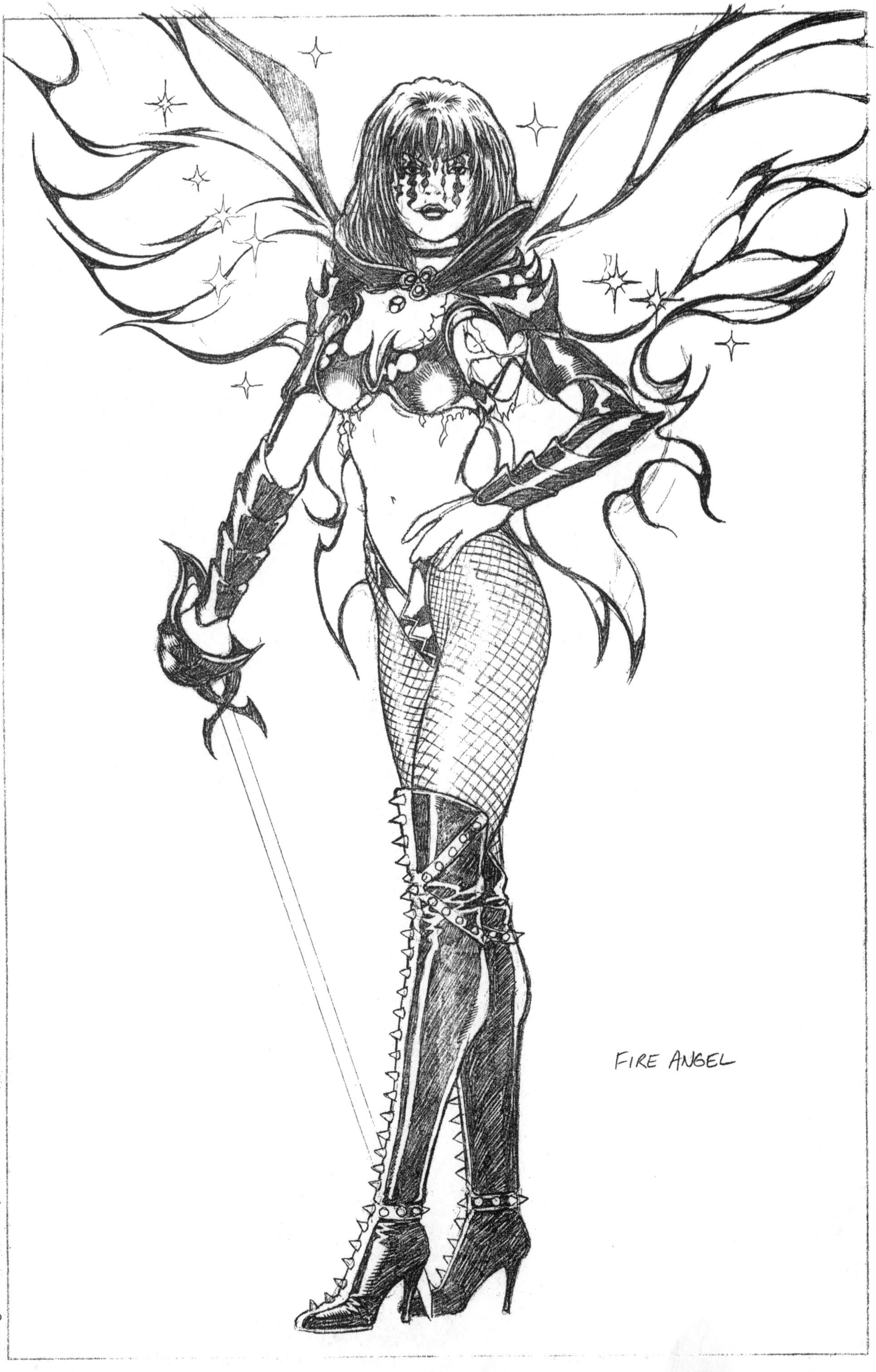
FIRE ANGEL

This Page and Next: Back in 1995, while Kevin was attending the San Diego Comic-Con, Jonathan Peterson asked him to come up with some development drawings for a Wildstorm project. These sketches are the result.

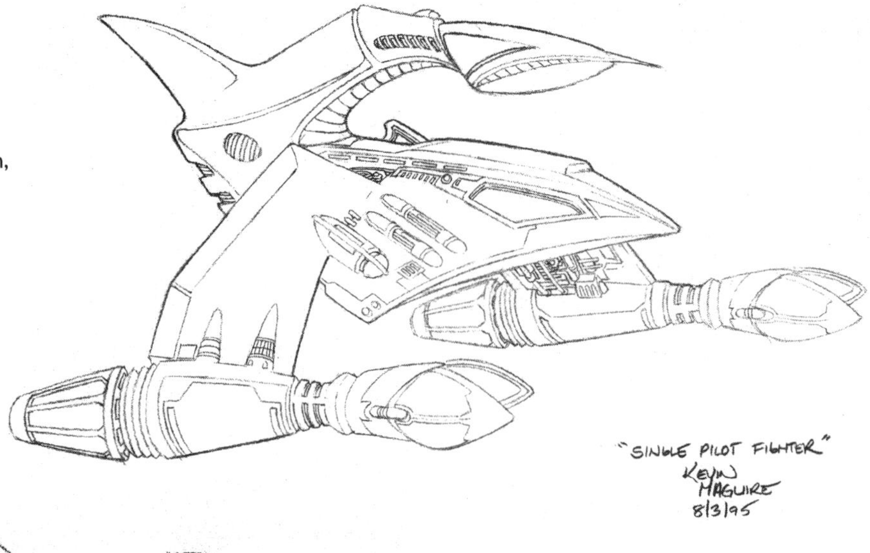
"SINGLE PILOT FIGHTER"
KEVIN MAGUIRE
8/3/95

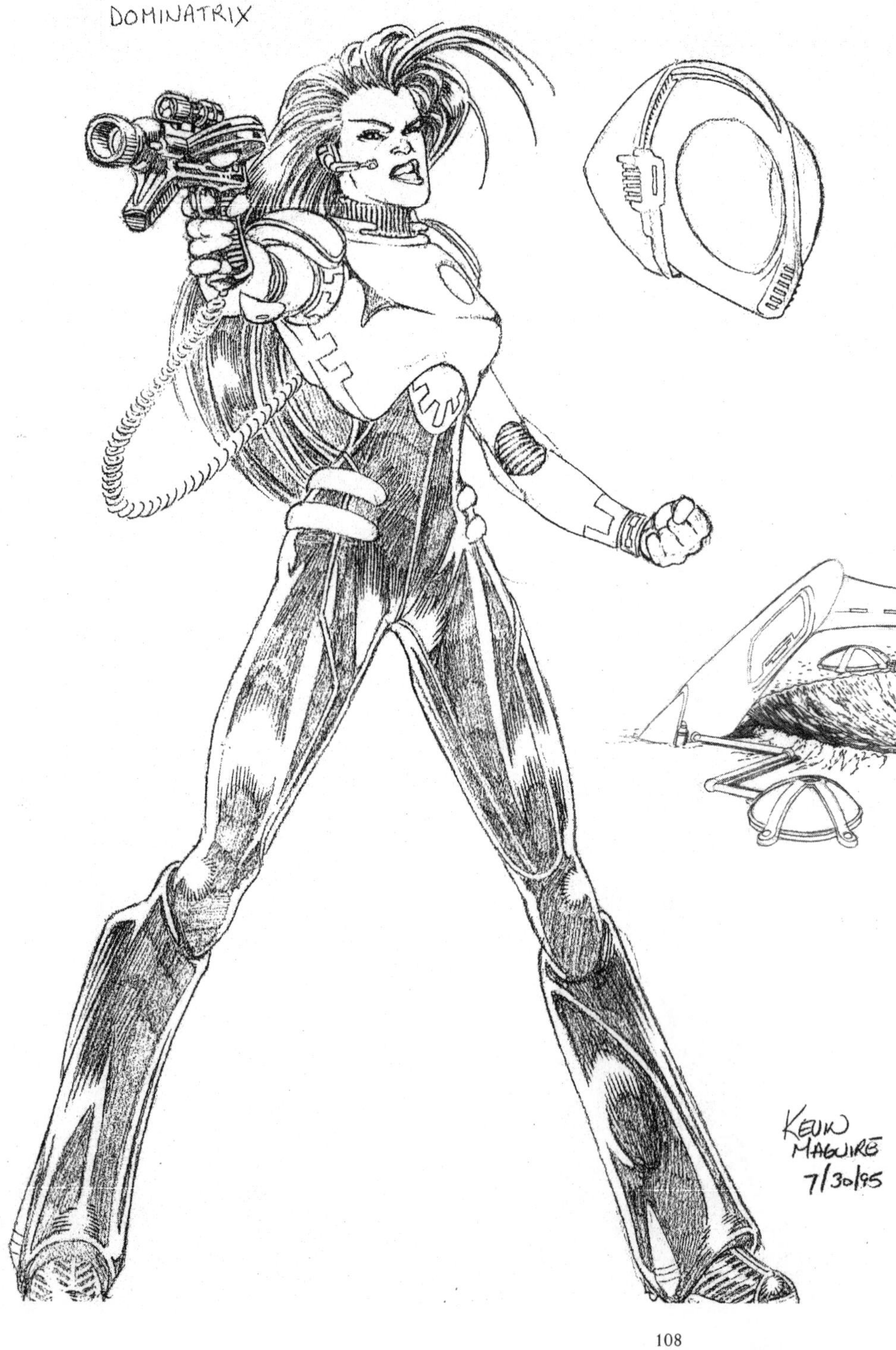
DOMINATRIX
KEVIN MAGUIRE
7/30/95

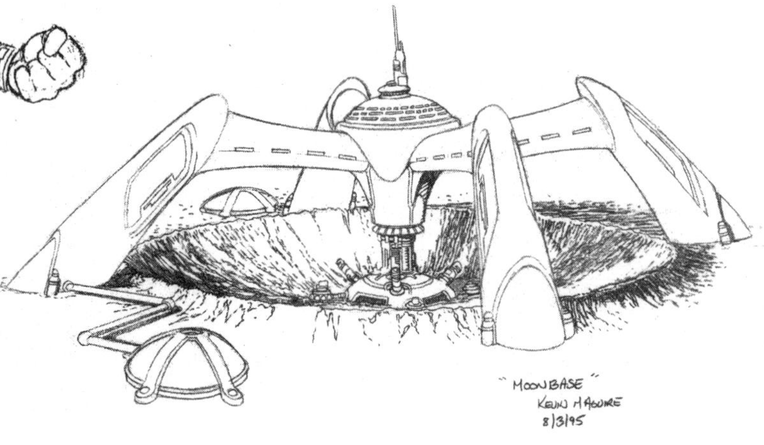
"MOONBASE"
KEVIN MAGUIRE
8/3/95

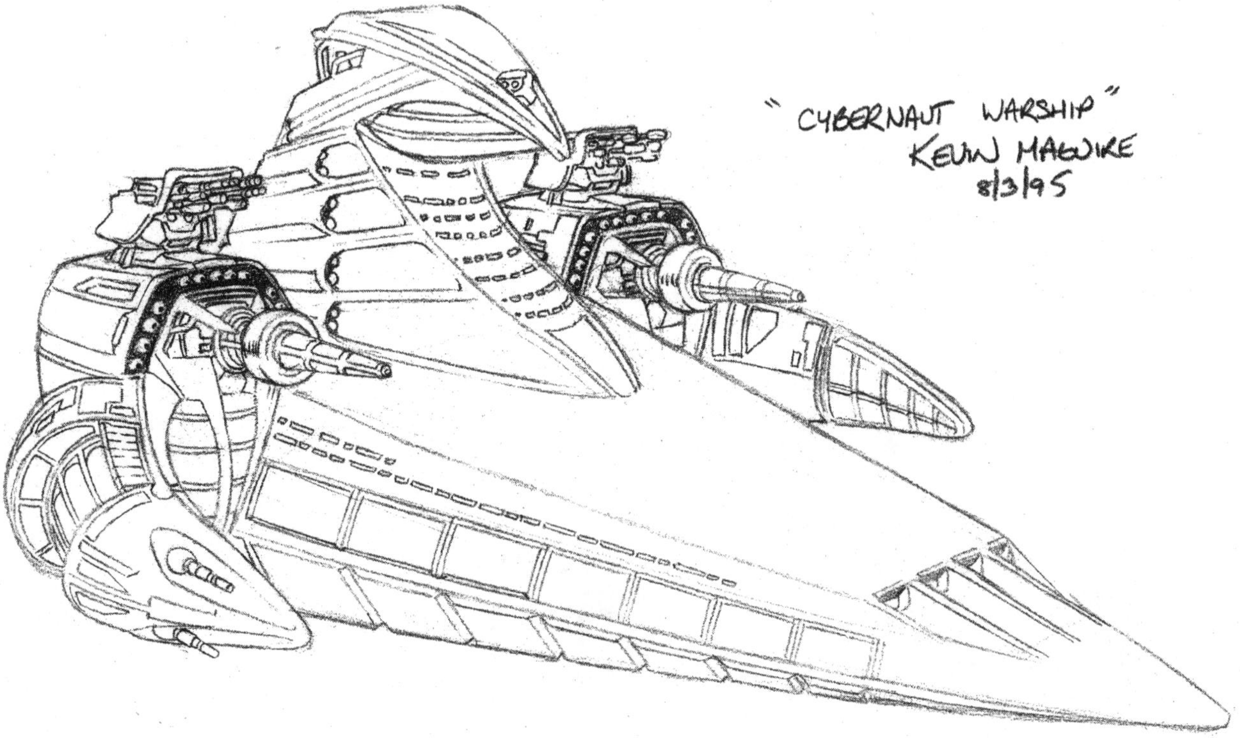
"CYBERNAUT WARSHIP"
KEVIN MAGUIRE
8/3/95

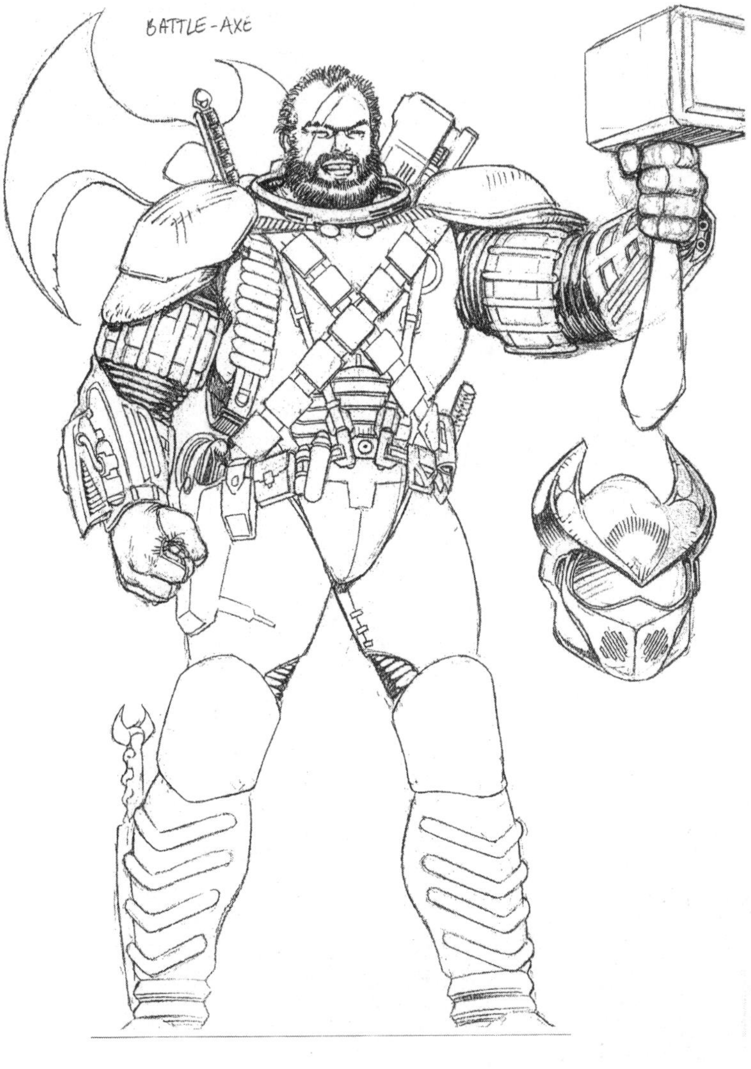
BATTLE-AXE

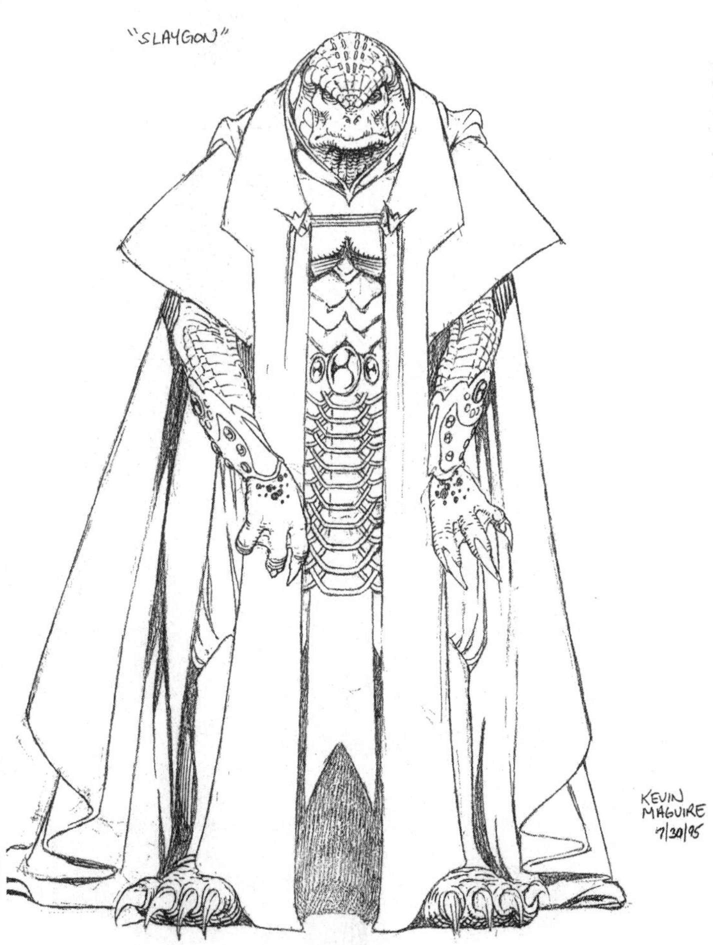
"SLAYGON"
KEVIN
MAGUIRE
7/30/95

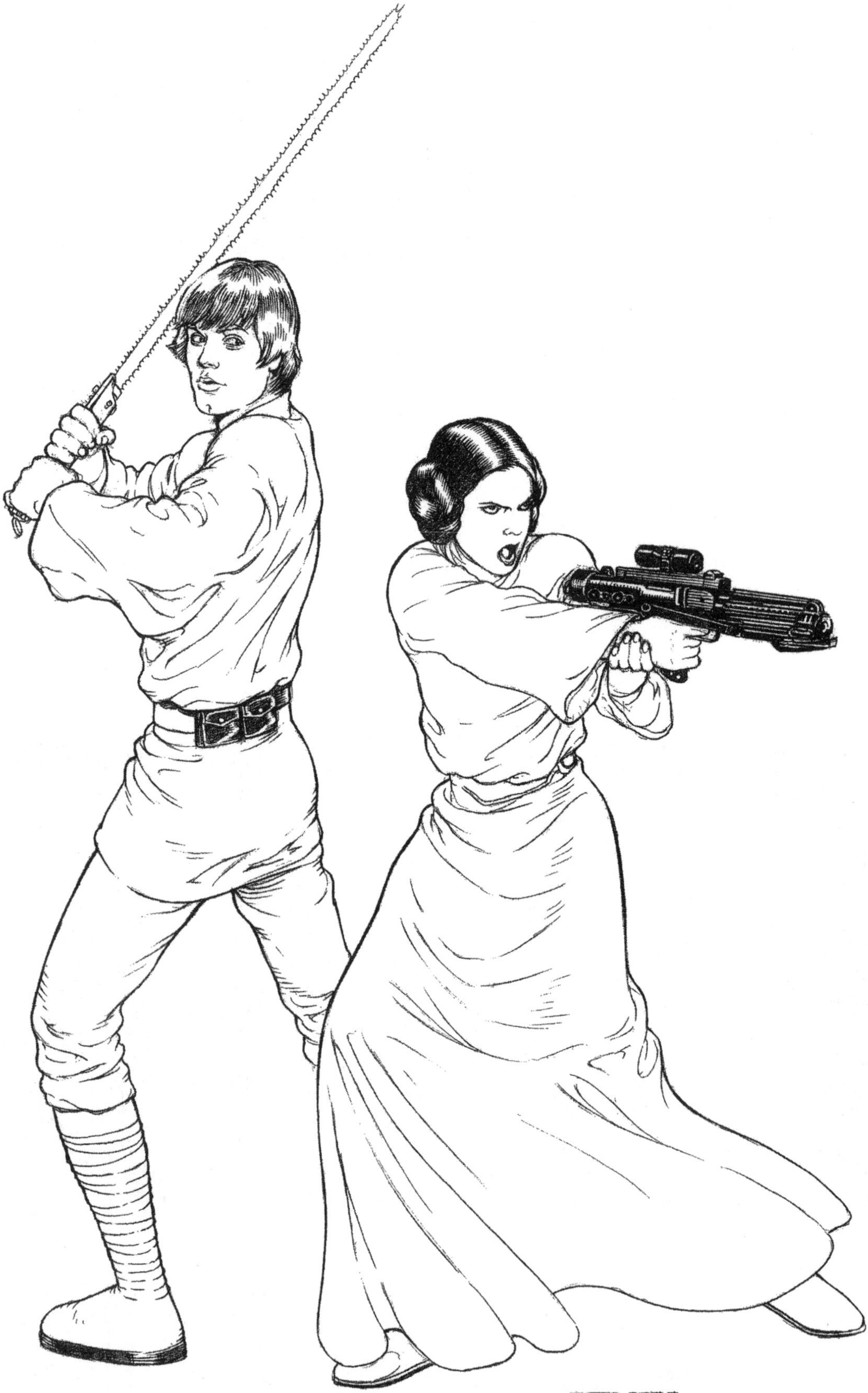

KEVIN MAGUIRE '03

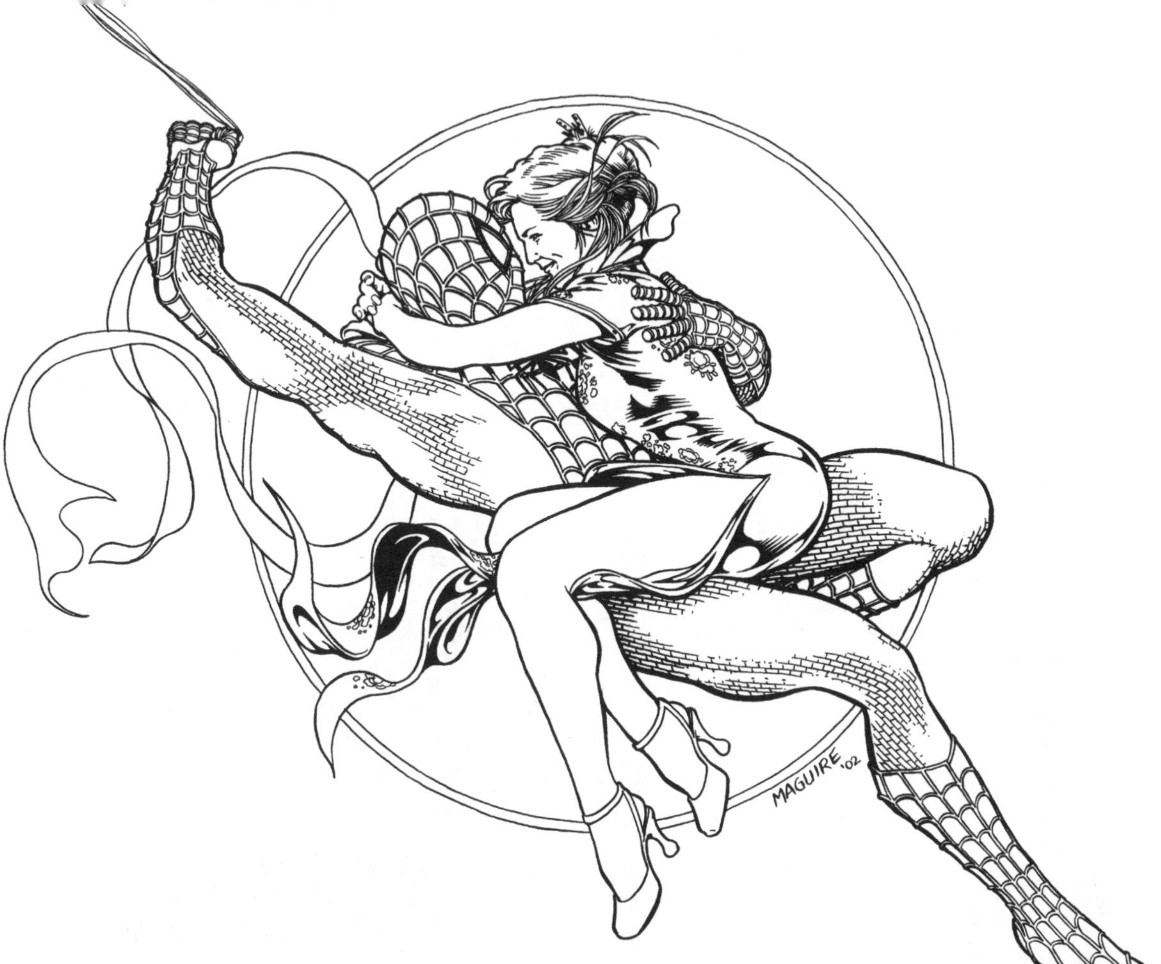
MAGUIRE '02

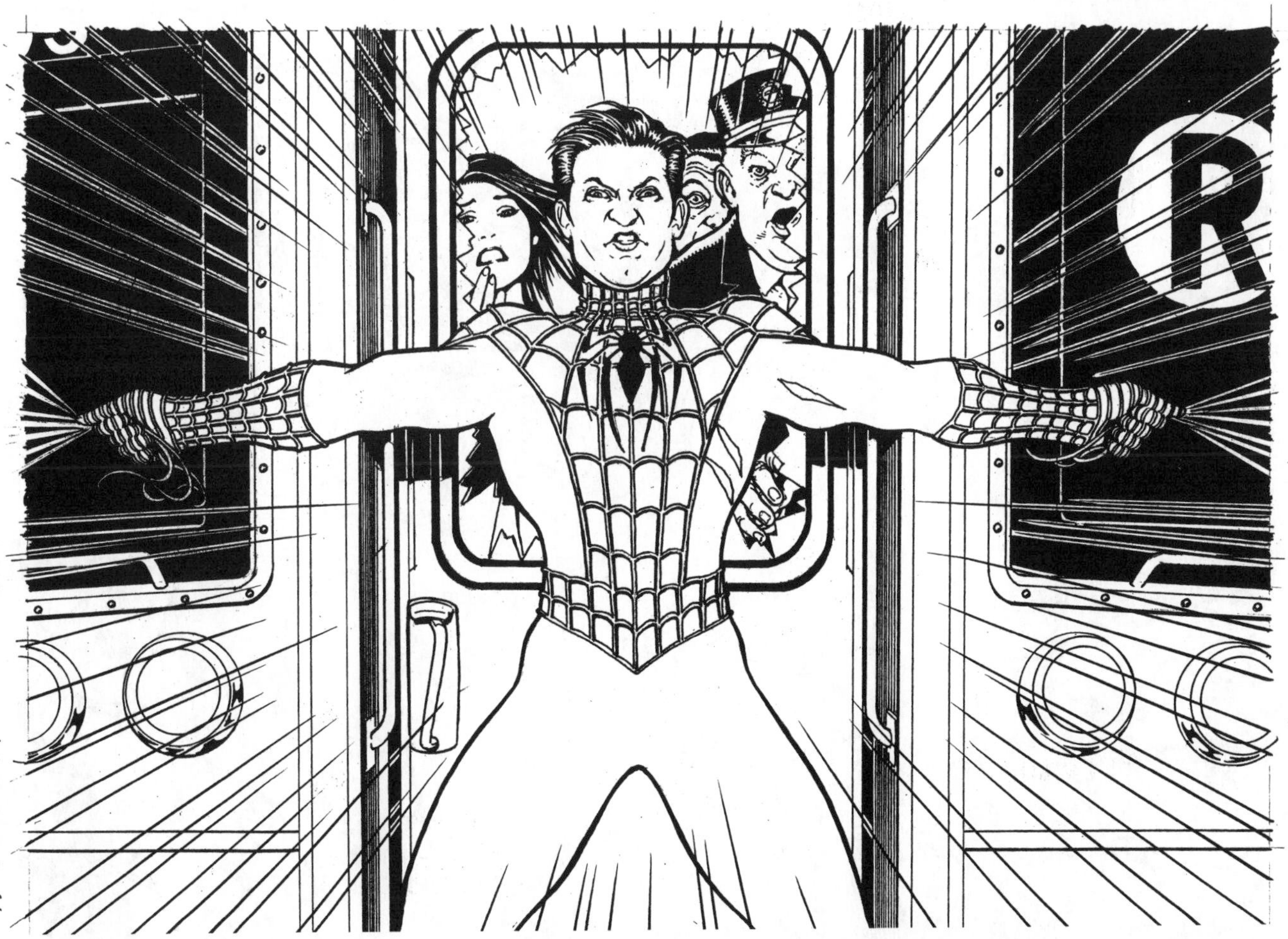

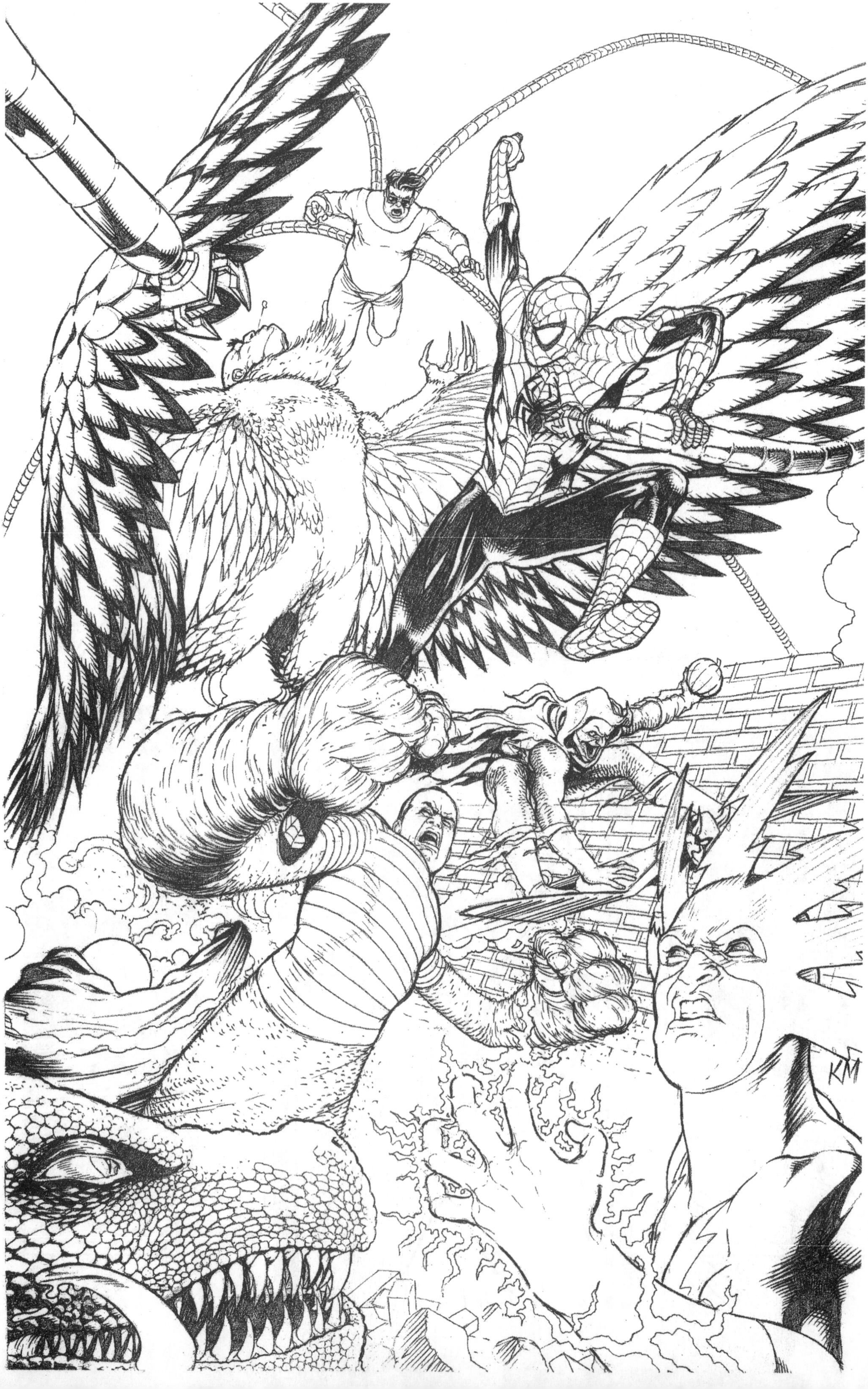
KM

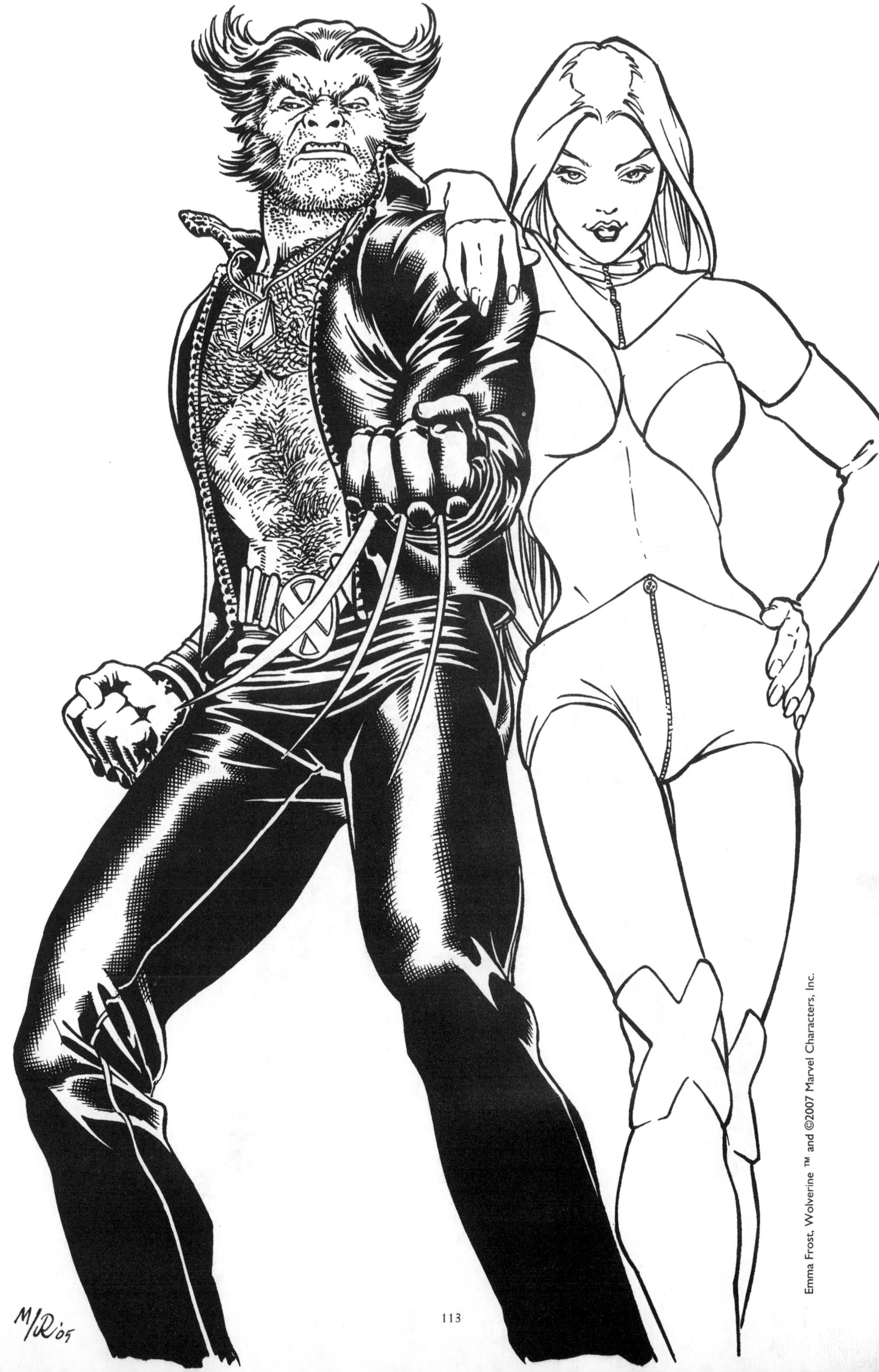
M/R '05

Black Widow ™ and ©2007 Marvel Characters, Inc.

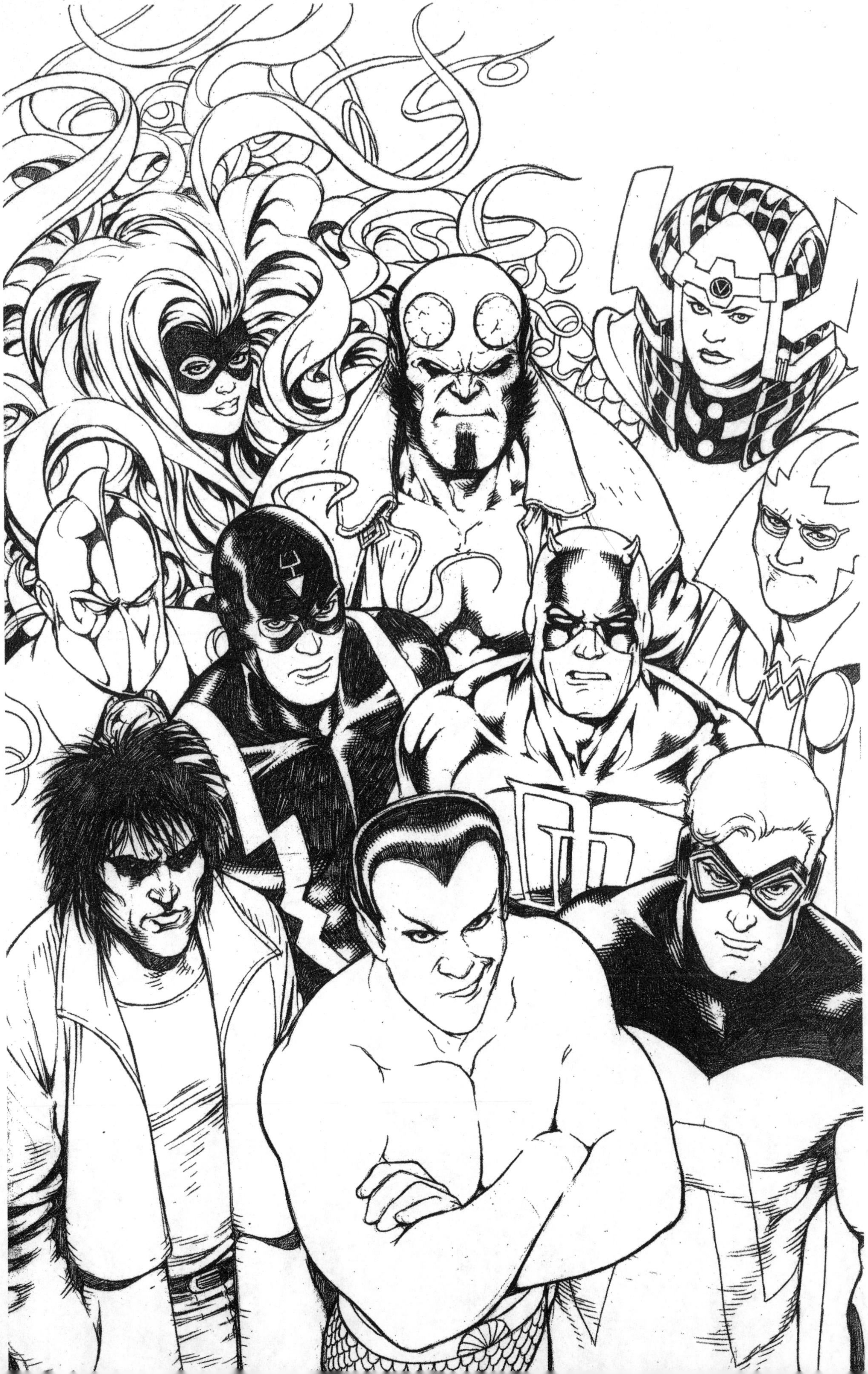

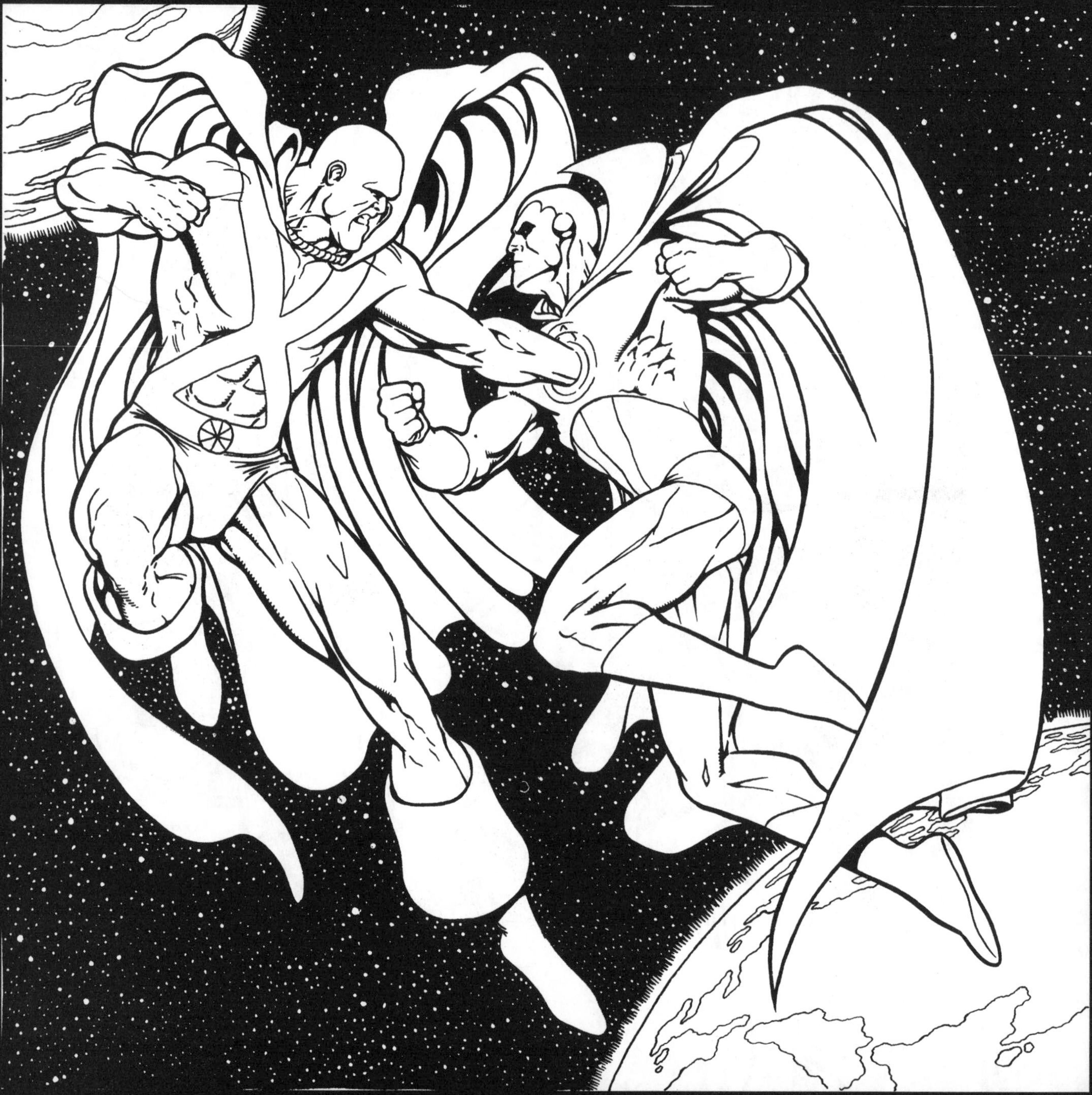

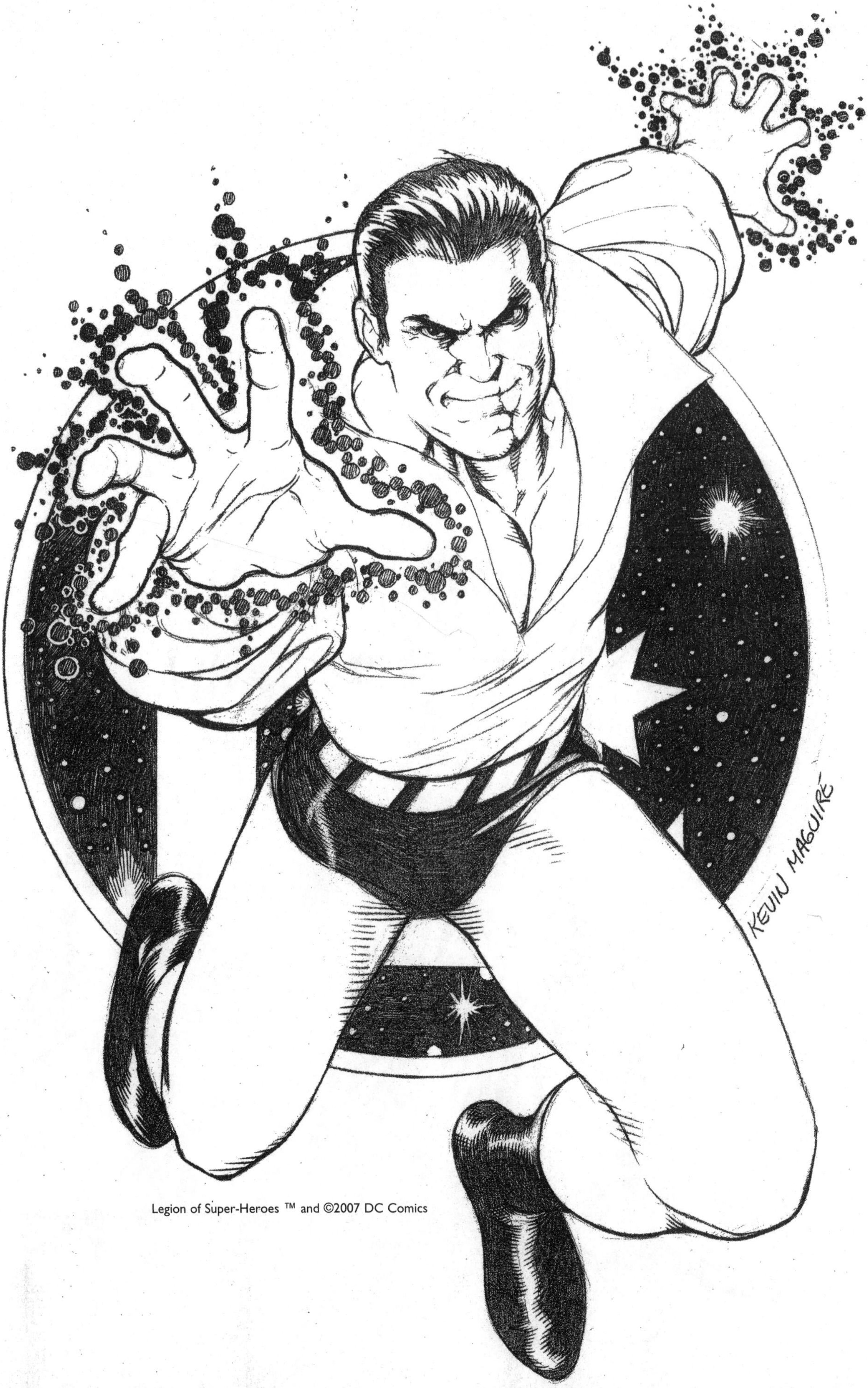
KEVIN MAGUIRE

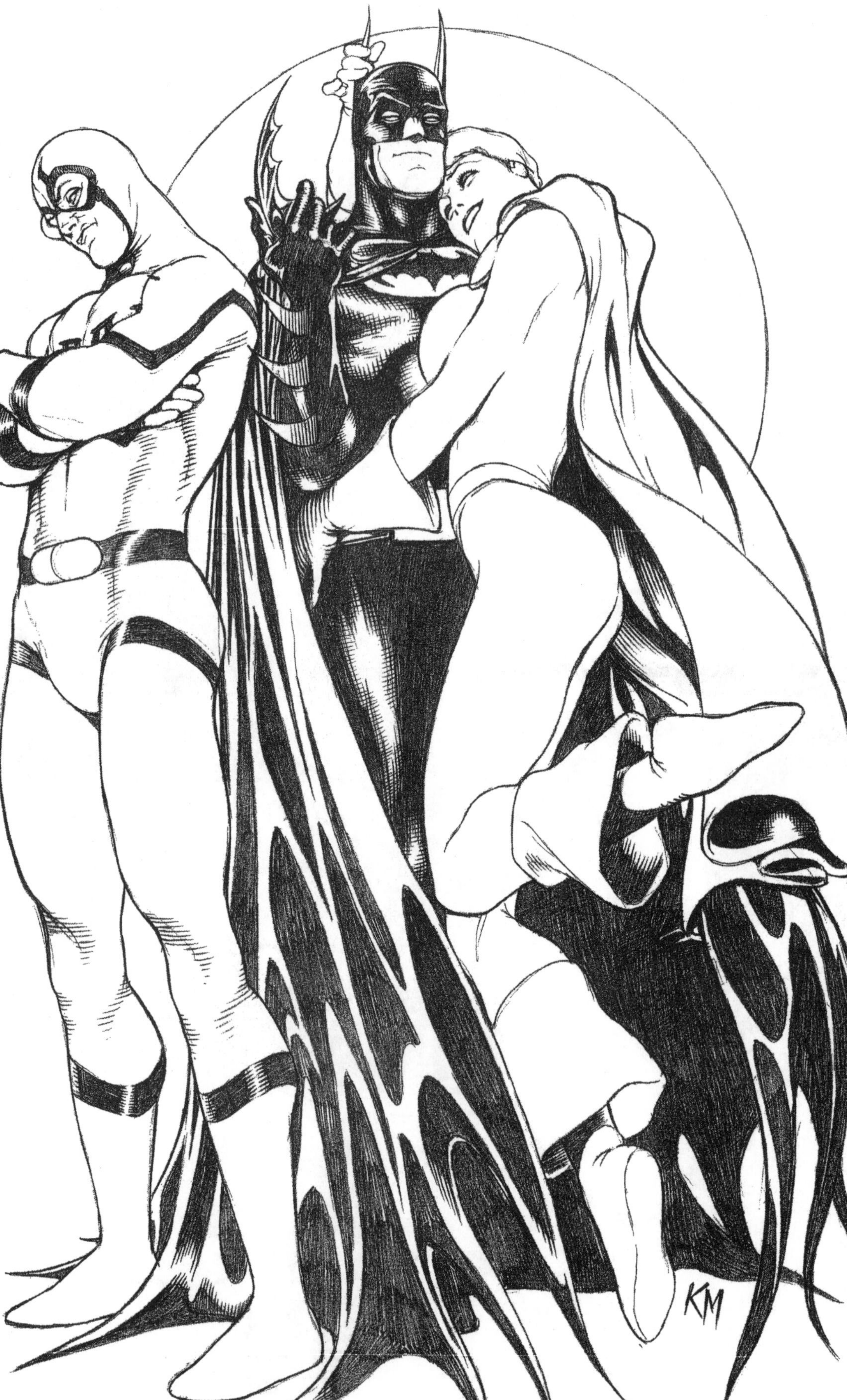
KM

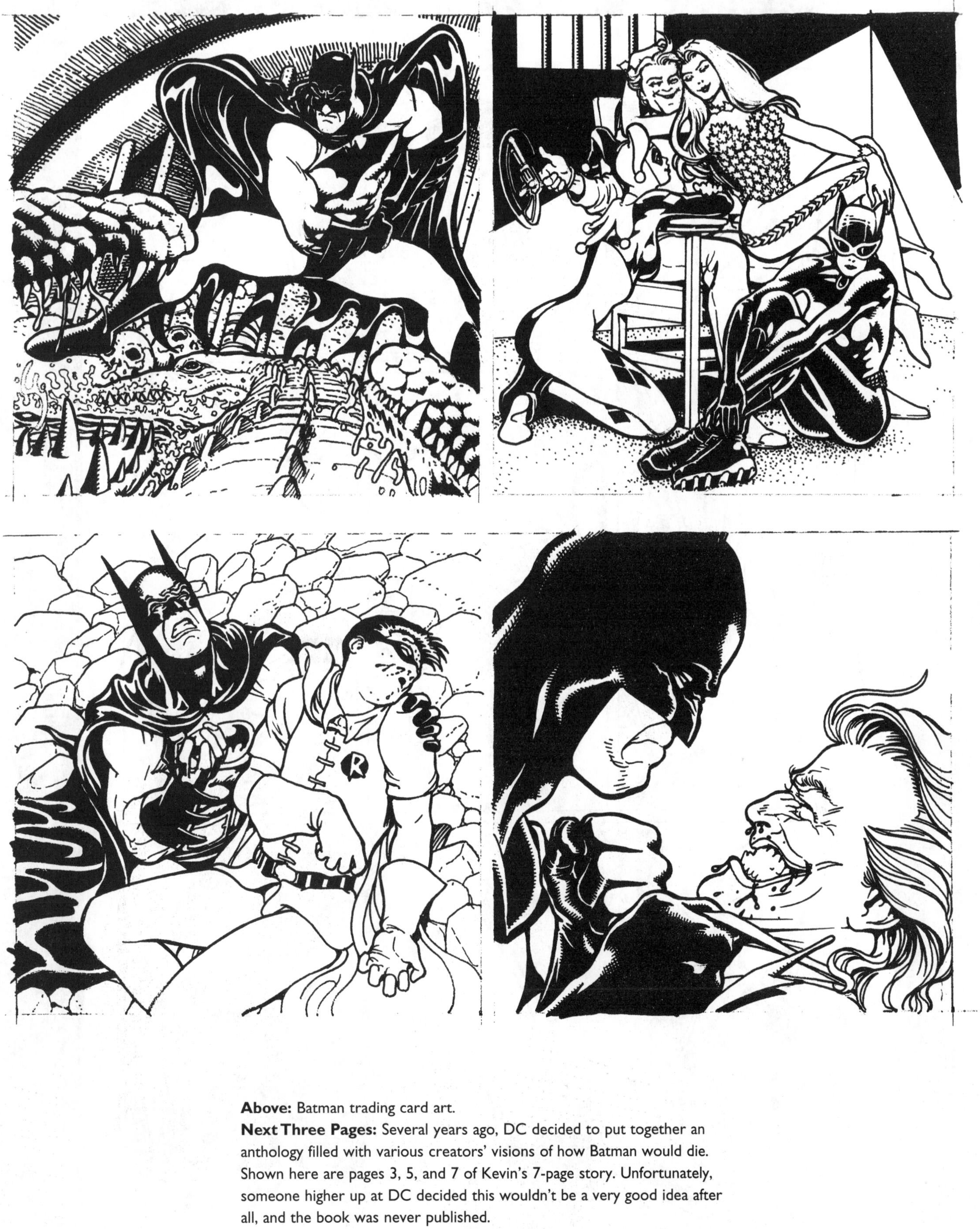

Above: Batman trading card art.
Next Three Pages: Several years ago, DC decided to put together an anthology filled with various creators' visions of how Batman would die. Shown here are pages 3, 5, and 7 of Kevin's 7-page story. Unfortunately, someone higher up at DC decided this wouldn't be a very good idea after all, and the book was never published.

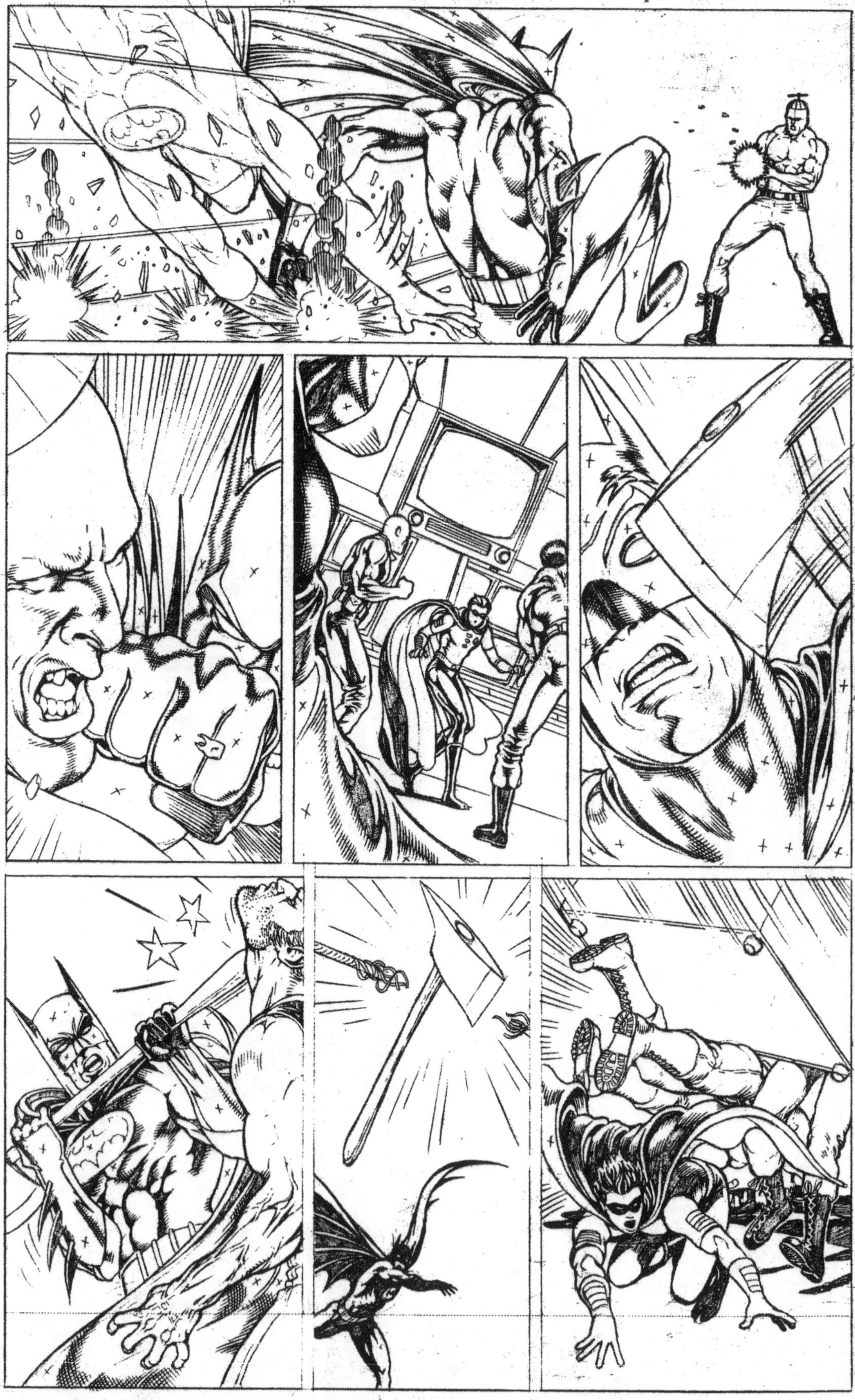

GRAIN ZIP
OR
ASPHALT TEXTURE

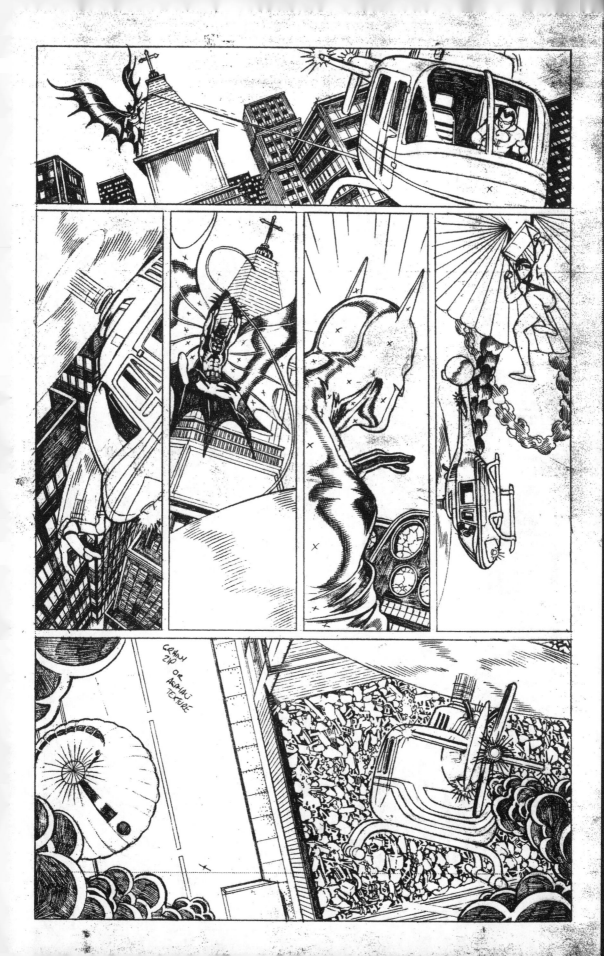

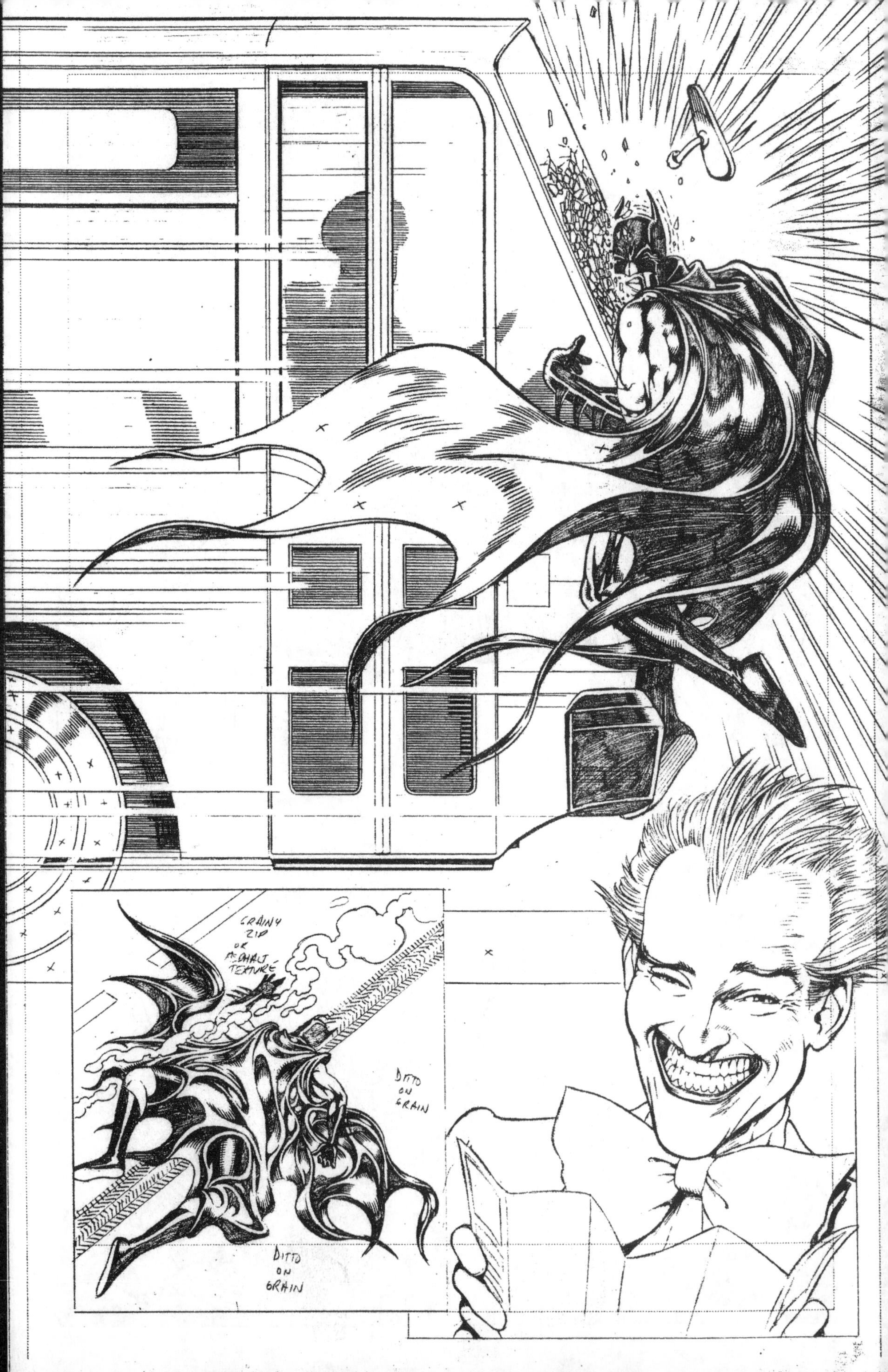
GRAINY ZIP OR ASPHALT TEXTURE
DITTO ON GRAIN
DITTO ON GRAIN

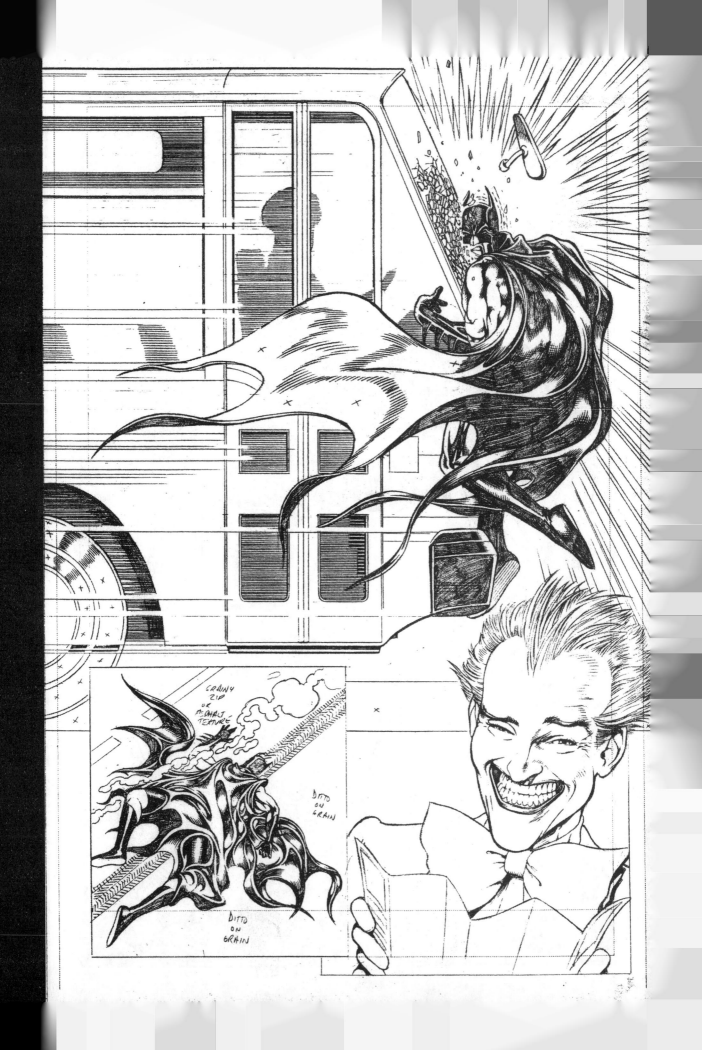

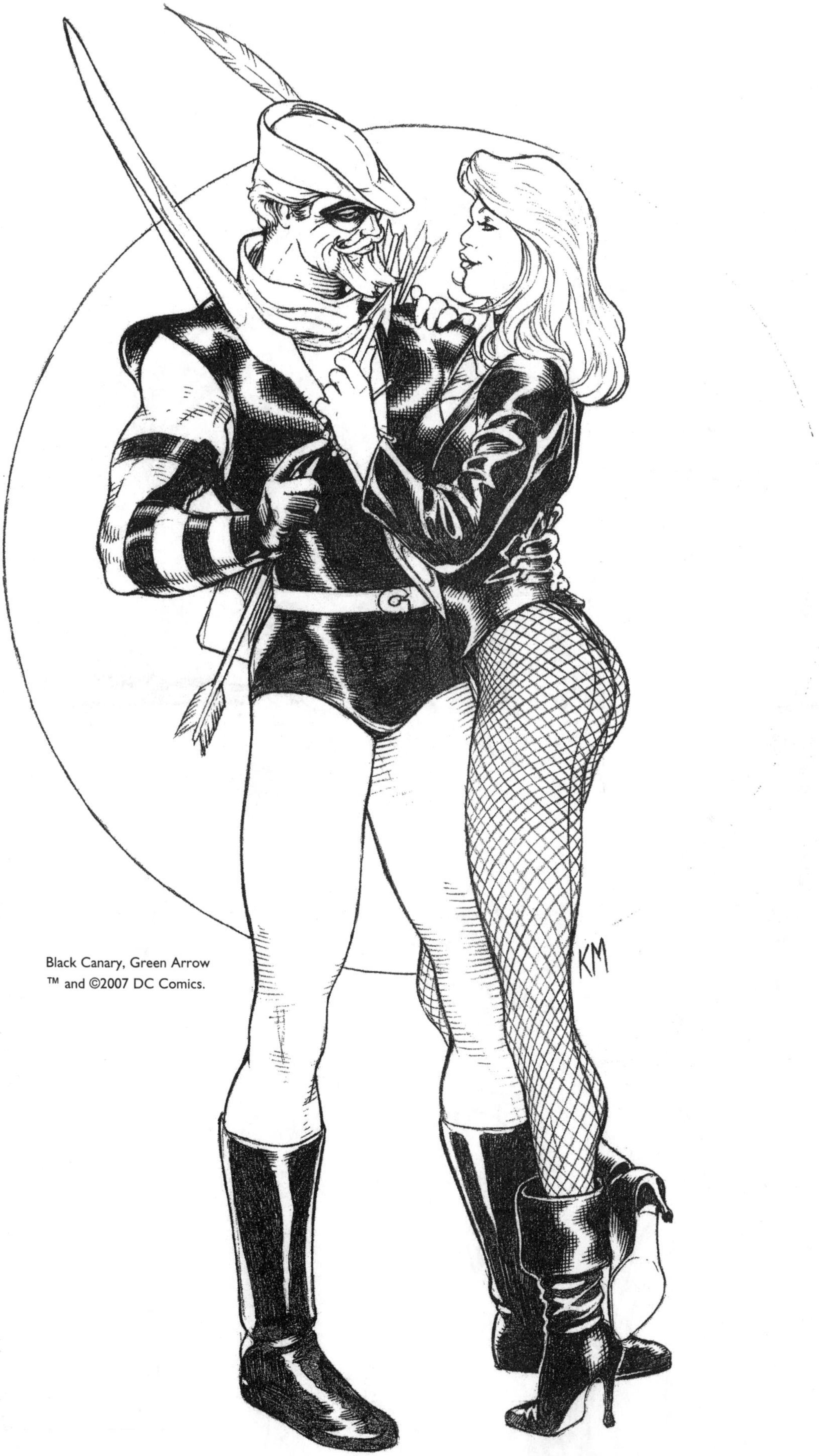
KM

Black Canary, Green Arrow
™ and ©2007 DC Comics.

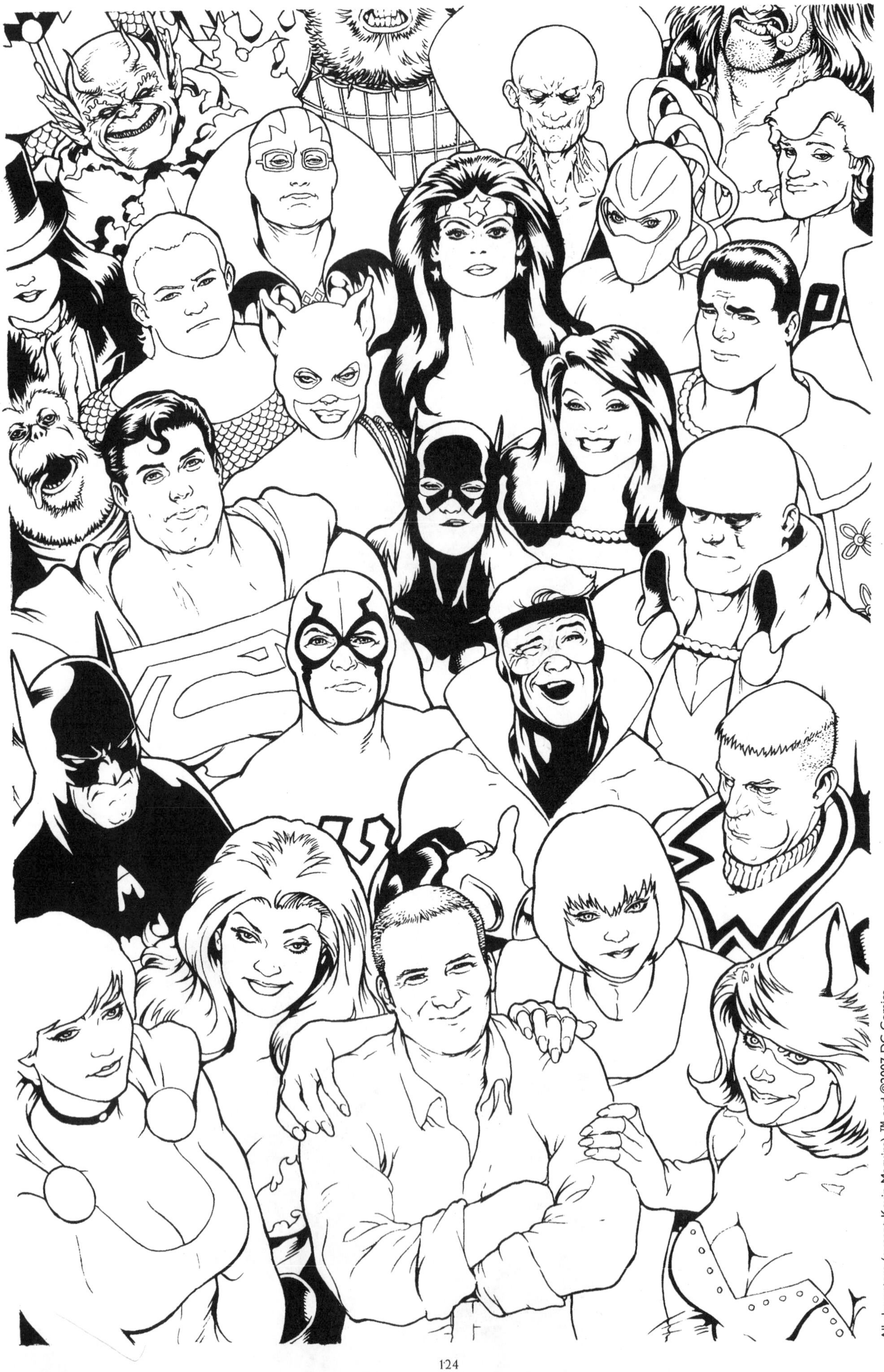

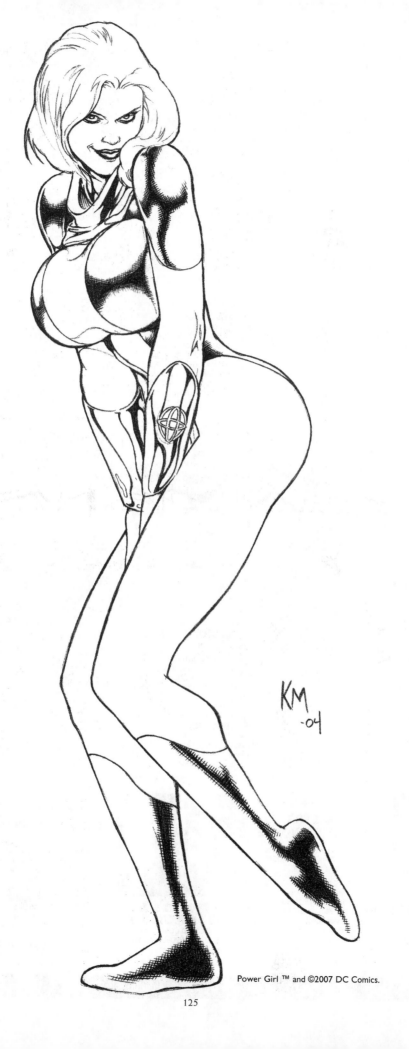

KM
-04

THE TWOMORROWS LIBRARY

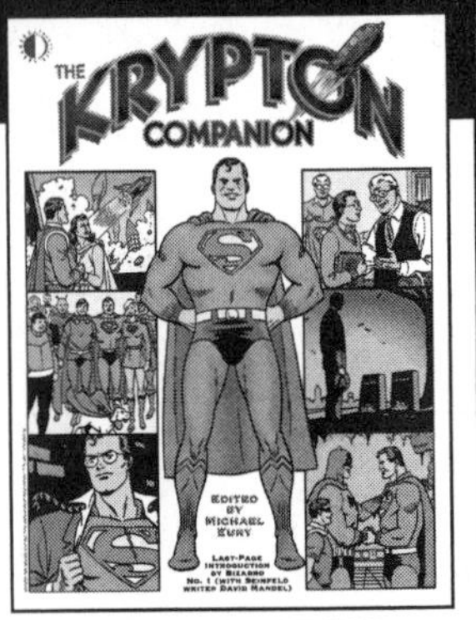
THE KRYPTON COMPANION
EDITED BY MICHAEL EURY

THE KRYPTON COMPANION

Unlocks the secrets of Superman's Silver and Bronze Ages, when kryptonite came in multiple colors and super-pets flew the skies! Features all-new interviews with **NEAL ADAMS, MURPHY ANDERSON, NICK CARDY, JOSÉ LUIS GARCÍA-LÓPEZ, KEITH GIFFEN, JIM MOONEY, DENNIS O'NEIL, BOB OKSNER, MARTY PASKO, BOB ROZAKIS, JIM SHOOTER, LEN WEIN, MARV WOLFMAN,** and others, plus tons of rare and unseen art! By **BACK ISSUE MAGAZINE'S** Michael Eury!

(224-Page Trade Paperback) **$29 US**

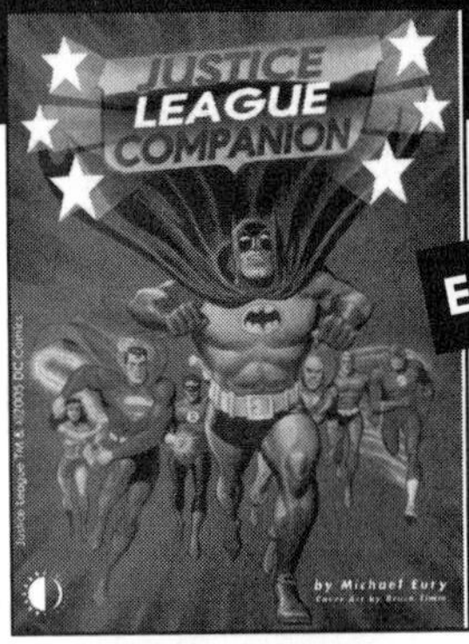
JUSTICE LEAGUE COMPANION
by Michael Eury

JUSTICE LEAGUE COMPANION VOL. 1

A comprehensive examination of the Silver Age JLA by **MICHAEL EURY**, tracing its development, history, and more through interviews with the series' creators, an issue-by-issue index of the JLA's 1960-1972 adventures, classic and never-before-published artwork, and other fascinating features. Contributors include **DENNY O'NEIL, MURPHY ANDERSON, JOE GIELLA, MIKE FRIEDRICH, NEAL ADAMS, ALEX ROSS, CARMINE INFANTINO, NICK CARDY**, and many, many others. Plus: An exclusive interview with **STAN LEE**, who answers the question, "Did the JLA really inspire the creation of Marvel's Fantastic Four?" With an all-new cover by **BRUCE TIMM** (TV's Justice League Unlimited)!

(224-page trade paperback) **$29 US**

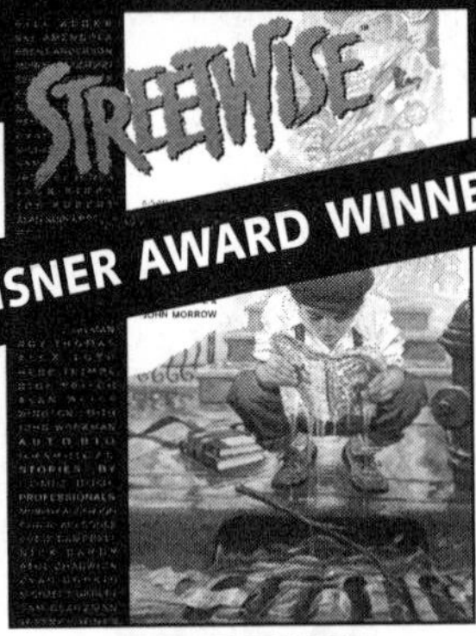
STREETWISE
EISNER AWARD WINNER!

STREETWISE TOP ARTISTS DRAWING STORIES OF THEIR LIVES

An unprecedented assembly of talent drawing **NEW** autobiographical stories:

- Barry **WINDSOR-SMITH** • C.C. **BECK**
- Sergio **ARAGONÉS** • Walter **SIMONSON**
- Brent **ANDERSON** • Nick **CARDY**
- Roy **THOMAS** & John **SEVERIN**
- Paul **CHADWICK** • Rick **VEITCH**
- Murphy **ANDERSON** • Joe **KUBERT**
- Evan **DORKIN** • Sam **GLANZMAN**
- Plus Art **SPIEGELMAN**, Jack **KIRBY**, more! Cover by **RUDE** • Foreword by **EISNER**

(160-Page Trade Paperback) **$24 US**

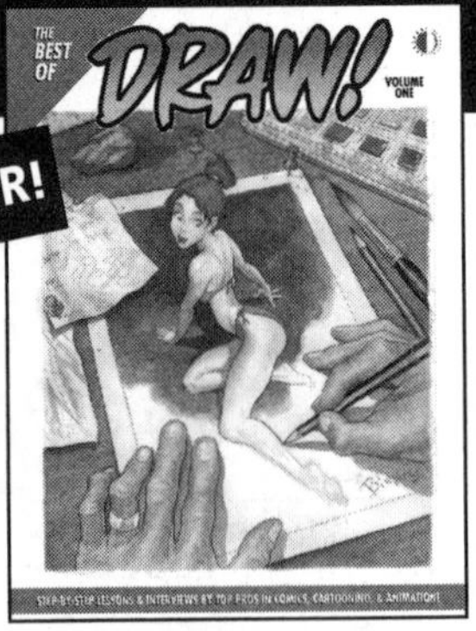
THE BEST OF DRAW! VOLUME ONE

BEST OF DRAW! VOL. 1

Compiles material from the first two sold-out issues of **DRAW!**, the "How-To" magazine on comics and cartooning! Tutorials by, and interviews with: **DAVE GIBBONS** (layout and drawing on the computer), **BRET BLEVINS** (drawing lovely women, painting from life, and creating figures that "feel"), **JERRY ORDWAY** (detailing his working methods), **KLAUS JANSON** and **RICARDO VILLAGRAN** (inking techniques), **GENNDY TARTA-KOVSKY** (on animation and Samurai Jack), **STEVE CONLEY** (creating web comics and cartoons), **PHIL HESTER** and **ANDE PARKS** (penciling and inking), and more!

(200-page trade paperback) **$26 US**

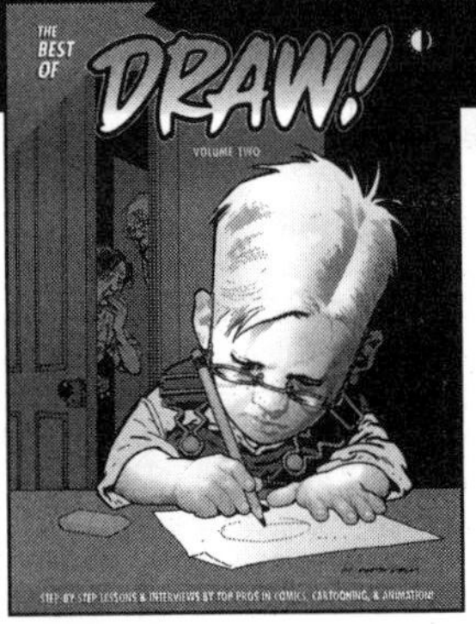
THE BEST OF DRAW! VOLUME TWO

BEST OF DRAW! VOL. 2

Compiles material from issues #3 and #4 of **DRAW!**, including tutorials by, and interviews with, **ERIK LARSEN** (savage penciling), **DICK GIORDANO** (inking techniques), **BRET BLEVINS** (drawing the figure in action, and figure composition), **KEVIN NOWLAN** (penciling and inking), **MIKE MANLEY** (how-to demo on Web Comics), **DAVE COOPER** (digital coloring tutorial), and more! Cover by **KEVIN NOWLAN**!

(156-page trade paperback) **$22 US**

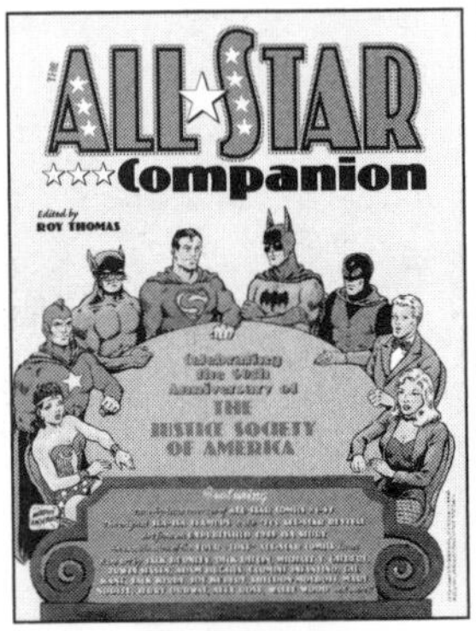
THE ALL-STAR companion
Edited by ROY THOMAS

ALL-STAR COMPANION VOL. 1

ROY THOMAS has assembled the most thorough look ever taken at All-Star Comics:

- Covers by **MURPHY ANDERSON!**
- Issue-by-issue coverage of **ALL—STAR COMICS #1—57**, the original **JLA—JSA** teamups, & the **'70s ALL—STAR REVIVAL!**
- Art from an unpublished **1945 JSA** story!
- Looks at **FOUR "LOST" ALL—STAR** issues!
- Rare art by **BURNLEY, DILLIN, KIRBY, INFANTINO, KANE, KUBERT, ORDWAY, ROSS, WOOD** and more!!

(208-page Trade Paperback) **$26 US**

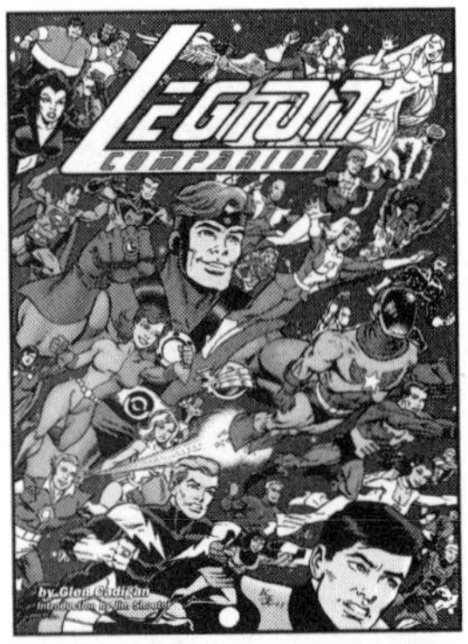
LEGION COMPANION

THE LEGION COMPANION

- A history of the Legion of Super-Heroes, with **DAVE COCKRUM, MIKE GRELL, JIM STARLIN, JAMES SHERMAN, PAUL LEVITZ, KEITH GIFFEN, STEVE LIGHTLE, MARK WAID, JIM SHOOTER, JIM MOONEY, AL PLASTINO**, and more!
- Rare and never-seen Legion art by the above, plus **GEORGE PÉREZ, NEAL ADAMS, CURT SWAN**, and others!
- Unused Cockrum character designs and pages from an **UNUSED STORY!**
- New cover by **DAVE COCKRUM** and **JOE RUBINSTEIN**, introduction by **JIM SHOOTER**, and more!

(224-page Trade Paperback) **$29 US**

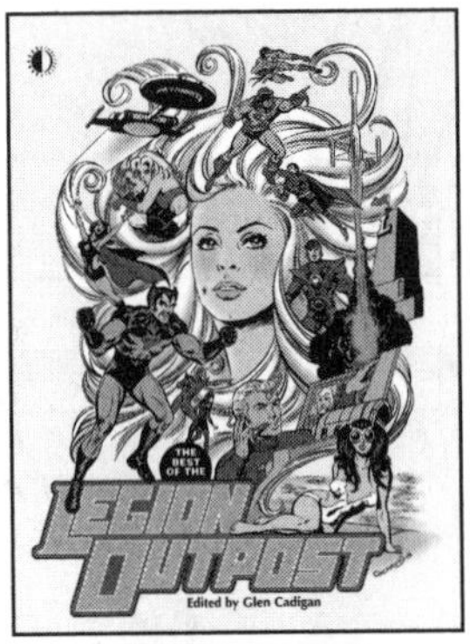
THE BEST OF THE LEGION OUTPOST
Edited by Glen Cadigan

BEST OF THE LEGION OUTPOST

Collects the best material from the hard-to-find **LEGION OUTPOST** fanzine, including rare interviews and articles from creators such as **DAVE COCKRUM, CARY BATES**, and **JIM SHOOTER**, plus never-before-seen artwork by **COCKRUM, MIKE GRELL, JIMMY JANES** and others! It also features a previously unpublished interview with **KEITH GIFFEN** originally intended for the never-published **LEGION OUTPOST** #11, plus other new material! And it sports a rarely-seen classic 1970s cover by Legion fan favorite artist **DAVE COCKRUM!**

(160-page trade paperback) **$22 US**

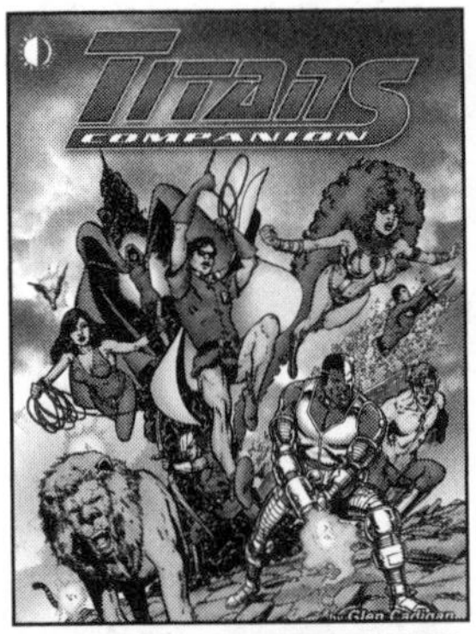
TITANS COMPANION

TITANS COMPANION

A comprehensive history of the **NEW TEEN TITANS**, with interviews and rare art by **MARV WOLFMAN, GEORGE PÉREZ, JOSÉ LUIS GARCÍA-LÓPEZ, LEN WEIN**, & others, a Silver Age section with **NEAL ADAMS, NICK CARDY, DICK GIORDANO**, & more, plus **CHRIS CLAREMONT** and **WALTER SIMONSON** on the **X-MEN/TEEN TITANS** crossover, **TOM GRUMMETT, PHIL JIMENEZ** & **TERRY DODSON** on their '90s Titans work, a new cover by **JIMENEZ**, & intro by **GEOFF JOHNS!** Written by **GLEN CADIGAN.**

(224-page trade paperback) **$29 US**

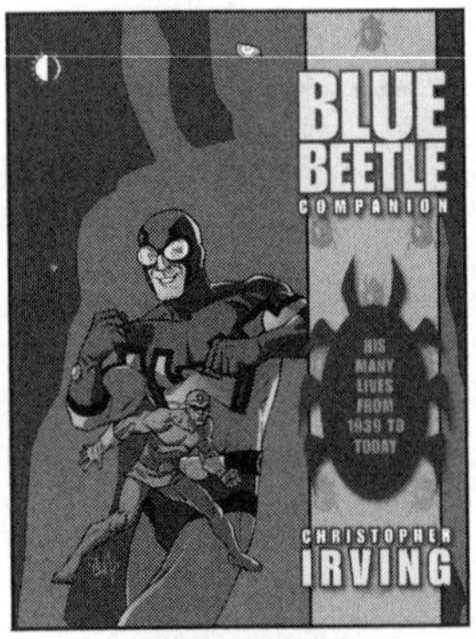
BLUE BEETLE COMPANION
HIS MANY LIVES FROM 1939 TO TODAY
CHRISTOPHER IRVING

BLUE BEETLE COMPANION

The history of a character as old as Superman, from 1939 to his tragic fate in DC Comics' hit **INFINITE CRISIS** series, and beyond! Reprints the first appearance of The Blue Beetle from 1939's **MYSTERY MEN COMICS #1**, plus interviews with **WILL EISNER, JOE SIMON, JOE GILL, ROY THOMAS, GEOFF JOHNS, CULLY HAMNER, KEITH GIFFEN, LEN WEIN**, and others, never-before-seen Blue Beetle designs by **ALEX ROSS** and **ALAN WEISS**, as well as artwork by **EISNER, CHARLES NICHOLAS, JACK KIRBY, STEVE DITKO, KEVIN MAGUIRE**, and more!

(128-page Trade Paperback) **$21 US**

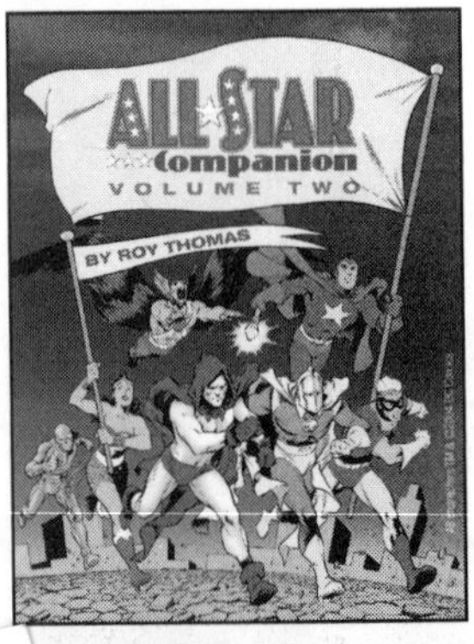
ALL-STAR companion VOLUME TWO
BY ROY THOMAS

ALL-STAR COMPANION VOL. 2

ROY THOMAS' new sequel, with more secrets of the **JSA** and **ALL-STAR COMICS**, from 1940 through the 1980s:

- Wraparound **CARLOS PACHECO** cover!
- More amazing information, speculation, and unseen **ALL-STAR COMICS** art!
- Unpublished **1940s JSA STORY ART** not printed in Volume One!
- Full coverage of the 1980s **ALL-STAR SQUADRON**, with scarce & never-published art!

(240-page Trade Paperback) **$29 US**

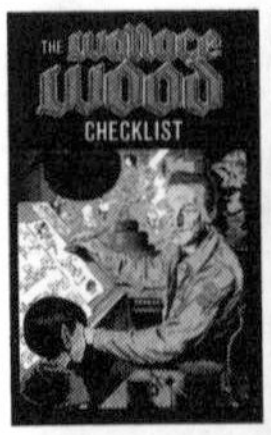
THE wallace wood CHECKLIST

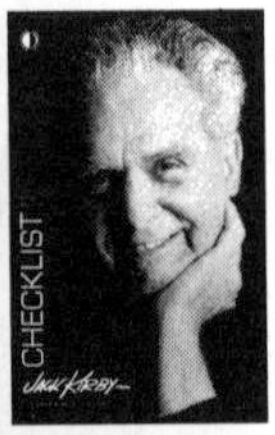
CHECKLIST

WALLY WOOD & JACK KIRBY CHECKLISTS

Each lists **PUBLISHED COMICS WORK** in detail, plus **ILLOS, UNPUBLISHED WORK**, and more. Filled with rare and unseen art!

(68/100 Pages) **$8 US EACH**

T.H.U.N.D.E.R. AGENTS COMPANION

The definitive book on **WALLACE WOOD**'s super-team of the 1960s, featuring interviews with Woody and other creators involved in the T-Agents over the years, plus rare and unseen art, including a rare 28-page story drawn by **PAUL GULACY, UNPUBLISHED STORIES** by **GULACY, PARIS CULLINS**, and others, and a **JERRY ORDWAY** cover. Edited by **CBA's JON B. COOKE.**

(192-page trade paperback) **$29 US**

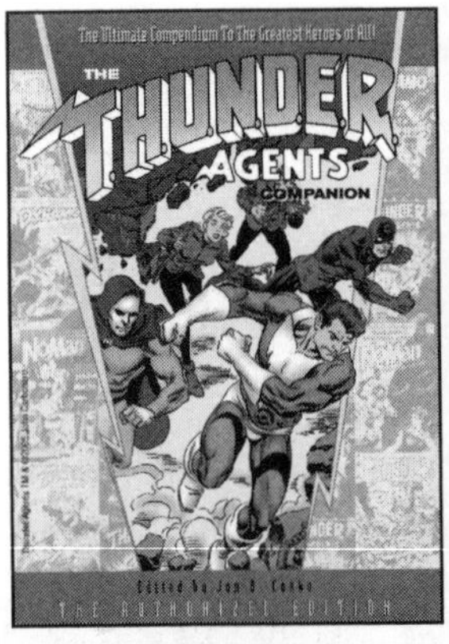
The Ultimate Compendium To The Greatest Heroes of All!
THE THUNDER AGENTS COMPANION

Prices include US Postage. Outside the US, **ADD PER ITEM**: Magazines & DVDs, $2 ($7 Airmail) • Softcover books, $3 ($10 Airmail) • Hardcover books, $6 ($15 Airmail)

HERO GETS GIRL!
The Life and Art of Kurt Schaffenberger
By MARK VOGER with photos by Kathy Voglesong

HERO GETS GIRL! THE LIFE & ART OF KURT SCHAFFENBERGER

MARK VOGER's biography of the artist of **LOIS LANE & CAPTAIN MARVEL!**

- Covers **KURT'S LIFE AND CAREER** from the 1940s to his passing in 2002!
- Features **NEVER-SEEN PHOTOS & ILLUSTRATIONS** from his files!
- Includes recollections by **ANDERSON, EISNER, INFANTINO, KUBERT, ALEX ROSS, MORT WALKER** and others!

(128-page Trade Paperback) **$19 US**

Secrets in the Shadows
The Art & Life of Gene Colan
by Tom Field

SECRETS IN THE SHADOWS: GENE COLAN

The ultimate retrospective on **COLAN**, with rare drawings, photos, and art from his nearly 60-year career, plus a comprehensive overview of Gene's glory days at Marvel Comics! **MARV WOLFMAN, DON MCGREGOR** and other writers share script samples and anecdotes of their Colan collaborations, while **TOM PALMER, STEVE LEIALOHA** and others show how they approached the daunting task of inking Colan's famously nuanced penciled pages! Plus there's a **NEW PORTFOLIO** of never-before-seen collaborations between Gene and such masters as **JOHN BYRNE, MICHAEL KALUTA** and **GEORGE PÉREZ**, and all-new artwork created specifically for this book by Gene! Available in Softcover and Deluxe Hardcover (limited to 1000 copies, with 16 extra black-and-white pages and 8 extra color pages)!

(168-page softcover) **$26 US**
(192-page trade hardcover) **$49 US**

COMICS ABOVE GROUND
How Sequential Art Affects Mainstream Media

COMICS ABOVE GROUND
SEE HOW YOUR FAVORITE ARTISTS MAKE A LIVING OUTSIDE COMICS

COMICS ABOVE GROUND features top comics pros discussing their inspirations and training, and how they apply it in "Mainstream Media," including Conceptual Illustration, Video Game Development, Children's Books, Novels, Design, Illustration, Fine Art, Storyboards, Animation, Movies & more! Written by **DURWIN TALON** (author of the top-selling **PANEL DISCUSSIONS**), this book features creators sharing their perspectives and their work in comics and their "other professions," with career overviews, never-before-seen art, and interviews! Featuring:

- **BRUCE TIMM**
- **BERNIE WRIGHTSON**
- **ADAM HUGHES**
- **LOUISE SIMONSON**
- **DAVE DORMAN**
- **GREG RUCKA & MORE!**

(168-page Trade Paperback) **$24 US**

COMIC BOOKS AND OTHER NECESSITIES OF LIFE
A COLLECTION OF POV COLUMNS BY MARK EVANIER
CARTOONS BY SERGIO ARAGONES

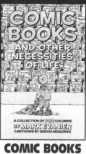

COMIC BOOKS & OTHER NECESSITIES OF LIFE

WERTHAM WAS RIGHT!

SUPERHEROES IN MY PANTS!

Each collects **MARK EVANIER'S** best essays and commentaries, plus new essays and illustrations by **SERGIO ARAGONÉS!**

(200-page Trade Paperbacks)
$17 US EACH
ALL THREE BOOKS: $34 US

THE DARK AGE
Grim, Great & Gimmicky Post-Modern Comics
By MARK VOGER
with photos by Kathy Voglesong

THE DARK AGE

Documents the '80s and '90s era of comics, from **THE DARK KNIGHT RETURNS** and **WATCHMEN** to the "polybagged premium" craze, the **DEATH OF SUPERMAN**, renegade superheroes **SPAWN, PITT, BLOODSHOT, CYBERFORCE**, & more! Interviews with **TODD McFARLANE, DAVE GIBBONS, JIM LEE, KEVIN SMITH, ALEX ROSS, MIKE MIGNOLA, ERIK LARSEN, J. O'BARR, DAVID LAPHAM, JOE QUESADA, MIKE ALLRED** and others, plus a color section! Written by **MARK VOGER**, with photos by **KATHY VOGLESONG.**

(168-page trade paperback) **$24 US**

DICK GIORDANO
CHANGING COMICS, ONE DAY AT A TIME
by Michael Eury

DICK GIORDANO CHANGING COMICS, ONE DAY AT A TIME

MICHAEL EURY's biography of comics' most prominent and affable personality!

- Covers his career as illustrator, inker, and editor, peppered with **DICK'S PERSONAL REFLECTIONS** on his career milestones!
- Lavishly illustrated with **RARE AND NEVER SEEN** comics, merchandising, and advertising art (includes a color section)!
- Extensive index of his published work!
- Comments & tributes by **NEAL ADAMS, DENNIS O'NEIL, TERRY AUSTIN, PAUL LEVITZ, MARV WOLFMAN, JULIUS SCHWARTZ, JIM APARO** & others!
- With a Foreword by **NEAL ADAMS** and Afterword by **PAUL LEVITZ!**

(176-pg. Paperback) **$24 US**

Alter Ego
COLLECTION VOLUME 1

ALTER EGO COLLECTION, VOL. 1

Collects the first two issues of **ALTER EGO**, plus 30 pages of **NEW MATERIAL!** JLA Jam Cover by **KUBERT, PÉREZ, GIORDANO, TUSKA, CARDY, FRADON, & GIELLA**, new sections featuring scarce art by **GIL KANE, WILL EISNER, CARMINE INFANTINO, MIKE SEKOWSKY, MURPHY ANDERSON, DICK DILLIN**, & more!

(192-page trade paperback) **$26 US**

'70s MARVEL MANIA / INDEPENDENT COMICS OF THE '80s
COMIC BOOK ARTIST
COLLECTION VOLUME 3
PAUL GULACY STEVE GERBER MICHAEL T. GILBERT STEVE RUDE DON SIMPSON & MORE!

COMIC BOOK ARTIST COLLECTION, VOL. 3

Reprinting the Eisner Award-winning **COMIC BOOK ARTIST** #7 and #8 ('70s Marvel and '80s independents), featuring a new **MICHAEL T. GILBERT** cover, plus interviews with **GILBERT, RUDE, GULACY, GERBER, DON SIMPSON, CHAYKIN, SCOTT McCLOUD, BUCKLER, BYRNE, DENIS KITCHEN**, plus a **NEW SECTION** featuring over 30 pages of previously-unseen stuff! Edited by **JON B. COOKE.**

(224-page trade paperback) **$29 US**

THE ART OF GEORGE TUSKA

ART OF GEORGE TUSKA

A comprehensive look at Tuska's personal and professional life, including early work with Eisner-Iger, crime comics of the 1950s, and his tenure with Marvel and DC Comics, as well as independent publishers. The book includes extensive coverage of his work on **IRON MAN, X-MEN, HULK, JUSTICE LEAGUE, TEEN TITANS, BATMAN, T.H.U.N.D.E.R. AGENTS**, and many more! A gallery of commission artwork and a thorough index of his work are included, plus original artwork, photos, sketches, previously unpublished art, interviews and anecdotes from his peers and fans, plus George's own words!

(128-page trade paperback) **$19 US**

TRUE Brit
A Celebration of the Great Comic Book Artists of the UK
SMUT
BRIT PROS REVEAL ALL

TRUE BRIT
CELEBRATING GREAT COMIC BOOK ARTISTS OF THE UK

A celebration of the rich history of British Comics Artists and their influence on the US with in-depth interviews and art by:

- **BRIAN BOLLAND**
- **ALAN DAVIS**
- **DAVE GIBBONS**
- **BRYAN HITCH**
- **DAVID LLOYD**
- **DAVE MCKEAN**
- **KEVIN O'NEILL**
- **BARRY WINDSOR-SMITH**

and other gents!

(204-page Trade Paperback with COLOR SECTION) **$26 US**

HOW TO CREATE COMICS
FROM SCRIPT TO PRINT

REDESIGNED and **EXPANDED** version of the groundbreaking **WRITE NOW! #8 / DRAW! #9** crossover! **DANNY FINGEROTH** & **MIKE MANLEY** show step-by-step how to develop a new comic, from script and roughs to pencils, inks, colors, lettering—it even guides you through printing and distribution, & the finished 8-page color comic is included, so you can see their end result! **PLUS:** over 30 pages of **ALL-NEW** material, including "full" and "Marvel-style" scripts, a critique of their new character and comic from an editor's point of view, new tips on coloring, new expanded writing lessons, and more!

(108-page trade paperback) **$18 US**

(120-minute companion DVD) **$35 US**

Learn To WRITE and DRAW like the pros!
HOW TO CREATE COMICS
From Script To Print
Danny Fingeroth & Mike Manley
From The Editors of Write Now! & DRAW!

BY JACK "KING" KIRBY
SILVER STAR
GRAPHITE EDITION
THE COMPLETE VISUAL NOVEL IN PENCIL FORM

SILVER STAR: GRAPHITE

JACK KIRBY'S six-issue "Visual Novel" for Pacific Comics, reproduced from his powerful, uninked pencil art! Includes Kirby's illustrated movie screenplay, never-seen sketches, pin-ups, & more from his final series!

(160 pages) **$24 US**

COLLECTED JACK KIRBY COLLECTOR, VOL. 1-5

See what thousands of comics fans, professionals, and historians have discovered: The King lives on in the pages of **THE JACK KIRBY COLLECTOR!** These colossal **TRADE PAPERBACKS** reprint the first 22 sold-out issues of the magazine for Kirby fans!

- **VOLUME 1:** Reprints **TJKC #1-9** (including the Fourth World and Fantastic Four theme issues), plus over 30 pieces of Kirby art never before published in TJKC! • (240 pages) **$29 US**
- **VOLUME 2:** Reprints **TJKC #10-12** (the Humor, Hollywood, and International theme issues), and includes a new special section detailing a fan's private tour of the Kirbys' remarkable home, showcasing more than 30 pieces of Kirby art never before published in TJKC! • (160 pages) **$22 US**
- **VOLUME 3:** Reprints **TJKC #13-15** (the Horror, Thor, and Sci-Fi theme issues), plus 30 new pieces of Kirby art! • (176 pages) **$24 US**
- **VOLUME 4:** Reprints **TJKC #16-19** (the Tough Guys, DC, Marvel, and Art theme issues), plus more than 30 pieces of Kirby art never before published in TJKC! • (240 pages) **$29 US**
- **VOLUME 5:** Reprints **TJKC #20-22** (the Women, Wacky, and Villains theme issues), plus more than 30 pieces of Kirby art never before published in TJKC! • (224 pages) **$29 US**

COLLECTED JACK KIRBY COLLECTOR VOL. 1

CALL, WRITE, OR E-MAIL FOR A FREE COLOR CATALOG!

MODERN MASTERS SERIES

Edited by **ERIC NOLEN-WEATHINGTON**, these trade paperbacks and DVDs are devoted to the **BEST OF TODAY'S COMICS ARTISTS!** Each book contains **RARE AND UNSEEN ARTWORK** direct from the artist's files, plus a **COMPREHENSIVE INTERVIEW** (including influences and their views on graphic storytelling), **DELUXE SKETCHBOOK SECTIONS**, and more! And **DVDs** show the artist at work!

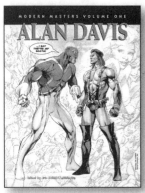  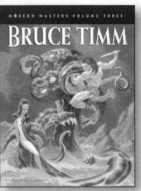  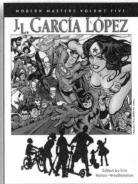

VOL. 1: ALAN DAVIS
(128-Page Trade Paperback)
$19 US

V.2: GEORGE PÉREZ
(128-Page Trade Paperback)
$19 US

V.3: BRUCE TIMM
(120-Page TPB with COLOR)
$19 US

V.4: KEVIN NOWLAN
(120-Page TPB with COLOR)
$19 US

V.5: GARCÍA-LÓPEZ
(120-Page TPB with COLOR)
$19 US

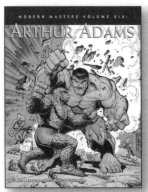    

V.6: ARTHUR ADAMS
(128-Page Trade Paperback)
$19 US

V.7: JOHN BYRNE
(128-Page Trade Paperback)
$19 US

V.8: WALTER SIMONSON
(128-Page Trade Paperback)
$19 US

V.9: MIKE WIERINGO
(120-Page TPB with COLOR)
$19 US

V.10: KEVIN MAGUIRE
(128-Page Trade Paperback)
$19 US

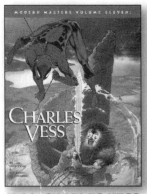  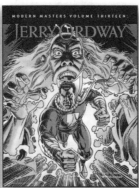 

V.11: CHARLES VESS
(120-Page TPB with COLOR)
$19 US
SHIPS FEBRUARY 2007

V.12: MICHAEL GOLDEN
(120-Page TPB with COLOR)
$19 US
SHIPS JUNE 2007

V.13: JERRY ORDWAY
(120-Page TPB with COLOR)
$19 US
SHIPS AUGUST 2007

MODERN MASTERS STUDIO DVDs
GEORGE PÉREZ (NOW SHIPPING)
MICHAEL GOLDEN (SHIPS JULY '07)
(120-minute Std. Format DVDs) $35 US EACH

 TwoMorrows. Bringing New Life To Comics Fandom.

TwoMorrows • 10407 Bedfordtown Drive • Raleigh, NC 27614 USA • 919-449-0344 • FAX: 919-449-0327 • E-mail: twomorrow@aol.com • www.twomorrows.com